THE
EARTH
FIRST!
READER

THE EARTH FIRST! READER

TEN YEARS OF RADICAL ENVIRONMENTALISM

EDITED BY
JOHN DAVIS
FOREWORD BY
DAVE FOREMAN

GIBBS·SMITH PUBLISHER

PEREGRINE SMITH BOOKS
SALT LAKE CITY

First edition
94 93 92 91 8 7 6 5 4 3 2 1
Foreword © 1991 by Dave Foreman
Introduction and editor's updates © 1991 by
John Davis
Articles by Gary Nabhan, Gary Snyder, and
Dave Foreman are copyrighted by them. All
other individual copyrights remain the prop-
erty of *Earth First! Journal.*

This is a Peregrine Smith Book, published by
Gibbs Smith, Publisher
P.O. Box 667
Layton, UT 84041

Design by J. Scott Knudsen
Manufactured in the United States of America

**Library of Congress Cataloging-in-
Publication Data**
The Earth first! reader : ten years of radical
environmentalism / John Davis, editor ; fore-
word by Dave Foreman.
        p. cm.
    ISBN 0-87905-387-9 (pbk.)
      1. Environmental policy—United States—
Citizen participation.
2. Environmental protection—United
States—Citizen participation.
3. Green movement—United States. I. Davis,
John, 1963- .
II. Earth first! journal.
HC110.E5E22 1991
363.7'057'0973-dc20   91-11206
                                       CIP

CONTENTS

6

FOREWORD

AROUND THE CAMPFIRE

In *Confessions of an Eco-Warrior,* I discuss the events and ideas that sparked the Earth First! flame in 1980, what I believe the resulting movement accomplished during the decade of the 1980s, and the circumstances that led to its breakup in 1990. But what about the *Earth First! Journal,* as opposed to the Earth First! movement? How did it begin? What did it do? Where has it gone? That's the cigar I'd like to chew on around this campfire. And maybe the smoke rings I blow into the night will carry an understanding of the distinction between the sprawling, sometimes unfocused Earth First! movement and the more tightly drawn publication entitled the *Earth First! Journal,* from which the pieces in this anthology are drawn.

A newspaper bearing the name *Earth First!* did not come into being until nearly two years after the formation of the movement with the same name, but its direct antecedents stretch back to the first announcement of Earth First! Following the decision by myself and four others in March 1980 to establish an uncompromising wing of the wilderness preservation movement, Howie Wolke circulated a memo to a select group of conservation activists. Following the original Round River Rendezvous at Wyoming's T-Cross Ranch that July, I mailed out a short, photocopied newsletter entitled "Nature More" (from Byron's poetic line, "I love not man the less, but nature more") to over five hundred conservationists culled from my Rolodex and various other lists of activists.

The response was encouraging enough to launch a regular newsletter. Still photocopied, that fall, I entitled it simply "Earth First" (the exclamation point came later) and gave Vol. 1, No. 1 the date November 1, 1980 (Samhain), proposing to issue it eight times a year on pagan Europe's nature holidays. Susan Morgan, the former education director for The Wilderness Society, accepted editorship and published it from her home in Breckenridge, Colorado, until she moved to Seattle in 1981, where she continued publication of the newsletter.

At the second Round River Rendezvous in Moab, Utah, I met a local journalist and photographer, Pete Dustrud, who suggested transforming the photocopied newsletter into a tabloid newspaper with headlines, photographs, and all the trimmings. Ken Sanders, owner of Dream Garden Press in Salt Lake City, offered to hire Pete as his shipping clerk and give him a place to live and office facilities for the

Earth First! tabloid. Pete produced the first issue of the newspaper-style *Earth First! Newsletter* in the winter of 81–82. This issue was filled with Pete's powerful black-and-white photos of Earth First! activities and activists, and headlined the coast-to-coast Road Show that Johnny Sagebrush and I had just completed. Pete also assumed the business management duties that Susan had been handling from Seattle, and expanded our line of T-shirts and bumper stickers.

After the third Round River Rendezvous at Little Granite Creek, Wyoming, Pete resigned as editor in a dispute over the "Dear Ned Ludd" column, which I edited. He feared the publication of monkeywrenching tips, particularly an installment on spiking roads. With Pete's resignation, Bart Koehler and I became co-editors of *Earth First!*. We were living in Ely, Nevada, at the time with Bart's partner, Wildcat Annie (whose government job pretty much supported us and our Earth First! organizing in those days). We commuted to Salt Lake City for paste-up in the Dream Garden office and to have our tabloid printed. In 1983, I moved to Chico, California, along with the publication and growing T-shirt business. Nancy Morton, a cardiac care nurse who later married me, inherited the task of supporting the *Earth First! Journal*. A year later Nancy and I moved the whole operation to Tucson, Arizona, where she planned to attend graduate school.

Soon after moving to Tucson, I received a letter from a Midwest college student named John Davis, who was graduating and wanted to volunteer for the newspaper. I tried to put him off, but he was insistent. He wrote me that he was moving to Tucson and would find a place to live, a part-time job to support himself, and would do whatever I wanted him to do for the paper. John proved himself such a priceless asset to the newspaper, and such a rich source of gossip thanks to his expertise in urban hunting and gathering, that I offered him a full-time job as managing editor. I yet don't know how someone of John's generation (he's still not 30) managed to learn grammar so well. I have grown so dependent on his editing that I feel uncomfortable sending out anything without his careful review. The serious writers who contributed to the *Earth First! Journal*, many of whom are represented in this anthology, overwhelmingly agreed with my trust in John's editing.

In Ely, I had begun a regular editorial and gossip column "Around the Campfire." In its first appearance, I suggested that the *Earth First! Newsletter* was now a full-fledged *newspaper*. I also outlined the role I conceived for the *Earth First!* newspaper—as distinguished from the Earth First! movement.

I offered three areas of concentration:

1) To offer a forum for internal discussion within the conservation movement about strategy, organization, and the like, and to criticize specific environmental groups for compromise and co-optation when necessary;

2) To offer a forum for discussion of biocentric philosophy—Deep Ecology—in a non-technical way for grassroots wilderness activists; and

3) To present ambitious, ecological wilderness proposals and discussion of conservation issues from an uncompromising standpoint.

A fourth emphasis soon developed from the third as the Earth First! movement stepped into the physical defense of the natural world. News coverage of environmental direct action regularly occupied our front page. Over the next couple of years, this slowly initiated a division in the movement as some began to feel that the sole role of the *Earth First! Journal* was to publicize their direct action campaigns and to channel support to them to continue such efforts.

When we formed Earth First! in 1980, we decided not to establish a formal organization. We wanted a looser structure—without formal officers and the administrative overhead that goes with an organization. It quickly became obvious, however, as Pete Dustrud cranked out a real newspaper and as subscriptions mushroomed, that some formal organization was necessary to cash checks, acquire a bulk mailing permit, and carry on the other necessary business activities associated with a regular publication. Our solution was for Pete to set up a sole proprietorship in his name for the newspaper as a separate entity within the Earth First! movement, which would remain without any encompassing formal structure. After he left, the sole proprietorship was transferred to my name and I maintained it as an entity distinct from the growing Earth First! movement until December 1988, when I transferred ownership to a non-profit corporation composed of the newspaper's staff of four people—John Davis, Kris Sommerville, Nancy Zierenberg, and Dale Turner. They continued this policy.

The *Earth First! Journal* ceased publication in December 1990, an early casualty of the breakup of the Earth First! movement. A newspaper with the name "Earth First!" that bears a superficial resemblance to the *Earth First! Journal* is now being published out of Missoula, Montana, but it is not a continuation of the *Earth First! Journal*. It is an entirely new and separate publication, as is the *Wild Earth* magazine that John Davis and I are now publishing.

The separation between the *Earth First! Journal* and the Earth First! movement was difficult for some to grasp. Nonetheless, I always felt that it was vital to maintain that separation. Running a two-hundred-thousand-dollar-a-year business (which the *Earth First! Journal* became) requires good management and careful accounting, but the nature of the Earth First! movement made it just as important that such a centralized administration never be established over everything that was contained under the name "Earth First!" Moreover, I felt that Earth First! would remain better focused on its initial goals of wilderness preservation if editorial control was retained by a small group of people who held a common vision of what Earth First! meant and who were committed to a fair exchange of ideas within those parameters, than if such editorial oversight was diffused to a wider, but less responsible, community.

There, in the smoking of our stogies, is a sketch of the history and the set-up of the *Earth First! Journal*.

But what did the *Earth First! Journal* (and its newsletter precursor) accomplish during its decade-long lifespan? Did it live up to the role I assigned it back in September 1982? That is not for me to judge. In the last chapter of *Confessions of an Eco-Warrior*, I offer my analysis of what the Earth First! movement overall achieved during the 1980s. I could argue that much of that legacy was supported by the *Earth First! Journal* and that the best ideas, most courageous actions, and most expansive vision within the entire environmental movement were given eloquent voice by the writers, artists, supporters, and staff of the *Earth First! Journal*.

But I say that to you only around this wilderness campfire that is quickly burning down to embers, as we listen to hunting owls and scampering rodents, as we finish our cigars and drain the last of the Kahlua. I leave the public judgment of the *Earth First! Journal*, 1980–1990 RIP, to others.

But here—before I leave you—here you hold in your hands the essence of the heart and the mind of a remarkable publication and of an extraordinary movement. It is with fond recollection that I review these selections from now-yellowing copies of the *Earth First! Journal*. There is magic here. Vision. And boldness.

Happy Trails,
Dave Foreman,
PICO PINACATE, MARCH 1991

ACKNOWLEDGMENTS

We are grateful to all who have written for *Earth First! Journal.* You have made the Journal and this book possible—and have done so without remuneration. In particular, we wish to thank those who wrote frequently for us: Christopher Manes; George Wuerthner; Howie Wolke; Dolores LaChapelle; Bill Devall; Lynn Jacobs; Robert Mueller; Leon Czolgosz; Bart Koehler; Roger Featherstone; Rod Mondt; John Patterson; Jean Eisenhower; Julia Fonseca; Roland Knapp; Sally Miller; Karen Wood; John Seed; Rick Davis; Paul Watson; Mike Roselle; Lone Wolf Circles; T. O. Hellenbach, head of Joaquin; Chim Blea; Barb Dugelby; Karen Pickett; Robert Streeter; Dale Turner; Reed Noss; Ned Mudd; Jasper Carlton; Jamie Sayen; Jeff Elliott; Mary Davis; Leslie Lyon; Trudy Frisk; and our poetry editor, Art Goodtimes.

We also thank the many activists who provided the impetus for the *journal*—especially the Tucson EF! activists who provided the impetus for getting the journals to the post office eight times a year! Special thanks go to *EF! Journal's* business and merchandise managers, Kris Sommerville and Nancy Zierenberg, without whom production would have faltered. Finally, gratitude is owed Dave Foreman, Howie Wolke, Ron Kezar, Bart Koehler, and Mike Roselle—Earth First!'s five co-founders—for starting a movement that revitalized the broader conservation movement in this country.

INTRODUCTION

This book is an attempt to encapsulate a significant part of the Earth First! movement, as represented over the past decade by *Earth First! Journal*. It is, of necessity, a representative, rather than a comprehensive, anthology of *Earth First! Journal* articles. It includes articles from the earliest issues printed on newsprint in 1982 through the journal's last year, 1990. (Previous issues, dating back to 1980, were xeroxed, stapled pages.)

We have striven to choose writings that best fulfill several criteria: continuing timeliness, informativeness, lucidity, and lasting value to the conservation movement. We have included neither Dave Foreman's nor Chim Blea's essays, because they comprise, in part, a new book by Dave entitled *Confessions of an Eco-Warrior* (Crown Books, 1991). Nor have we included EF! Wilderness proposals. These are so fundamental, and lengthy, that we hope to expand and consolidate them into a comprehensive North American Wilderness Recovery Strategy, after activists have completed the additional mapping and research needed to finish this project.

Lack of space (and the editor's admitted ineptness at judging poetry) prevented us from placing in this book more than a few poetic writings, book reviews or letters, despite the importance of each of these types of writing in *EF! Journal*. Readers who find this book rewarding would do well to read the periodicals that have arisen to replace the journal: *Wild Earth* (POB 492, Canton, NY 13617) and *Earth First!* (POB 5176, Missoula, MT 59806). We have also omitted from the book most of the "WHAT YOU CAN DO" sections that generally accompanied news articles in *EF!J*. Though these sections are important for helping readers involve themselves in the issues, readers can peruse the new journals for information on where letters and blockades are now needed.

We have somewhat arbitrarily divided the book into seven chapters. Within these chapters, articles are placed in chronological order.

You'll notice what may seem to you bizarre edition names above ·each article along with the year of publication: Brigid for February, Eostar for March, Beltane for May, Litha for June, Lughnasadh for August, Mabon for September, Samhain for November, and Yule for December. These are the names of the old Pagan holidays and correspond to major seasonal events (e.g., Eostar = Spring Equinox). We finally dropped the names in 1990, since they were hard to spell and harder to pronounce.

Before beginning this anthology, it is necessary to mention the expiration of *Earth First! Journal* and what is arising in its stead. As discussed in the last chapter of this book, the Earth First! movement has undergone a division of sorts, and the original *EF! Journal* has ended. Or, to use Dave Foreman's apt analogy, Earth First! has undergone speciation. The movement and the journal have evolved into multiple species.

To carry Dave's biological analogy a little farther, it is fair to add that this anthology displays something of a founder effect. The book represents strains of thought common to Earth First!'s founders and early protagonists, which prevailed in Earth First! until the last couple of years; and it does not give much space to the views of the more socially-oriented elements that now seem to be gaining strength in EF!.

The reasons for the split in EF! are many and complex and discussed elsewhere. Here suffice it to say that as the Earth First! movement grew in size and effectiveness, it attracted an increasing diversity of people, including FBI agents and informers, and social change activists who wanted EF! to expand its focus. Many of us who still want to focus on wilderness and biodiversity issues, and to leave social issues to other groups, have therefore decided to let the EF! movement go where it will and continue our work under different banners.

Nonetheless, uncompromising coverage of wilderness issues will continue. Dave Foreman and I have started a new journal, *Wild Earth*, concentrating on wilderness and wildlife. Most of the writers in this book will be writing for *Wild Earth*. A new Earth First! publication, *Earth First!*, is coming out of Missoula, Montana. It reflects the expanded EF! movement. (Addresses above.)

That this book is more representative of the "old guard" of the Earth First! movement than it is of the newer elements is not to denigrate the new efforts. Diversity will ensure lasting strength for the broader ecology movement. This book is an attempt to preserve for future environmentalists some of the thoughts of a small but disproportionately strong part of that movement, and, more importantly, to help preserve the planet's remaining wildlands.

John Davis
JANUARY 1991

CHAPTER 1

Earth First! Actions

EARTH FIRST! AS A MOVEMENT AND A TRIBE, *defined itself through its actions as well as its philosophy. Indeed, Dave Foreman, Earth First! co-founder, once said, "Let your actions set the finer points of your philosophy."*

Given that action articles tend to become dated quite quickly, however, we cannot do justice in this anthology to Earth First!'s tradition of exciting action coverage. We merely include here articles on four of Earth First!'s many dramatic campaigns.

The campaigns chosen represent some of the finest in overt EF! activity. The Bald Mountain blockades at least temporarily saved Bald Mountain from destruction, made old-growth a national issue, and thrust Earth First! into the forefront of the environmental movement. The Four Notch battles publicized the decadence, deceptiveness, and destructiveness of the US Forest Service. The sinking of Iceland's whaling boats by activists from the Sea Shepherd Conservation Society—"Earth First!'s Navy," in the words of Sea Shepherd founder Paul Watson—dealt a devastating blow to Iceland's whaling industry. Sea Shepherd's recent encounter with the Japanese drift-net fleet slowed and exposed the largest slaughter of wildlife in the world today—drift-net fishing.

We chose these campaigns not only because of their significance in the history of environmental activism, but also because the issues remain hot. Oregon's old-growth is still being cut; the Texas National Forests are still being cleared; commercial whalers are threatening to rear their ugly heads again; and drift-net fishers are expanding to heretofore relatively unexploited parts of the seas.

KALMIOPSIS CAMPAIGN
KALMIOPSIS/BALD MOUNTAIN BACKGROUND
Beltane 1983
by Chant Thomas

Bald Mountain has become the focus and symbol of the continuing battle to save the intact old growth forest ecosystems of the Pacific Northwest. The Illinois River flows through one of the wildest and most inaccessible canyons in the Northwest as it makes a 20-mile detour around Bald Mountain before turning north toward the Rogue River. The present official Kalmiopsis Wilderness boundary runs along the crest of Bald Mountain. To the south, brushy slopes drop into the protected area; to the north, lushly forested slopes drop into the unprotected North Kalmiopsis country, over 160,000 acres of wilderness in jeopardy, the largest unprotected wildland on the West Coast.

The North Kalmiopsis needs Wilderness protection. It is home to Black Bear, Cougar, Wolverine, Bald Eagle, and Osprey, and to rare trees and flowers. Here are the clearest, coldest tributaries of the Illinois River, essential habitat and spawning grounds of the salmon and steelhead which make the lower Illinois and Rogue Rivers a mecca for anglers. The canyons of Silver and Indigo Creeks may be the wildest in Oregon.

It is along the Illinois River Trail on Bald Mountain that the US Forest Service is building the Bald Mountain Road. If the road is built, other roads on the drawing boards will soon become reality and the North Kalmiopsis will be severed from the rest of the wilderness.

BLOCKADE BEGINS
Beltane 1983

"The Forest Service is an outlaw agency. If we don't stop them in the Kalmiopsis, there won't be any old growth forest left on the Pacific Coast outside of currently designated Wilderness and parks."

So said Marcy Willow of Eugene as Oregon Earth First! launched a nonviolent blockade of construction of the Bald Mountain Road along the northern boundary of the Kalmiopsis Wilderness Area in southwest Oregon's Siskiyou National Forest.

The controversial Forest Service road is designed to snake along the high ridge from Flat Top out to Bald Mountain between the

Illinois River and Silver Creek and "open up" 160,000 acres of rugged country for clearcutting. The road will wipe out portions of the popular Illinois River Trail and come within six inches of the Kalmiopsis Wilderness boundary. The Silver Creek country to the north of Bald Mountain has long been proposed for addition to the Kalmiopsis Wilderness, but opposition from Senator Mark Hatfield has prevented its protection.

The vast Kalmiopsis country has been under Forest Service attack for several decades. Despite the diversity and lushness of the forest, much of the area is poorly forested due to highly mineralized soils, and the soils are highly susceptible to destruction if disturbed.

The blockade to halt this destruction was organized by Earth First! affinity groups from Grants Pass, Medford, Eugene and Corvallis, with help from the Bigfoot Preservation Society. "We're in this for the long run," said Mike Roselle. "If necessary, we'll be here 'til snow flies in the fall."

BLOCKADERS ASSAULTED BY BULLDOZER
Litha 1983

Foreman Run Down by Truck

"If you don't get out of the way, I'm going to kill you!" screamed Plumley Company bulldozer operator Fred Brown to five Earth First!ers blocking his path at the end of the remote road in the Siskiyou National Forest near Grants Pass, Oregon. But the five stood firm even as Brown charged them time and again with his machine. Finally, he buried them with dirt from the blade. The fight for the North Kalmiopsis was, in Mike Roselle's words, "getting gnarly."

The fight to save 160,000 acres of primeval forest had begun two weeks earlier on April 25 when Mike Roselle, Steve Marsden, Pedro Tama and Kevin Everhart shut down operations on the Bald Mountain Road for over three hours until Josephine County sheriff's deputies arrived to arrest them. They were charged with disorderly conduct and spent the night in jail.

Nine days later, seven Oregonians blockaded construction at the same site—but with a twist. They handcuffed and chained themselves to the bulldozer when the police arrived. They thus shut down operations for four hours. They were released from jail that day on their own recognizance.

Then on May 12, Dave Willis and Dave Foreman set up a road-
block on the access road 10 miles from the construction area to stop
the Plumley workers on their way to work. With their support team,
they pulled a downed tree into the road in front of themselves
because, as Foreman said, "I don't want to be a hood ornament on a
Plumley truck."

At 6 AM, a sheriff's deputy arrived and asked them to move. They
refused. The deputy then winched the log out of the way and parked
50 feet in front of them. Willis, missing both hands and feet from
frostbite, was in his wheelchair. At 6:15, the Plumley sixpac pickup
carrying five workers arrived and drove around the deputy's vehicle.
The workers tried to pass Willis on the inside of the road cut but
Foreman stepped over and blocked their path. They then drove to the
outside of the road bend. Foreman stepped back in place.

For a moment the blockaders faced off the truck. Then it shot forward, hitting Foreman in the chest and knocking him back five feet.
Again truck and man faced off. The truck pushed against Foreman. He
pushed back. Les Moore, the driver, accelerated. Foreman had to
backpedal to keep from being run over. He finally lost his balance and
went down. He held on to the bumper for a few seconds and the truck
finally stopped . . . after having pushed him a distance later measured
at 103 yards.

The five construction workers piled out of the truck and surrounded Foreman, who was lying half under it. "You dirty communist
bastard," yelled Les Moore, "Why don't you go back to Russia where
you came from?"

"But, Les," Foreman replied, "I'm a registered Republican."

The deputy then dashed up, handcuffed Foreman and dragged him
away, under arrest for disorderly conduct. The construction workers
heaped abuse on the media people present, warning them not to take
further photographs "or else."

Foreman was bailed out of jail that afternoon. The Sheriff's
Department told the media that there had been no assault, that
Foreman had stepped in front of a moving vehicle and had been
knocked down and that the truck had immediately stopped. However,
a UPI reporter had witnessed the entire incident and two TV stations
had filmed it. The Forest Service and Sheriff's Department were
caught in their cover-up when the TV news aired that evening. The

question remaining was: had the authorities encouraged the construction workers to intimidate the blockaders?

Due to the negative publicity from the assaults, the Plumley
Company on May 13 ordered its employees to refrain from further violence. Accepting that in good faith, the blockaders decided not to
press assault charges unless further violence took place. Arraignment
also took place on May 13. Foreman pled not guilty and was released
on his own recognizance until his trial, with the bizarre order that he
not set foot in National Forest. The judge was not moved by his
protestations that there were 180 million acres of National Forest in
the US. The previous blockaders pled not guilty and were ordered not
to enter National Forest land in Josephine County until their trial.

Undaunted, Earth First! and the Kalmiopsis Action Alliance were
planning larger blockades for the near future.

BALD MOUNTAIN ROAD STOPPED!
Lughnasadh 1983

On July 1, US District Judge James Redden of Eugene, Oregon,
ordered the US Forest Service to immediately halt construction of the
Bald Mountain timber road slicing through wilderness of the North
Kalmiopsis Roadless Area in southwestern Oregon. Judge Redden was
responding to a request for a temporary restraining order (TRO) as
part of a suit filed June 30 by Roseburg attorney Neal Kagan for Earth
First!, the Oregon Natural Resources Council and nine southern
Oregon residents.

The historic suit is the first filed by environmental groups against
the Forest Service's second Roadless Area Review and Evaluation
(RARE II). Earlier this year, the Ninth Circuit Court of Appeals in
San Francisco ruled that the Forest Service's 1979 final environmental
impact statement on RARE II was inadequate in considering the environmental impact of development on roadless areas not selected by
the Forest Service (FS) for Wilderness recommendation. The court
ordered the FS not to undertake development activities in such areas
until they had fully complied with the National Environmental Policy
Act (NEPA). Managers of many National Forests immediately suspended development plans but the Siskiyou National Forest
management insouciantly proceeded to grant a construction contract
for the Bald Mountain timber road in the 160,000-acre North
Kalmiopsis Roadless Area.

Ric Bailey of Oregon EF! said that Judge Redden's decision should be grounds for overturning Oregon State Judge O'Neill's decisions in ordering blockaders to pay restitution to Plumley Construction Company for downtime caused by the blockade (no one has yet paid restitution) and prohibiting them from entering National Forests for a year. (In a clearly unconstitutional ruling, Judge O'Neill prohibited Dave Foreman from setting foot on any National Forest land in the US and has ordered several other blockaders to stay off all National Forest land in Oregon.)

Dave Foreman suggested that, given Judge Redden's ruling, Siskiyou Forest Supervisor Bill Covey should be the one in jail and the Forest Service should be required to pay restitution to the blockaders for all their expenses in fighting the criminal acts of the Forest Service. He said Earth First! would be happy to bid on a FS contract to reclaim the illegal road.

On July 6, Judge Redden heard testimony from Plumley Company on why the TRO should not be continued. He continued the TRO until July 13. On that day, he issued an injunction against construction of the Bald Mountain Road.

RETURN TO BALD MOUNTAIN
Eostar 1987

by Chant Thomas

The Second Battle for the Kalmiopsis

The vast old growth forest of the Kalmiopsis is once again being viciously attacked. The Siskiyou National Forest has reneged on an agreement to postpone logging within the North Kalmiopsis Roadless Area until the Forest Plan is completed. Now a full scale federal blitzkrieg is under way with 24 timber sales active, imminent, or planned in this world-class natural treasure.

Important chapters in the history of citizen resistance to federal forest destruction have been written here in the past, and the newest chapters in the continuing saga have now begun. It took a place as incredibly wild, as amazingly unique, and as severely threatened as the Kalmiopsis to lure the still-embryonic Earth First! movement out of the Rocky Mountains and over to the continent's western edge in early 1983. The local Sierra Club had lost its appeals and lawsuits attempting to stop the nefarious Bald Mountain Road. A handful of Oregon's original Earth First!ers realized that the direct actions of "Mother Nature's Army" were the last hope. The second EF! Road Show came to southwestern Oregon. Radical activists from the peace movement provided non-violent direct action training sessions. People were inspired. The result was a precedent-setting series of seven direct actions. Violence unveiled its ugly visage in the third action when protesters were pushed by a bulldozer and the fourth action where Dave Foreman was run over by a logger's crummy before being arrested.

A total of 44 brave folks were arrested in the historic Bald Mountain Road Blockades in 1983. Those actions not only served as models and inspirations for later actions in the Pacific Northwest Coastal Rainforest (at Millennium Grove, the Sinkyone, and Breitenbush), but also generated a greater awareness of the US government's forest destruction programs. Furthermore, the blockades led to a successful lawsuit by Earth First! and the Oregon Natural Resources Council (EF! and ONRC v. Block), in which the Siskiyou National Forest road-building activities were declared illegal.

However, in 1984 Oregon's Senator Mark "timber pimp" Hatfield rammed his Oregon Wilderness (Destruction) bill through Congress. Hatfield's motto is "Not one more acre" of Kalmiopsis Wilderness, and his bill's language released the West's largest and most diverse old growth conifer forest to the timber beasts. Once again Siskiyou Earth First! is rising to meet the challenge.

The Kalmiopsis is a spur range of the Siskiyou Mountains in far southwestern Oregon and northwestern California. Although relatively low in elevation (from a few hundred feet in the canyons to 5000 feet on the highest peaks), the area is extremely rugged and is the least explored major mountain region in the lower 48. Running through the area are the Rogue and Illinois Rivers, both in the National Wild and Scenic River System; smaller rivers and creeks called Indigo, Silver, Chetco, and North Fork of the Smith are nominees. Most river canyons are too rugged to accommodate even a trail; vast areas of the Kalmiopsis region are trailless.

In the center of the Kalmiopsis region is the Pacific Coast's largest wilderness, covering 640 square miles: 180,000 acres of *protected* Wilderness and 230,000 acres of *unprotected* roadless area, with Bald Mountain Ridge straddling the boundary between. Only a few logging roads separate this wild core from other roadless areas, including the

Wild Rogue Wilderness to the north, and the North Fork Smith Roadless Area to the south.

Annual rainfall in the Kalmiopsis is up to 200 inches, and its complex geology creates extremely varied vegetative communities. It is one of the oldest continuously vegetated regions in western North America. The plant communities have evolved for many millions of years without catastrophic interruptions such as submersion, glaciation, or volcanic devastation. Many of its plants, including *Kalmiopsis leachiana*, are plentiful here, but rare or nonexistent elsewhere.

The southern Kalmiopsis is predominantly sparsely-vegetated redrock barrens—the largest peridotite deposit (a red form of serpentine) in North America. The central Kalmiopsis, especially the Chetco watershed, is rocky with fire-induced deciduous vegetation. The northern Kalmiopsis is richly endowed with a vast old growth forest, where streams of pure water provide the base for the fabled fisheries of the Illinois and Rogue Rivers.

Forest ecologists believe conifer forests have grown here for many millennia, undisturbed by the great glaciations of higher and more northern regions. Some ecologists believe this area to be one of the places where modern conifer forests first evolved and then migrated across the continent and the world. Most of this vast old growth forest grows unprotected in the 110,000-acre North Kalmiopsis Roadless Area, and it is here where the non-violent Mother Nature's Army will fight the blitzkrieg of federal logging roads and clearcuts.

Preparations have begun. It will take an extended series of direct actions to slow the devastating progress of Reagan's Raiders, and to generate the public awareness and money to make the Kalmiopsis a national issue. Siskiyou EF! is planning several events to culminate in direct actions, including logging road blockades, old growth tree sit-ins, logging site occupations, plus sit-ins and demos at Siskiyou NF headquarters in Grants Pass, Region 6 headquarters in Portland, and in Washington, DC! Meanwhile, the Kalmiopsis is included in a proposal for a Siskiyou National Park.

Winter Demonstrations Kick off Earth First! Kalmiopsis Campaign

On November 20, Earth First!ers from the Williams, Applegate, and Ashland areas of southwestern Oregon descended from the sunny

Siskiyou Mountains into the frozen fog of the Rogue Valley to initiate this year's Kalmiopsis Campaign. About 50 folks, half of them children, demonstrated in front of BLM district headquarters in Medford, where several timber sales were being auctioned, including the Rum Creek and Hewitt Creek Sales adjacent to the Wild and Scenic Rogue River corridor.

Timber company buyers had to walk the gauntlet of children clutching large helium balloons, painted with slogans such as "Would you cut down your grandmother?" and "Little kids love big trees." Bald Mountain Blockade veterans Mary Beth Nearing and Steve Marsden (disguised as the Kalmiopsis premier resident, Bigfoot) described the issues to the media. Some of the children were interviewed for TV, explaining why they hate clearcuts.

The demonstration ended with a moving song by the Siskiyou Earth First! Children's Choir to the tune of "Old McDonald Had a Farm":

> BLM had a tree farm ee i ee i oh
> and on this farm they had some clearcuts ee i ee i oh
> with a clearcut here and a clearcut there
> here a cut, there a cut, everywhere a clearcut
> BLM had a tree farm ee i ee i oh

After more verses about slash burns and bulldozers, the choir ended with:

> And on this farm they had no animals ee i ee i oh
> with no deer here and no bear there
> no owls flying anywhere
> BLM had a tree farm ee i ee i NO!

After the choral performance, several demonstrators entered the timber sale auction room with their banners and balloons, to witness the selling of millions of board feet of our precious forest.

The BLM demonstration whetted the appetites of many who'd never participated in an Earth First! activity before. So, three weeks later, over 100 folks, including students and staff of Horizon School, staged a rally at the entrance to the Siskiyou NF headquarters in Grants Pass. After an unemployed timber faller stopped by (in his 1987 Corvette!) to complain about "environmentalists," the mob paraded behind Santa Claus (llama-outfitter Chant Thomas) up to the headquarters, singing songs such as "Tree Reggae" and a reworded "Jingle Bells," accompanied by drums, flutes, and bagpipes.

The throng assembled around the American flagpole, and Santa narrated a skit in which a logger cut down an old growth tree and handed the Forest Service "timber revenues" to Ronald Ray-gun, who sneakily passed the tree-dollars on to our own bearded Khomeini character, who laundered the money into weapons and handed them to a Contra!

This drama was followed by more singing and then a tree-planting ceremony on the Freddie lawn amidst pomp and ceremony. Overcome at last by the message of the children and the power of life, Ray-gun promised to change his ways and ripped his money in half.

This demonstration was extensively covered by the media throughout western Oregon, as was a simultaneous demo in Portland, led by Bald Mountain sage Lou Gold. The media was also interested in a letter sent to the Siskiyou NF headquarters from Denver. The letter was signed "Sierra Clubbers who aren't whimps" and claimed that trees in the Hobson Horn Timber Sale had been spiked with 1.5-inch diameter hardrock drill cores. The Freddie PR men commented that the spikers "had to eat a lot of Cheerios to drill 1½ inch holes into big old trees." We wonder where Sierra Clubbers would get such an idea. . . .

Meanwhile, more demonstrations are planned for the Siskiyou-Kalmiopsis area. Siskiyou Earth First! has learned that such events attract much media attention when composed of many children, mothers, and famous personalities such as Santa Claus, Ronnie Ray-gun, Bigfoot, Spotted Owl, and Smokey the Bear. The children were wonderfully effective. Can you picture a cop or Freddie trying to snatch a helium balloon adorned with anti-government slogans away from a 4-year old kid?

Kalmiopsis-Wild Rogue Region Proposed for a Siskiyou National Park

The vast wild areas of southwestern Oregon in and around the Kalmiopsis and Wild Rogue Wilderness Areas are included in a proposal for a 750,000-acre Siskiyou National Park, being spearheaded by David Atkin and the Oregon Natural Resources Council.

Establishment of the Park would continue the regional change of focus from timber and mining to fisheries, tourism, and recreation. The Park idea is gaining popularity in southwestern Oregon and northwestern California, the West Coast's most depressed area, which is in dire need of economic diversification.

The Park study area contains 280,459 roadless acres which would be protected as de facto wilderness with National Park status. Also included within the Park would be 200,000 acres of roaded and partially clearcut forests located between the Roadless Areas and Wilderness Areas. Some present roads would be upgraded, but no new roads would be built. Park status would create more stringent management requirements for environmental and scenic quality on federal lands adjacent to the Park. However, Siskiyou Earth First! would prefer a National Park of millions of acres.

Editor's update: In 1991, the struggle over the Kalmiopsis has not yet been resolved. The Forest Service still wants to cut the unprotected Kalmiopsis wildlands. Through direct actions and legal challenges, wilderness proponents have thus far been able to stop most of the cutting. However, after forest fires burned part of the Kalmiopsis in 1988, Senator Mark Hatfield (R-OR) placed on the 1989 Senate Interior Appropriations Bill a rider that barred court challenges to "salvage" timber sales in the Silver Fire burn area of Oregon's North Kalmiopsis Roadless Area. Subsequently, forest that should have been added to the Kalmiopsis Wilderness was logged.

This cutting, and attempts to renew construction of the Bald Mountain road, met renewed Earth First! resistance, resulting in numerous arrests, cutting delays, and a lawsuit by the timber firm against six blockaders (the Sapphire Six). The lawsuit signaled a growing trend among land exploiters to use SLAPPs—strategic lawsuits against public participation—as a means to intimidate activists, who are generally impecunious and cannot afford court costs.

TEXAS EARTH FIRST! FIGHTS FREDDIE GODZILLA
Samhain 1986
by Barbara Dugelby

East Texas once was a land rich in woods and wildlife, with contiguous miles of upland forests, prairies, grassy glades, and fertile bottomlands. Beneath the shade of magnolias, white oaks and towering pines, the woods

*came to life with foxes, deer, raccoons, gray squirrels, wild turkeys. But
these days of unspoiled wilderness are gone. In their stead are neat rows of
slash and loblolly pines, planted to fill a society's ever growing need for lumber. Among these trees the squirrels no longer play, and where are the
wolves and bears? They've vanished from the land.* (From the introduction to *Land of Bears and Honey,* by Daniel Lay.)

Lay was right. East Texas is no longer the "Land of Bears and
Honey." The little remaining wilderness is being chewed apart by the
United States Forest Service (FS) in unsuccessful efforts to protect
pine plantations. While the FS claims to have turned a "barren East
Texas land into one of the 'national treasures' of our country," actually
for 50 years these "stewards" have raped, scraped, sawed, and mauled
some of the most biologically rich lands of North America.

In 1984 the Forest Service was caught cutting hundreds of acres
of newly established Wilderness, for the sake of protecting from the
Southern Pine Beetle the pine plantations that surround these tiny
islands of diversity. A lawsuit was filed, and the FS was shaken by the
outcry. But in the end the agency only got its hand slapped. We are
still losing pieces of our Wilderness Areas in the name of "pine beetle control."

Recently, the Farced Circus chose the Four Notch Area of the
Sam Houston National Forest, once part of a Wilderness proposal, to
try (again unsuccessfully) to stop a beetle infestation. Over 3600 acres
have been cut in the Four Notch area, with more falling every day.

The FS's latest maneuver in the Four Notch area has been to
"crush," with a machine as big as a house, what hardwoods and other
vegetation survive. There still remain many undamaged hardwoods,
among them 70-90 year old White Oaks, sweetgums, hickory, and
holly. To the FS this is trash, however, and thus they have crushed
over 1000 acres, on their way to ravaging over 2500 acres. They have
not attempted to market the hardwoods or protect wildlife in the area.

So, what will the Forest Service do with thousands of acres of
crushed debris? NAPALM it!! Helicopters equipped with torches and
a petroleum product called Alumagel, a napalm-like substance, are the
FS's newest toys for sculpting National Forest into a toilet paper pulp
farm! The napalm contract, the cover of which ironically features a
picture of Smokey the Bear leaning on a sign saying "Help Prevent
Forest Fires," will be awarded October 22 and the torching may occur

shortly thereafter, depending on weather conditions and moisture content of the wood. The FS has admitted that "animals will die as a result of the fire," as they burn the areas from the outside inward in concentric circles. But they don't feel that it is "much of a problem."

This is GENE-OCIDE! As scientists around the world proclaim the need to preserve biological diversity in the tropics, we destroy it in our own backyard. Texas Earth First! intends to stop this sterilizing of our National Forests on October 21. We plan to greet the giant tree crusher at dawn, chained to trees in its path. If necessary, EF!ers will enter the NAPALM FIRE ZONE to protect the remnants of diversity in the Sam Houston National Forest.

Acre after acre, the FS invites the very infestation that it is combating by replacing biological diversity with monoculture pine plantations. They operate at a deficit to the government and thus to the taxpayer, and to the environment . . . because they are pawns of the timber industry.

The Biological Crossroads of North America are not doomed yet, however. There remain wild areas—hardwood bottomlands, old growth pine stands and bogs that the FS has not reached with its greasy chainsaws. The battle will not end when they put us in jail.

LATE TEXAS NEWS
Samhain 1986

by Leon Czolgosz

After most of this issue of *Earth First!* had already gone to the typesetter, Barbara Dugelby called us from Austin with the stunning announcement that the Forest Service had just agreed to a 7-day moratorium on crushing and burning in the Four Notch. The moratorium came in response to pressure from the Texas State EPA and the office of the Attorney General of Texas.

As a direct result of the bold action of Texas Earth First! in exposing Forest Service practices in the Four Notch to public scrutiny, Nancy Lynch, Chief Attorney for the EPA, notified the Sam Houston National Forest of the EPA's intention to file suit to halt the crushing and burning. Shortly thereafter, Attorney General Jim Mattox suggested to the Forest Service an alternative to an immediate lawsuit; namely, that the FS voluntarily halt their activities while the Attorney General's office made an on-site investigation to determine if further action was warranted.

In response, Forest Supervisor Mike Lannan announced the 7-day moratorium, to run from October 31 to November 7. During this period a team from the EPA and Mattox's office will tour the Four Notch, accompanied by both Forest Service officials and representatives of the Texas environmental community. We can only hope that the state officials resist the pious blandishments of the Freddies and listen to the voice of reason. But whatever the ultimate outcome, the moratorium is clear proof of what can be accomplished by courgeous direct action, after all other means of appeal to the bureaucracy have failed.

Editor's update: Through deceit and treachery, the Forest Service eventually managed to destroy Four Notch. During Earth First!'s campaign to save Texas National Forest land, several activists were physically abused; but the FS's nefarious deeds were exposed to the nation, and the agency has since had to show more restraint in Texas.

RAID ON REYKJAVIK
Yule 1986
by Captain Paul Watson

Hold it right there. Before you begin to read the narrative that follows, let's get something straight. If you are a self-righteous tight-ass who gets morally indignant about correct tactics, then do yourself and us a favour and read *Time* or the *Greenpeace Examiner* instead. This article does not contain scenes of excessive violence nor does it contain sexually explicit material (unfortunately). It does, however, advocate the destruction of property because I believe that respect for life takes precedence over respect for property which is used to take lives.

Let's get something else straight. The killing of whales in 1986 is a crime. It is a violation of international law, but more importantly it is a crime against nature and against future generations of humanity. So, I don't want any crappy letters about tradition, livelihood or Icelandic rights.

With that said, we can begin the story.

August 1985: The *Sea Shepherd* stops in Reykjavík while on route to the Faroe Islands. We berth directly behind the Greenpeace ship *Sirius*. Across the harbour, we see the Icelandic whaling fleet tied together. Our plan is to take on provisions before heading to the Faroes. While there, pictures are taken, port facilities surveyed, security measures observed and a few crew tour the site of a whale processing plant 50 miles from the city.

Our arrival did not go unnoticed. The Icelandic police post a 24
hour guard at our gangway and police divers investigate the hulls of
the whalers every few hours. Some of this activity is the fault of our
reputation and some of it results from a Greenpeace conference where
we were accused of being terrorists. Greenpeace made it clear that
they were not associated with us in any way. We hold our own press
conference to say that we are not associated with the wimps on the
Sirius in any way. A bunch like that can give us a bad name. At the
same time, we deliver a warning to Iceland through the media: We
have not come to interfere with Icelandic whaling at the moment; but
if Iceland intends to violate the moratorium on commercial whaling
set to begin in 1986, then Iceland can expect to see the enforcement
of International Whaling Commission (IWC) regulations.

We then left Iceland and Greenpeace. Greenpeace workers were
relieved to see us leave. They were "networking" with the whalers—
giving tours of their ship and sharing beer with whale-killers. My crew
were not allowed on their ship. When we left, Greenpeace warned us
to stay out of Icelandic waters. Quaking in our deck-boots, we scurried
away from Iceland in mortal fear and proceeded to the Faroe Islands to
save a few whales.

June 1986; Malmo, Sweden: The *Sea Shepherd* sails from
Plymouth, England, to Sweden. We berth a few blocks from where the
meeting of the IWC is taking place. Ben White is our official observer
at the meeting. He is not happy. "The whalers intend to keep whaling.
They say that Icelandic and Norwegian whaling is not commercial
and must continue for scientific purposes."

The objective for continuation of scientific whaling would be
almost funny were it not so tragic. The Icelanders requested a scientific permit to kill whales so as to determine the reasons for a
decline in Fin and Sei Whale populations in the North Atlantic. The
scientific committee rejected the proposal. One committee member
stated, "Iceland is seeking to prostitute science in an attempt to mask
a commercial venture."

Iceland left the meeting vowing to kill whales despite IWC disapproval. The established approach had failed. A decade of work to
bring about a moratorium was all for nothing. With the moratorium in

effect, whales continued to be slaughtered by the Soviet Union, Japan, Iceland, Norway, and South Korea. We were ready to act against these pirates; but, still, the forces of moderation screamed, "We still have an ace in the hole, the Packwood-Magnuson Amendment."

The Packwood-Magnuson Amendment is a wonderful piece of legislation designed to protect whales through economic sanctions against nations that do not comply with IWC regulations. This meant that Iceland, Norway, Japan and South Korea would have to stop whaling or face the ire of the US. To keep whaling would be to lose fishing rights in US waters and to lose the right to market fish in the US. Sounds too good to be true, and it was. President Reagan announced that the US would not impose sanctions on a NATO ally. By choosing to discriminate in the application of the Amendment, the President made a mockery of the law and sacrificed whales on the altar of NATO. To add insult to injury, the President then struck a deal with the Icelanders that would allow them to sell 49% of their whale meat to Japan without US interference. The price—permission to use Iceland as a staging platform for the Soviet-US summit.

July 1986; the North Atlantic: On route back to Britain after our second summer of interfering with Pilot Whale killing in the Faroe Islands, the kid approaches me. You might remember the kid from the last article I wrote for *Earth First!*. Rod Coronado is a young Californian, an articulate, dedicated whale warrior. He is not satisfied with being jailed and shot at in the Faroe Islands. He has a plan and a damn good one to boot—a commando raid of Reykjavik.

We don't discuss details or strategy. If the kid has an idea, that's all the detail I want to know. We do review, however, the Sea Shepherd Society guidelines for direct action in the field. We have five rules: 1) No explosives. 2) No utilization of weapons. 3) No action taken that has even a remote possibility of causing injury to a living thing. Respect for life must always be our primary consideration. 4) If apprehended, do not resist arrest in a violent manner. 5) Be prepared to accept full responsibility and suffer the possible consequences for your actions. Could he operate within the guidelines? Yes. End of discussion. He and David Howitt were now on their own as Sea Shepherd field operatives.

15 October 1986: Rod and David arrive in Reykjavik and book into the Salvation Army Youth hostel. Hey, our guys travel first class.

They find jobs in the local fish processing plant. There are more jobs than citizens in Iceland, so securing employment as a non-citizen is relatively easy.

They spend three weeks scouting the sites and determining the schedule of the security watches. They wait for an opportunity.

November 8: A stormy day and night in Iceland. Rod and David drive the 50 miles to the whale processing plant. It is Saturday night and the watchman has gone home, leaving the station abandoned.

The two Sea Shepherd agents break into the plant. The tools are there—sledge hammers, acid and, ah yes, two monkeywrenches. The objective is to inflict as much economic destruction as possible.

The refrigeration machinery is destroyed, after which six diesel engines are dismantled and the plant's pumps destroyed. Engine parts are tossed into the deep waters of the fjord along with flensing knives and tools. The laboratory is demolished. The computers are trashed thoroughly and cyanic acid poured into the diskette files and filing cabinets. After eight hours, the plant looks as if it suffered a bomb blast. Damage was later estimated at 1.8 million US dollars.

Our two merry eco-commandos then drive back to Reykjavík in the early morning. They go directly to the three whaling ships tied in the harbour. A fourth is in dry dock. Both men go through all the cabins on board the ships. On the third ship, they locate a sleeping watchman. They decide to spare the third ship so as to avoid possible injury to the watchman. The wind is howling and the water is choppy and the noise provided by nature covers the activities of the two men below decks. They spend nearly two hours in preparation. The removal of 14 bolts from the salt water sea valve flange results in a massive volume of water spewing into the engine compartment of the ship. The other ship is dealt with in a similar manner a few moments later. The third ship is cut adrift so as not to be dragged down with the two now mortally wounded killer boats.

The crew then calmly walks down the dock and drives to the airport at Kleflavik 30 miles away. The ships sink within 40 minutes. The police discover the results at 0600 hours.

At about the same time, our crew is stopped by a routine road-block on route to the airport. Both men are questioned and given a breath analyzer test to determine if they have been drinking. They have not and are allowed to proceed. They board an Icelandic airlines flight to Luxembourg and leave at 0745 hours.

Back in Vancouver, early Sunday morning: My phone rings. It is Sarah Hambley, our director for the United Kingdom. Calmly she says, "Paul, we have two on the bottom."

The raid on Reykjavík had been a success. Rod and David had brought the Icelandic whaling industry to its knees and then kicked it in the teeth. The damage to the ships was later estimated at $2.8 million, to add to the $1.8 million of damage to the plant. The Hvalur of Hvalfjordur whaling company received a reprimand to their pirate whaling activities which has cost them $4.6 million, in addition to canceling their insurance, and increasing their future security costs. The destruction of the refrigeration unit spoiled the stockpile of whale meat. The Japanese were not happy to discover that the Icelanders had refrozen the thawed meat and were attempting to sell it.

The news of the raid on Reykjavík was greeted enthusiastically throughout most of the world. Of course, we had our critics. The ever dependable Greenpeace crowd condemned the act as terroristic, foolish, simplistic . . . *ad nauseum*. I understand their position. After all, there are more anti-whalers employed in the world than there are whalers; and shucks, actually ending whaling might lead to, *shudder*, no more work for anti-whalers. One has to feel sorry for all the Greenpeace Fuller Brush men who would suffer. They have a good thing going—hundreds of salesmen knocking on doors throughout North America, peddling eco-business for 35% of the take. I say, throw the bums out. A more realistic reaction came from Dr. Roger Payne, one of the world's leading whale researchers. Speaking a week after the incident, Dr. Payne said, "I have given up thinking it (whaling) can be handled through international agreements. These whaling nations are willing to cheat, lie, use the name of science—whatever is necessary. They're completely unethical."

Another positive result of Sea Shepherd activities is that people have been aroused from their complacency and apathy over whaling. Most people thought whaling was a thing of the past. After all, we have a moratorium in effect. Our actions shook the world awake on this issue and delivered a message: Whaling continues despite international regulations. The whaling nations Iceland, Norway, South Korea, Japan, and the Soviet Union are in contempt of international regulations.

Norway responded to the raid in Iceland by throwing a fit of para-noia. Believing that Sea Shepherd hit squads were poised for attack, the country increased their security budget, thus increasing their costs and cutting into illegal whaling profits. The security won't help. When the first opportunity arises, the whaling ships of Norway will be converted to submersibles by Sea Shepherd agents.

Rod has returned to the US. David is back in merry old England. Iceland has issued warrants for their arrest through Interpol but extra-dition is not possible due to the illegality of Iceland's whaling operation. I am being investigated by Canadian authorities for possible conspiracy charges, but I'm not losing any sleep over the noise from Ottawa. Our legal ass is covered.

We have important things to do, including further enforcement of international regulations against offending whaling nations. We are also preparing an expedition to the North Pacific in the summer of 1987 to confront the drift-net fishermen of Japan, Korea and Taiwan. Each summer, they send about 2000 ships to the North Pacific to set monofilament nets that range from 8 to 35 miles in length. The incidental kills in these nets include approximately 150,000 marine mammals and one to two million sea birds each year; plus they have a severe impact on populations of salmon, billfish, squid and other finny types.

Editor's update: Through the above and subsequent actions, Sea Shepherd essentially killed the Icelandic whaling industry. Unfortunately, however, Icelandic whalers hope to restart whaling operations soon. If they do, we can expect more daring Sea Shepherd exploits at their expense.

TORA! TORA! TORA!
November 1990
by Captain Paul Watson

Editor's note: On 13 August 1990, Paul Watson and his crew of 23 on the Sea Shepherd II *rammed two Japanese drift-net fishing boats and chased the fleet of six out of the North Pacific fishing grounds. Here the Captain tells the story.*

On December 7, 1941, the Imperial Japanese First Naval Air fleet launched a surprise attack against the US Naval base at Pearl Harbor on the Hawaiian island of Oahu.

As the Japanese planes swooped in low, their wing commander gave his orders. The Japanese words "tora, tora, tora" crackled through the cockpits of the torpedo bombers.

"Attack, attack, attack." Such was the battle cry of a people who had mastered the martial strategies of Asia. The attack was swift, surprising, ruthless, and effective.

As an ecological strategist, I have faced the Japanese as adversaries on numerous occasions. For this reason, I have studied Japanese martial strategy, especially the classic work entitled *A Book of Five Rings* written by Miyamoto Musashi in 1648. Musashi advocated the "twofold way of pen and sword," which I interpret to mean that one's actions must be both effective and educational.

In March 1982, the Sea Shepherd Conservation Society successfully negotiated a halt to the slaughter of dolphins at Iki Island in Japan. Contributing to this success was our ability to quote Musashi and talk to the Japanese fishermen in a language they could understand—the language of no compromise confrontation.

During our discussion, a fisherman asked me, "What is of more value, the life of a dolphin or the life of a human?"

I answered that, in my opinion, the life of a dolphin was equal in value to the life of a human.

The fisherman then asked, "If a Japanese fisherman and a dolphin were both caught in a net and you could save the life of one, which would you save?"

All the fishermen in the room smirked. They had me pegged a liberal and felt confident that I would say that I would save the fisherman, thus making a mockery of my declaration that humans and dolphins are equal.

I looked about the room and smiled. "I did not come to Japan to save fishermen; I am here to save dolphins."

They were surprised but not shocked by my answer. All the fishermen treated me with respect thereafter.

Why? Because the Japanese understand duty and responsibility. Saving dolphins was both my chosen duty and my responsibility.

Sea Shepherd had already established a reputation in Japan as the "Samurai protector of whales." This came in an editorial that appeared in the Tokyo daily *Asahi Shimbun* in July 1979, a few days after we rammed and disabled a Japanese owned pirate whaler, the *Sierra*, off the coast of Portugal.

That incident ended the career of the most notorious outlaw whaler. In February of 1980, we had the *Sierra* sunk in Lisbon harbor. A few months later, in April, our agents sunk two outlaw Spanish registered whalers, the *Isba I* and the *Isba II*, in Vigo Harbor in northern Spain.

We then gave attention to two other Japanese pirate whalers, the *Susan* and the *Theresa*. Given the controversy of the *Sierra*, and the fact that the *Susan* and the *Theresa* were owned by the same Japanese interests, South Africa, which had just publicly denounced whaling, did not want the stigma of harboring illegal whaling ships. The South African Navy confiscated and sunk the *Susan* and *Theresa* for target practise after we publicly appealed to them to do so, in 1980.

The last of the Atlantic pirate whalers, the *Astrid* was shut down after I sent an agent to the Spanish Canary Islands with a reward offer of 25,000 US dollars to any person who would sink her. The owners saw the writing on the wall and voluntarily retired the whaler.

Because of these actions many have labeled us pirates ourselves. Yet we have never been convicted of a criminal charge, and we have never caused injury or death to a human. Nor have we attempted to avoid charges. On the contrary, we have always invited our enemies to continue the fight in the courts. Most times they have refused and the few times they complied, they lost.

Vigilante buccaneers we may well be, but we are policing the seas where no policing authority exists. We are protecting whales, dolphins, seals, birds, and fish by enforcing existing regulations, treaties and laws that heretofore have had no enforcement.

In November 1986, when two Sea Shepherd agents, Rod Coronado and David Howitt, attacked the Icelandic whaling industry, they were enforcing the law. The International Whaling Commission (IWC) had banned commercial whaling, yet Iceland continued to whale without a permit. We did not wish to debate the issue of legality with the Icelanders. We acted instead. Coronado and Howitt destroyed the whaling station and scuttled half the Icelandic whaling fleet.

Iceland refused to press charges. I traveled to Reykjavik to insist that they press charges. They refused and deported me without a hearing. The only legal case to result from the incident is my suit against Iceland for illegal deportation.

Sea Shepherd campaigns have protected many other species as well. In March of 1983, the crew of the *Sea Shepherd II* were arrested under the Canadian Seal Protection Regulations, an Orwellian set of rules which actually protected the sealing industry. The only way to challenge these unjust rules was to break them. We did and at the same time we chased the sealing fleet out of the nursery grounds of the Harp Seals. We beat the charges and in the process helped the Supreme Court of Canada in its decision to dismiss the Seal Protection Act as unconstitutional.

In the years since, we have intervened against the Danish Faeroese fishermen in the North Atlantic to save the Pilot Whales they kill for sport. We have shut down seal hunts in Scotland, England and Ireland. We have confronted Central American tuna seiners off the coast of Costa Rica in an effort to rescue dolphins.

In 1987, we launched our first campaign to expose drift-net operations in the North Pacific. Our ship the *Divine Wind* voyaged along the Aleutian chain documenting the damage of the drift nets and ghost nets (abandoned nets). We helped convince Canada to abandon plans to build a drift-net industry.

For new supporters who do not know what drift nets are, I will briefly explain. Drift nets are to the Pacific Ocean what clearcuts are to the Amazon Rainforest or the Pacific Northwest Temperate Rainforest. Drift-netting is strip-mine fishing.

From May until late October, some 1800 ships each set a net measuring from 10 to 40 miles in length! These monofilament nylon gill nets drift freely on the surface of the sea, hanging like curtains of death to a depth of 26 or 34 feet. Each night, the combined fleet sets 28,000 to 35,000 miles of nets. The nets radiate across the breadth of the North Pacific like fences marking off property. The nets are efficient. Few squid and fish escape the perilous clutches of the nylon. Whales and dolphins, seals and sea lions, sea turtles, and sea birds are routinely entangled. The death is an agonizing ordeal of strangulation and suffocation.

Drift nets take an annual incidental kill of more than one million sea birds and a quarter of a million marine mammals, plus hundreds of millions of fish and squid. A few short years ago, the North Pacific fairly teemed with dolphins, turtles, fur seals, sea lions, dozens of species of birds and uncountable schools of fish. Today it is a biological wasteland.

The Japanese say their nets are taking fewer incidental kills now than a few years ago. This is true, but the reason the kills are down is simply that there are now fewer animals to kill.

For many years, governments and environmental groups have talked about the problem. Nobody actually did anything about it. Sick of talk, the Sea Shepherd Conservation Society decided to take action.

The *Sea Shepherd II* moved to Seattle, Washington, in September 1989 to prepare for an expedition to intercept the Japanese North Pacific drift net fleet. We set our departure date for June 1990. Overhauls and refitting were completed by May to meet the targeted date.

We were unable to leave Seattle. One of our crew was a paid infiltrator working, we believe, for the Japanese fishing industry. He successfully sabotaged our engine by pouring crushed glass into our oil, destroying our turbo-charger, and destroying electrical motors. Although we discovered the damage and identified the saboteur, we faced extensive repairs.

The saboteur fled to Britain. We asked Scotland Yard to track him down and investigate the incident. However, the damage was done and we were hardly in a position to cry foul. After all, we had already been responsible for destroying six whaling ships ourselves. The enemy had succeeded in striking a blow—it was as simple as that. We were down, but not for long.

We immediately set to work to repair the damage. Thanks to an appeal to Sea Shepherd Society members, funds were raised to purchase a replacement turbo-charger.

The *Sea Shepherd II* was prepared for departure again on August 5. We left Seattle and stopped briefly in Port Angeles on the Olympic Peninsula. Port Angeles resident and Sea Shepherd veteran David Howitt stopped by to visit us. He could not bring himself to leave. The ship departed with David on board. He had left his job and an understanding wife on the spur of the moment. We needed him and he knew it and that was reason enough to return to the eco-battles. He took the position of 1st Engineer.

It was with confidence that I took the helm of our ship and headed out the Strait of Juan de Fuca for the open Pacific beyond. I had a good crew, including many veterans.

Myra Finkelstein was 2nd Engineer. A graduate zoologist, Myra had worked for weeks in the bowels of the engine room to repair the damage to the engine. She was a veteran of the 1987 drift-net campaign and the 1989 tuna dolphin campaign. In addition she had been a leader of the Friends of the Wolf campaign in northern British Columbia where she had parachuted into the frigid and remote wilderness to interfere with a government sponsored wolf kill.

Sea Shepherd Director Peter Brown was on board with the camera gear to document the voyage. Peter was also helmsman and my deputy coordinator for the expedition.

Marc Gaede, who had sailed with us a year ago on the campaign off the coast of Costa Rica, returned as our photographer. Trevor Van Der Gulik, my nephew, a lad of only 15 from Toronto, Canada, became—by virtue of his skills—our 3rd Engineer. Trevor had helped to deliver the *Sea Shepherd* from Holland to Florida in 1989.

Also sailing with us this summer was Robert Hunter. Bob and I had both been founders of Greenpeace and he had been the first President of the Greenpeace Foundation. Bob had been the dynamic force behind the organization and ultimate success of Greenpeace. Like myself, he had been forced out of Greenpeace by the marauding bureaucrats who in the late 1970s ousted the original activists and replaced us with fund-raisers and public relations people.

With Bob on board, I felt a little of the old spirit which got us moving in the early 70s. We had no doubts: we would find the drift-net fleets.

Five days out to sea, we saw a military ship on the horizon, moving rapidly toward us. We identified her as a large Soviet frigate. The frigate hailed us and asked us what we were about. I replied that we were searching for the Japanese drift-net fleet and asked if they had seen any Japanese fishing vessels.

The Russians said they thought the Japanese were a few days to the west. Then, surprisingly, the Soviet officer, who spoke impeccable English, said, "Good luck, it is a noble cause that you follow. We are with you in spirit."

Eco-glasnost? Only a few years ago we battled the Russian whalers. In 1975 Bob Hunter and I had survived a Russian harpoon fired over our heads by a Soviet whaler we had confronted. In 1981, we had invaded Siberia to capture evidence on illegal whaling by the

Russians. We had narrowly escaped capture. Now, here we were being hailed by the Soviets with a statement of support. We have indeed made progress.

In fact, the Soviets were allies in more than just words. On 29 May 1990, the Russians had seized a fleet of North Korean fishing boats with drift nets in Soviet waters. Japan was diplomatically embarrassed when it was discovered that the 140 supposedly North Korean fishermen in Soviet custody were in fact Japanese.

On the eighth day out from Seattle, I put the *Sea Shepherd II* on a course of due west and decided not to correct the drift. I felt that the drift would take us to the outlaws. Slowly we began to drift north of the course line. Forty-eight hours later, my intuition proved itself right. The sea herself had taken us directly to a drift-net fleet.

At 2030 Hours on August 12, we sailed into the midst of six Japanese drift netters. The fleet had just completed laying their nets—more than 200 miles of net in the water. The Japanese ships were each about 200 feet long, equal in size to our own.

As we approached, the Japanese fishermen warned us off, angrily telling us to avoid their nets. Our ship is a large 657 ton North Atlantic trawler with an ice strengthened bow and a fully enclosed protected prop. We were able to cruise harmlessly over the lines of floating nets. We made close runs on the vessels to inspect them closely.

With darkness rapidly closing in, we decided to wait until morning before taking action against the ships. The Japanese vessels had shut down for the night. They drifted quietly. We waited out the night with them.

An hour before dawn they began to move. We moved with them. For three hours, we filmed the hauling in of mile after mile of net from the vessel *Shunyo Maru #8*. We watched the catch of two-foot-long squids being hauled into the boat along with incidental kills of sharks, sea birds and dolphins. The catching of the sea birds violated the Convention for the Protection of Migratory Birds, a treaty signed between the US and Japan in 1972. The nets impact more than 22 species of birds, 13 of which are protected by the treaty. It was to enforce this treaty that our ship and crew had made this voyage.

The fishing boats were brilliantly illuminated and the work on the deck could be adequately filmed. As the power blocks pulled in the nets, the bodies of squid, fish and birds fell from the nets to the deck or back into the sea.

We had the evidence we needed. We had seen the bodies of protected species in the net. For the next step we needed more light. It was painful to continue watching but it was imperative that we wait for dawn and the light we needed to properly film events.

At 0540 Hours, there was enough light. We prepared the deck and the engine room for confrontation. We positioned our cameramen and photographers. I took the wheel. We brought the engine up to full power and charged across the swells toward the *Shunyo Maru #8* whose crew was still hauling in nets. Our objective was to destroy the net retrieval gear. To do so, we had to hit her on an angle on her port mid-side.

We sounded a blast on our horn to warn the Japanese crew that we were coming in. I piloted the *Sea Shepherd II* into position. We struck where intended. The ships ground their hulls together in a fountain of sparks amidst a screeching cacophony of tearing and crushing steel. The net was severed, the power blocks smashed. We broke away as the Japanese stood dumbfounded on their decks.

One fisherman, however, hurled his knife at photographer Marc Gaede. The knife missed Marc and hit the sea. The same fisherman grabbed a second knife and sent it flying at cameraman Peter Brown. Peter's camera followed it as it came toward the lens. It fell at his feet.

As we pulled away, I looked with satisfaction on the damage we had inflicted. One ship down for the season. On board our own ship, a damage control party reported back that we had suffered minimal injury. The Japanese ships were no match for our steel reinforced hull.

We immediately targeted a second ship, the *Ryoun Maru #6*. The Japanese were attempting to cut a large shark out of the net. Looking up, they saw us bearing down at full speed upon them. Eyes wide, they ran for the far deck.

We struck where intended. Again to the roaring crescendo of tortured metal, the power blocks and gear were crushed; the deck and gunnels buckled. The net was severed.

We broke off and immediately set out for the third ship. By now, the Japanese realized what was happening. The first and second ships had been successfully Pearl Harbored. The third was not to be surprised. As we approached, she dropped her net and fled. We pursued.

We then turned and targeted a fourth ship. She also fled, dropping her net in panic. We stopped and pulled up alongside the radio beacon marking the abandoned net. We confiscated the beacon. We then grappled the net, secured a ton of weight to one end and dropped it, sending the killer net to the bottom, two miles beneath us. We watched the cork line drop beneath the surface, the floats disappearing in lines radiating out from our ship toward the horizon.

On the bottom the net would be rendered harmless. Small benthic creatures would literally cement it to the ocean floor over a short period of time.

We cleaned up the remaining nets and then returned to the chase. For the next twenty hours, we chased the six ships completely out of the fishing area.

The next morning, we could look at what we had achieved with pleasure. Two ships completely disabled from further fishing, a million dollars worth of net sunk and destroyed and all six ships prevented from continued fishing and running scared.

We had delivered our message to the Japanese fishing industry. Our tactics had been both effective and educational. Effective in that we directly saved lives by shutting down a fleet, and educational in that we informed the Japanese fishing industry that their greed will no longer be tolerated.

Our ship was only slightly damaged. Most importantly, there were no injuries on any of the ships involved.

I turned the bow of our ship southward to Honolulu to deliver the documentation to the media and to begin again the tedious task of fund-raising which will allow us to mount further attacks against these mindless thugs slaughtering our oceans.

As we headed south, we stopped repeatedly to retrieve drifting remnants of nets. In one we found 54 rotting fish. In another a large dead mahi-mahi. In another a dead albatross. These "ghost nets" present an additional problem for life in the sea. Each day the large fleets lose an average of six miles of net. At present an estimated 10,000 plus miles of ghost nets are floating the seas. These non-biodegradable nets kill millions of fish and sea creatures each year. Decaying fish attract more fish and birds . . . a vicious cycle of death and waste ensues.

Arriving in Honolulu, we berthed at pier eleven, ironically just in front of two fishery patrol vessels, one from Japan, the other from Taiwan. The crew of each scowled at us.

We were prepared for the Japanese to attempt to lay charges against us or failing that to publicly denounce us. Instead, they refused to even recognize that an incident took place.

We contacted the Japanese Consulate and declared that we had attacked their ships and had destroyed Japanese property. We informed the Consulate that we were ready to contest charges, be they in the International Court at the Hague or in Tokyo itself. The Consulate told us he had no idea what we were talking about.

The Japanese realize they have nothing to gain by taking us to court and much to lose. Which means that we must return to the oceans and must escalate the battle.

The Taiwanese drift netters are beginning to move into the Caribbean Sea. We must head them off. We must continue to confront the Japanese fleets, and we must take on the Koreans.

Each net we sink will cost the industry a million dollars. Each vessel we damage will buy time for the sea animals. Each confrontation we mount will embarrass the drift-net industry.

This summer, we won a battle. However, the war to end high seas drift-netting continues.

The Japanese, Taiwanese, and Korean drift-net fleets can be driven from the oceans. We need only the will, the courage, and the financial support to do so.

Editor's update: Sea Shepherd is seeking crew for upcoming campaigns. Crew members are needed for both the Sea Shepherd II *and the Society's new craft, the* Edward Abbey. *Especially needed are experienced navigators, engineers, mechanics, welders, electricians, cooks and medics. If interested, write for a crew application. To help end drift-netting, contribute to Sea Shepherd Conservation Society, POB 7000-S, Redondo Beach, CA 90277.*

CHAPTER 2

Land Use and Conflicts

THE FEDERAL LAND MANAGEMENT AGENCIES OF THIS COUNTRY—*the United States Forest Service, Bureau of Land Management, National Park Service, and Fish & Wildlife Service—were frequently the subject of attacks in EF! Journal. These agencies manage—nay, mismanage—vast acreages: Forest Service, 190 million acres; BLM, 340 million (almost half of it in Alaska); NPS, 90 million; and FWS, 90 million (mostly in Alaska). The Defense Department controls another 25 million acres, mostly in the West, and is still seeking more.*

None of these agencies has adequately protected the land; all are beholden to private exploitive interests. The Forest Service serves timber companies and ranchers. The BLM serves ranchers and miners. The Park Service serves concessionaires and motorized tourists. The Fish & Wildlife Service serves hunting and fishing interests (including the National Rifle Association). All these agencies allow, on at least some of their lands, off-road vehicle driving, trapping, mining, and other land abuses. The Defense Department, of course, serves its own exploitive ends, using countless natural areas across the West for bombing ranges and war games.

Not surprisingly, then, conservationists often find themselves at odds with these agencies, as the articles in this chapter show. However, conservationists generally favor continued federal control of these lands; we simply want them protected as Wilderness. Indeed, as Jamie Sayen explains in this chapter, in northern New England, environmentalists are working for federal acquisition of private timber lands. So our relationship with public land agencies has been somewhat ambivalent.

The threats discussed here remain at least as serious today as when the articles were written. The corporations and agencies are as errant in their behavior as ever, but they are facing increasing opposition from a growing grassroots conservation movement.

THE BLM

Samhain 1982
by Clive Kincaid

The Bureau of Land Management's wilderness inventory of 22 million acres of public land in Utah handed "Corporate America" a virtual *carte blanche* to the most scenic and mysterious landscape in North America.

This wild public land that was once yours has been "sold down the river" to Exxon, Gulf, AMAX, Phillips, Chevron, Getty, Kaiser, Texaco, Tenneco, Cotter, Plateau, and other industrial giants by the BLM's indefensible inventory decisions. The future of Utah wilderness could be forever crippled by this arrogant government deception. Why did it happen?

AN ANSWER: Thousands of pieces of corroborating evidence now point conclusively to what really occurred in Utah. *The BLM orchestrated a systematic prostitution of the wilderness inventory, basing its subjective determination of wilderness character on countless bits of extraneous non-wilderness data.* Wherever BLM managers were apprised of another resource value or private company interest that might conflict with a roadless area, either that area was re-defined in such a way as to eliminate the errant parcels or it was dropped entirely from further review. The BLM has defended its innumerable inconsistent boundary adjustments with the notion of purported flexibility or "gray areas" built into the inventory procedures themselves, and has spent thousands of man-hours developing detailed explanations to counter public challenges. As one Utah BLM staff professional explained privately, "The Manager's deliberate scheme is to bury the public record in so much bureaucratic bullshit that no one will ever figure it all out."

At this writing, at least 60 instances have been discovered where otherwise arbitrary and inexplicable BLM boundaries mysteriously coincide with the presence of documented resources. Potential conflicts now rest conveniently outside the roadless area and no significant conflict remains inside the roadless area—yet the true roadless area encompasses both.

No, there is no single paper trail evincing illegal actions on the part of the BLM. There is no "smoking gun." Yet the preponderance of evidence points to a deliberate systematic exclusion of wilderness lands.

Not unlike other types of legal construction, absenting the ability to prove literal *intent*, it may well be possible to prove *effect*. And there is one fatal flaw in the Utah inventory that comes close to proving both. The Utah BLM decided that the very government procedures that they bent so well in scores of cases were not "flexible" enough for their tawdry manipulations. There were a few large roadless areas so much in the public eye that the BLM could not safely play fast and loose with the inventory procedures. The Bureau couldn't bear not to clear away those unwanted troubles and maybe feather a few nests besides.

So the BLM in Utah asked Washington feds for an "exception" to the process. Not one of the other 10 western states needed "exceptional" treatment. Every other BLM office managed to work within the procedural framework imposed by government policy.

The State Director of the BLM in Utah wrote two memoranda to Washington, DC, which said, "We request that an exception be granted to adjust boundaries . . . due to the lack of outstanding characteristics in part of the unit. Each of these inventory units exhibit a high degree of character change . . . " The DC office made the allowance, admonishing the state office to take great care in utilizing this "variation from the general policy." BLM then proceeded to butcher seven large roadless areas, justifying an average reduction of 35,000 acres on the basis of this exception. In each case where BLM wielded this criminal "exception" scalpel, it simultaneously removed significant jeopardizing private interests.

WILD LANDS SLASHED: Mt. *Ellen* was a 156,000-acre area in the Henry Mountains. BLM field notes suggested that over 140,000 acres were roadless, but BLM only identified a 24,600-acre Wilderness Study Area (WSA). A major part of the deleted roadless area contains recoverable coal, and is controlled by AMAX Corporation (BLM was just beginning its coal suitability study). Public furor forced a reinstatement of 33,800 acres of the Blue Hills badlands; but BLM cited the new "exception" for the deletion of the remaining 55,000 acres (actually 80,000 acres—BLM never has cited accurate acreage figures). The boundaries of the now 54,480-acre Study Area coincide *precisely* with the geological formation bounding the known recoverable coal reserves. This parsimonious reinstatement eliminated 16,000 acres of the roadless area claimed by Schauss Exploration; 11,000 acres claimed (in May 1980, just six months prior to BLM's decision) by Exxon; and 2000 acres claimed by Homestake Mining. In the final BLM study area, only a few hundred acres with some 30-year-old non-corporate claims remained.

Mt. Pennell is the sister peak in the Henry Mountains and a 159,650-acre inventory unit. BLM could not acknowledge the wilderness character in Mt. Ellen without also acknowledging Mt. Pennell. This area contained the magnificent Swap Mesa adjacent to the Capitol Reef proposed wilderness, and has long been coveted by the National Park Service. So BLM capriciously inventoried one non-existent road, refused to "cherry-stem" another, and illegally divided the area—dismissing 70,000 roadless acres including Swap Mesa. Then BLM applied the new "exception" to delete the remaining 20,000 offending acres (actually over 30,000 acres) and reduced the true 130,000-acre roadless area to a 27,300-acre WSA. The final boundary approximated the geological formation containing the known strippable coal reserves. This administrative line eliminated 11,000 acres claimed by Plateau Resources; 23,000 acres claimed by Ranchers Exploration and Development Corporation; and 33,000 acres claimed by Exxon Corporation.

Fiddler Butte was a 101,310-acre area adjacent to NPS proposed wilderness on the Dirty Devil in Glen Canyon. Again illegally, and this time without even an offending road as an excuse, BLM divided the roadless area in two and dismissed the eastern 45,000 acres as non-wilderness. Of the 56,000 acres to the west, BLM identified a 27,000-acre Study Area and eliminated 20,000 acres based on the "exception." BLM removed from the western half 13,000 acres of Cotter Corporation claims, 3000 acres of Fischer-Watt claims, and 5000 acres of Buttes Resources claims. The entire eastern deletion resided within a geologic formation containing the hottest deposit of tar sands in Utah, called the "Desert Tar Sands Triangle."

Desolation Canyon was originally the largest BLM roadless area in the state (over 475,000 acres). The devious tricks used to fragment it included nicking off 82,000 acres by calling a pack-trail a road; identifying impassable boulder-strewn dry washes as roads; establishing a 40,000-acre roadless zone-of-influence around the magnificent Book Cliffs escarpment; and using the "exception" to eliminate 50,000 acres, including lands claimed by the BLM to be too flat and open and other lands claimed to be too rugged and steep to merit Wilderness designation. Along the edge of the roadless area was a Getty Corporation oil and gas field. The geological formation defining the potential for further hydrocarbon discovery (the Thompson-Jack's Canyon deposit) corresponded with BLM's special exception/character change/too steep-flat deletion.

The *Paria-Hackberry* roadless area was originally 196,431 acres. BLM identified 148,584 acres as roadless. But again that was too big an area to avoid trouble spots. BLM needed a 12,726-acre "exception." The area of the headwaters of the Paria River consists of slickrock/sandstone formations, and ridges and canyons with sparse pine forests eventually rising in 1000-foot cliff faces to the surrounding mesa tops thickly covered in pinyon and juniper. The forested mesa tops are an obvious character change. But why eliminate eight separate surrounding mesas from the roadless areas? An answer can be found in BLM's draft Kanab-Escalante grazing environmental impact statement, which shows a 100-percent coincidence between the "exceptional mesas" and mesas previously targeted by the same BLM office for chaining and seeding.

The *750,000-acre Kaiparowits* is an area conservation groups have successfully fought to protect for decades. Yet BLM identified there only two Wilderness Study Areas, and finally added a third after a storm of public protest. It is clear that King Coal caused the demise of the Plateau. From close review of the *Development of Coal Resources in Southern Utah* EIS emerges a clear picture of proposed coal development.

If one overlays the boundaries of all the Kaiparowits inventory units on this map, it is apparent that there is significant conflict with all 10 units. But BLM could not eliminate the entire Kaiparowits. To do so might discredit their wilderness inventory.

The largest unit, Fifty-Mile Mountain, had historically been protected by BLM for its recreational values. To make it a WSA, BLM would have to "lock up" some existing coal leases. But luckily none of these leases were actual proposed mining areas with mining plans. So Fifty-Mile Mountain was not a serious problem.

The second problem inventory unit was Mud Springs Canyon. These colorful badlands were adjacent to Kodachrome Basin State

Park, named by Melville Grosvenor on a National Geographic expedition in the unexplored region in the 1920s. BLM would have an
equally difficult time dropping Mud Springs Canyon. This roadless
area was 10 miles from the nearest proposed coal mining area. The
only actual conflict was with the proposed location of a new Denver &
Rio Grande railroad line to carry coal trains north to Sevier. Because
of the difficult grade, that rail would have to loop through the south-
east third of the Mud Springs Canyon unit. Well, Mud Springs
Canyon did become a WSA. According to BLM, 56,150 acres were
roadless—yet only 38,075 are under study. Listen to BLM: "The solitude and primitive recreation characteristics are not present on 18,065
acres in the southeastern portion of the inventory unit. . . ."

BLM conceded the wilderness values in Fifty-Mile Mountain and
in a castrated Mud Springs Canyon, once there were no longer
conflicts with proposed coal development. But the rest of the plateau
had to go so as not to jeopardize the future of King Coal.

BLATANT DECEPTION: What has emerged from a thorough
investigation of all of the types of information easily available to the
BLM but virtually invisible to the general public is a shockingly clear
picture of what must have taken place: a total manipulation of the
inventory to illegally protect all the major, and innumerable minor,
private interests. To be sure, coincidences do occur. But coincidence
repeated *ad nauseum* ceases to be coincidence. It becomes instead cor-
relative. It is doubly dubious when coincidence regularly occurs within
the realm of an "exception to the general policy"—indeed a delicate
exception that is ultimately explained away by the government as a
subjective interpretation not readily debatable by the public.

There is no debating a concrete fact such as a corporate leasehold.
And it is precisely such facts that this "special exception" *systemati-
cally*, rather than coincidentally, represents. This is the fatal flaw.
Exactly where BLM required the use of some vague "exception" to the
Bureau's policies and procedures, it exercised some of its most blatant
deception, allowing it to circumvent public accountability. This suggests a deliberate intent to prostitute the wilderness program in Utah.
As for effect, more than one million acres of your finest wilderness
have thus disappeared and are now in the hands of corporate America.

It is no wonder that Utah BLM State Directors have had unwavering
praise for the "high professional standards" of their subordinates. The petty gov-

ernment officials are expert prevaricators. They have put forward a masterful, and until now, extraordinarily successful deception. Utah wilderness be damned, as the Bureau's wilderness program marches inexorably forward to Secretarial approval in a hastily advanced September 1984 deadline.

The rest is up to you! It took six years to put Interior Secretary Albert Fall in prison for the Teapot Dome scandal. One wonders what will happen to those responsible for this bloody mess.

Editor's update: Unfortunately, not much has changed at the Utah BLM. It remains intransigently opposed to Wilderness. Indeed, the Southern Utah Wilderness Alliance (SUWA, POB 518, Cedar City, UT 84721) fall 1990 newsletter quoted State Director James Parker as saying, "When I'm asked why northern Utah has all the hazardous waste sites and southern Utah has all the wilderness, I reply that northern Utah had first choice."

Since the above article was written, BLM roadless areas have continued to be marred by mining companies, off-road vehicles, and ranchers. The BLM has recommended less than 2 million of its 22 million acres in Utah as Wilderness. In 1986 Earth First! released a proposal that would protect over 16 million acres in the Great Basin and Canyon Country of Utah as Wilderness. The Utah Wilderness Coalition, in which SUWA is a key player, is supporting a bill (HR 1500) introduced by Representative Wayne Owens (D-UT) that would protect over 5 million acres as Wilderness. Unfortunately, some mainstream Utah environmentalists have refused to support even this moderate bill, and are asking for less than 4 million acres of Wilderness. Congress will probably determine the fate of these lands within the next few years.

The only state BLM wilderness bill to have passed by the end of the 101st Congress is for Arizona. Some mainstream environmentalists are hailing the Arizona Wilderness Bill as a favorable precedent, even though it will only protect about 1 million acres of BLM land, as well as about 1.2 million acres of US Fish & Wildlife Service land. This bespeaks the low expectations environmentalists have for the BLM wilderness study process, and does not bode well for Utah.

A FGHANIZATION OF THE AMERICAN WEST
Brigid 1985
by Leon Czolgosz

In what critics are terming the "Afghanization of the American West," the United States Air Force and Navy appear to be escalating their efforts to turn large areas of several western states into playgrounds for the latest supersonic fighter-bombers and other high-tech military hardware.

The problem surfaced several years ago, when the Air Force announced its intention to create two "SOAs," or supersonic operations areas, in the Southwest. One of these, the so-called Reserve SOA, covers large portions of Catron County, New Mexico (one of the most sparsely-populated counties in the lower 48), as well as adjacent portions of Arizona. The area impacted consists largely of public lands, much of which is National Forest, and includes much of the nation's first designated Wilderness, the Gila. The second proposed SOA was in west Texas, in an equally-sparsely populated area, but one containing no federal lands. This area was termed the Valentine SOA.

The proposals generated almost 100% opposition among the populations of both areas. After a series of public hearings and an inadequate environmental impact statement (EIS), the Air Force announced it was proceeding with the Reserve SOA (though it did agree to restrict flights to above 15,000 feet and to somewhat reduce the total number of missions). The west Texas area is being designated an "MOA," or military operations area, a designation which officially means that only subsonic flights will occur. In practice, however, sonic booms occur frequently in MOAs, too. Alarmingly, the military can and does create MOAs at will, without even going through the motions of notifying the public in advance.

During the fight against the Reserve and Valentine SOAs, local residents got little more than platitudes from their elected political representatives. Catron County, population 2500, could be safely ignored in favor of Alamogordo, population 25,000, home of Holloman Air Force Base, from whence the supersonic missions are flown. The New Mexico Congressional delegation took care not to offend the Air Force, lest the state lose the dubious boost to the economy bestowed by the air base.

It now appears that the Reserve and Valentine proposals were but the tip of an iceberg. They were the opening wedge in the military's campaign to grab large portions of the public domain (and some private land, too). In April of 1984 it was suddenly disclosed that the Air Force had seized, without public input or legal process, some 89,000 acres of Bureau of Land Management lands in the Groom Range of Nevada, for addition to the already gigantic Nellis Air Force Range and Nevada Test Site. (A considerably larger chunk of overlapping airspace is currently designated as the Desert MOA.) The Groom Range, a BLM Wilderness Study Area which is immediately adjacent to the incomparable 1.5-million acre Desert National Wildlife Range (and should have been added to it), is now totally closed to public entry.

The Groom Range seizure generated a spate of critical media attention, especially in Nevada, where bad-mouthing the federal government is popular. Nevertheless, the Navy soon dropped another bombshell, proposing an extensive SOA centered on the Dixie Valley, near Fallon, home of the Fallon Naval Air Station. As if this weren't enough, the Air Force is proposing a Gandy SOA, a 2800 square-mile area straddling the Utah-Nevada border between Ely and Wendover (much of which will be over the Goshute Indian Reservation).

Military operations areas supposedly cannot be created or expanded without approval from the Federal Aviation Administration (FAA). However, sometimes the public does not learn of the expansion of an MOA until after the fact (as happened recently with the Desert MOA). Currently, critics of the militarization of the West worry about expansion at two existing MOAs—the Sells MOA in southern Arizona and the Mountain Home MOA in Idaho. Some fear that expansion is only the first step, and that these areas, too, will eventually become SOAs.

The sudden land grab has received only spotty regional media coverage. The lack of national media attention is alarming, given the magnitude of the scheme. According to Charles S. Watson Jr., director of the Nevada Outdoor Recreation Association (NORA) and one of the most active opponents of the militarization of the West, the SOA proposals, in totality, recall the "Continental Operations Range" (COR) proposed by the Department of Defense in 1974 but rejected then as too grandiose and politically unfeasible. But now, with the Reagan Administration's swollen military services' budgets, the Air

Force and Navy apparently feel that they need more space in which to play their war games and squander the taxpayers' money. So they have decided to implement the once-discredited COR, this time in piece-meal fashion and via the back door.

At present, the most public attention is focused on the Fallon SOA proposal. The Fallon Naval Air Station has been around for a long time, and the Dixie Valley has been part of an MOA. However, not until 1982 did the Navy decide to upgrade the small facility into one of their major aviation training centers. Last year the Navy announced their proposal to designate an area of 5600 square miles as the Fallon SOA. Later it was disclosed that SOA designation was merely the first step: the Navy, it seems, is also seeking the withdrawal of 181,000 acres of public lands, a process which, if successful, will make the lands just another military base. The affected area includes, in addition to the Dixie Valley, portions of the Stillwater Mountains, including 23,000 acres of BLM WSAs (Wilderness Study Areas). The Stillwaters are important wildlife habitat; 45 Desert Bighorn Sheep were recently released there, and the BLM hopes to expand the herd further.

The Navy has *already* established four small, automated electronic sites within BLM WSAs—Desatoya Mountains WSA, Clan Alpine Mountains WSA (near the summit of Augusta Peak), Stillwater Range WSA, and Job Peak WSA. These sites are part of what the Navy calls the "Tactical Aircrew Combat Training System," or TACTS, which is supposed to monitor aircraft during training exercises. In addition to on-base facilities, TACTS will ultimately include 23 remote sites. Two of these will be large "Master Relay Stations," requiring road access. One of these is already operational (on Fairview Peak). The second is to be built on New Pass Peak, and will require upgrading an existing primitive road. The remaining 21 sites (ten are already either installed or being installed) involve remote solar powered transponder units put in place by helicopter. The Navy plans eventually to place at least two of these units in the Toiyabe National Forest, south of Austin.

All these developments are scheduled to take place regardless of the outcome of the land withdrawal proposal. It seems likely that if the Navy actually gains title to the land, future development will be on a much greater scale. The Navy maintains that a land withdrawal will not affect existing uses of the area, and that they do not plan to close the area to public access. (How many military bases do you know of that allow free public access?)

The Navy has just finished a draft EIS on the Fallon SOA proposal. The Navy will prepare a separate EIS on the withdrawal proposal.

The most vocal opponents of the SOA proposal are the Dixie Valley's 60-odd residents, mostly ranchers and retirees. They have already been subjected to over 200 sonic booms, even though the area at present is officially only an MOA.

Another group that has already had problems with Naval aviation in the Fallon area consists of civilian pilots. One of them, Dr. Richard Bargen, recently shut down his Morning Star Flying Doctor Service, saying that continued flying in the area was too risky. Bargen has been the medical link to the outside world for scores of patients from isolated ranches, hamlets and mining camps for the past four years.

Bargen and three others started a lawsuit against the Navy over the SOA proposal in 1983. After the suit was filed, the FAA suspended Bargen's pilot's license for 90 days for allegedly flying too close to a Navy radar installation, a charge he says is groundless.

Most of the Dixie Valley residents seem willing to be bought out by the Navy, although the military has made no move to do this yet. This seems to be the approach favored by Nevada's senators, Chic Hecht and Paul Laxalt. NORA's Charles Watson, however, warns that removing the residents would pave the way for the area to become the "Northern Nevada Test Site."

Curiously, the reaction of Nevada politicos, at both the state and federal level, has been mild, considering their usual anti-federal paranoia. The reaction of State Senator Alan Glover (D–Carson) is typical. He said that there isn't much the state can do about the situation: "As long as 86% of our land is controlled by the federal government, this problem is never going to go away." Clearly, in the land of the "Sagebrush Rebellion" the military establishment is a less popular target than the BLM and Forest Service.

In their Fallon proposal, the Navy ignores existing data on the effects of sonic booms. Studies of supersonic test flights taken in the 1960s to determine the impacts of the proposed American SST on people and structures on the ground found that pressures of 1.4 to 1.7 pounds per square foot from sonic booms were "intolerable" to most people. Yet the Navy is *admitting* that average pressures of 3.9 lbs./sq. ft.

will result from so-called "carpet" sonic booms, and that there will be occasional pressures up to 10.6 lbs./sq. ft. Pressures of 6 lbs./sq. ft. will crack plaster and break windows, and pressures of 10 lbs./sq. ft. can cause severe physical trauma, presumably for wildlife as well as people.

The situation regarding the Gandy SOA along the Utah/Nevada border is less clear at the moment. Presumably, the Air Force will do an EIS . The Gandy SOA will impact several BLM WSAs, and possibly several Forest Service RARE II areas.

In Arizona, as in Nevada, the military has already started supersonic operations despite the fact that the Sells area is not officially designated a SOA. Much of the Sells MOA lies over the Papago Reservation. The impacts of sonic booms over the Papago Reservation have been even more severe than those over Nevada. According to Watson, hundreds of windows have been broken and automobiles have reportedly been moved several feet from sonic boom pressures. Last summer, Watson says, a Papago Indian was permanently blinded when his horse bolted and trampled him after being startled by a sonic boom.

The Sells MOA is used by planes flying from Davis–Monthan Air Force Base in Tucson and Luke AFB near Phoenix, and by Marine aircraft flying from Yuma. Luke Air Force Base has overall authority for managing the MOA. When contacted, the Public Information Office at Luke stated that there were no plans to make the Sells MOA an SOA. However, they said that the Air Force was doing a draft EIS for the Sells MOA, because of expanded operations.

Persons concerned about the military takeover of the West should ask for information from Charles S. Watson, Nevada Outdoor Recreation Association, POB 1245, Carson City, NV 89702. They would also do well to write their senators and representatives to protest expanded military operations in the West.

Epilogue: As of late 1988, the militarization described above seems to have intensified, though as with most things military, secrecy is such as to preclude an accurate assessment of recent developments. The following are a few events and trends that indicate a worsening of the problem:

Dixie Valley residents have all departed. The Navy is burning the empty houses, and offering cash compensation—"ten cents on the dollar," according to one former resident.

The military is now threatening to expand Ft. Irwin in the

California desert. If the military succeeds, it will damage wild lands now held by the BLM.

Overflights continue to be a problem throughout the West, and even in some areas eastward. The Boundary Waters area of Minnesota, for example, has been called the "Snoopy MOA."

Pilots routinely violate what limited restrictions have been placed on them. For instance, planes in the Gila National Forest (Reserve SOA) frequently buzz at tree-top level, despite a 15,000 foot restriction.

In July 1988, 2 horseback riders were thrown to the ground in the Mt. Hood Wilderness of Oregon when their horses bolted as two air National Guard jets flew low over them. The couple suffered broken bones and lacerations. The military denied that the incident involved their jets.

Editor's update: The militarization of the West has continued since Leon wrote this article and epilogue. The Defense Department has attempted to expand its hegemony by millions of acres, most of it in the West but some in Maine and elsewhere east of the Mississippi. As of early 1991, the military appears to have retreated from its latest and biggest land grab effort, but the retreat may only be a way to quiet the intense opposition it faces from environmentalists and local citizens. In effect, the military canceled plans to expand many of its landholdings, but left a loophole whereby base commanders can be exempted from the cancellations if special circumstances require expansion.

ROAD FRENZY
Litha 1985
by Howie Wolke

Two hundred years ago, at least a hundred thousand Grizzly Bears roamed the forests, tundras, prairies, mountains and plains of what is now the western United States from the Pacific Ocean to the Mississippi River.

By the end of the 1800s, the Grizzly had all but disappeared from the Great Plains. The last reported Grizzly sighting (and killing) in Texas was in 1890; in North Dakota 1897. In California, the Grizzly was last seen in 1924. By 1950, the great bear was restricted in range to the high and remote wilds of Colorado, Wyoming, Idaho, Montana and northeastern Washington. Today, a mere 600–800 bears remain, dwindling still, predominantly in the Greater Yellowstone and Northern Continental Divide Ecosystems (the latter includes Glacier National Park and the adjacent Bob Marshall country), with only a handful of the bears in the mountains of north-central Idaho and extreme northwestern Montana.

The demise of the Grizzly in the lower 48 states has coincided—by no accident—with the demise of the American wilderness. The Grizzly is the quintessential wilderness species; for the most part, it cannot coexist with intensive agriculture, forestry, industrialization, or with civilization in general. Moreover, it is not the only species dependent upon a predominantly wilderness environment. Gray Wolves, Mountain Lions, Lynx, Black Bear, Bison, Elk, Bighorn Sheep, Jaguars, Cooper's Hawks, Pileated Woodpeckers, and scores of other native species all either require or thrive most in an undisturbed environment. Each road, clearcut, oil rig, uranium mine, subdivision, ski resort, or range "improvement" puts additional pressure on wild animals, threatening some with local or regional extinction, and effectively reducing the populations, and thus limiting the genetic and evolutionary possibilities, of nearly all indigenous species. Each new road built through wildlife habitat on our public lands further reduces the biological diversity—often in many ways we cannot even begin to understand—and therefore the stability and the general health of a portion of the planet.

The United States Forest Service, custodian of roughly 190 million acres of public lands, is on a road-building binge. Amidst widespread charges of scandal and conspiracy, the green-shirted bureaucrats, goose-stepping to the tune of multiple use, calmly go about their business of destroying the remaining unprotected American wilderness, largely by means of a *massive, publicly financed road-building program*. Forest Service road-building probably poses the greatest single threat to the natural environment of the United States of America today.

Forest roads are built for a variety of purposes: to gain access to timber stands, recreational sites, mines or drilling operations; to provide additional recreational access to designated Wilderness Areas (honest!); to eliminate roadless areas from Wilderness consideration; and to meet road mileage quotas and budgetary goals handed down from the Chief to his Regional Foresters, from Regional Foresters to Forest Supervisors, and from Supervisors to District Rangers. Most forest roads are built primarily for timber access.

Although some conservationists believe the Forest Service road-building binge to be largely the result of a massive Reagan Administration conspiracy, it is actually the result of three-quarters of a century of bureaucratic growth. It is also the inevitable result of a mind-boggling array of complex laws and regulations, a flawed intra-agency promotion policy, a militaristic style and structure within the agency, an almost religious belief in the anthropocentric idea of "multiple use," decades of overcutting the most accessible and productive forest timber stands, and the generally (there are exceptions!) low quality individuals who choose to find security and stability in a government career.

Certainly, Reagan Administration anti-environmentalism has worsened a bad situation. But the Forest Service road-building mania has been accelerating for some 50 years, and the reasons are as complex as the bureaucracy itself. The *destruction* of wildlife habitat, watersheds, and quality recreational opportunities is the common thread that binds together the Forest Service road-building program of past, present, and (unless we halt it) future.

As *Earth First!* has previously reported, the Freddies are planning to build approximately 33,000 miles of roads between 1985 and 1999 in Montana, Idaho, Wyoming, Utah, Nevada, Colorado, Arizona and New Mexico Roadless Areas. The figure for Washington and Oregon alone is roughly 30,000 miles!

Nationally, the agency is planning to crisscross our remaining roadless areas with well over 75,000 miles of new roads (three times Earth's circumference) during the next 15 years. The ecological ramifications of this program will be devastating.

On the average, each mile of Forest road constructed obliterates about 5 acres of natural habitat. Thus, the Forest Service plans to remove from its productive base approximately 375,000 acres of land during the next 15 years just from inventoried Roadless Areas. Imagine the socio-political brouhaha if a federal agency or corporation proposed a 375,000 acre strip mine! The political turkey would be shot dead in its tracks.

Of course, thus far we've only been looking at plans for inventoried Roadless Areas. By definition (due to the Wilderness Act's general requirement that a Wilderness be at least 5000 acres in size), roadless areas under 5000 acres are not included in these figures. In fact, essentially every new Forest road cuts through previously unroaded areas, however small. Often the value of even a small piece of roadless wildlife habitat, if it supplies critical escape cover, important food or water sources, or valuable breeding or birthing areas, is extremely high. Forest Service plans to further road and degrade these areas (about 100,000,000 acres of the National Forests are now classified as "roaded") will also have severe ecological consequences.

The specific impacts of Forest roads on the natural environment are complex and variable, but virtually always negative. In addition to driving sensitive "wilderness species" out of an area and obliterating productive forest and rangelands, Forest roads disturb soils and cause increased erosion and stream siltation, thus raising water temperature, altering the physical composition of the stream bed, and reducing the dissolved oxygen. The overall water quality and productivity of rivers and streams is often greatly reduced.

Forest roads also make more of the National Forest vulnerable to littering, off-road-vehicle abuse, man-caused fire, and poaching. Access also causes crowding of adjacent backcountry and Wilderness Areas; and each roadless area lost ultimately represents additional dispersed recreational pressure on remaining roadless areas and designated Wilderness units. Already, much of the National Wilderness Preservation System is suffering from overuse, often resulting in water pollution, erosion, local soil compaction, reduction in wildlife populations, and reduced opportunity for solitude. As more roadless areas are "developed," the quality of our remaining wilderness lands, designated and de facto, will decrease.

Furthermore, every constructed road reduces the political opportunity for Wilderness designation or administrative roadless management for adjacent lands, thus rendering large acreages of wild country vulnerable to various forms of multiple abuse, such as logging, mining, overgrazing, and off-road vehicles. (In 1980, approximately 66% of the National Forest System was open to off-road vehicle use.) Simply stated, FS road-building transforms the healthy natural forest into a scarred, eroding, artificially simplified industrial production zone.

In 1980, the Carter Administration Forest Service built 10,485 miles of road in our National Forests. Most of these roads (9562 miles) were built by timber purchasers, with the actual cost of the road being subtracted from the price the purchaser paid for the standing timber, thus resulting in timber companies paying artificially low prices for federal timber. In this way (known as the timber "Purchaser Credit Program"), the American taxpayer directly subsidizes thousands of miles of timber road construction each year, presenting the timber industry with a massive gift of federal timber. Many, if not most, of the timber sales in western National Forests would be uneconomical if timber companies had to pay for these logging roads. This is especially true in the high altitude slow-growing forests in the Rockies, where much of the remaining timber inventory is in rugged, roadless terrain, requiring extremely high financial investment (subsidies) for road access. The taxpayer-subsidized roads are a major reason for the now widely publicized issue of "below cost timber sales."

In 1980, taking into account all funding sources (including appropriated funds from the Federal Treasury and Purchaser Credit dollars subtracted from the stumpage price of timber), the Forest Service road-building program cost the American taxpayers approximately 500 million dollars!

During the Reagan Administration years, the percentage of road construction directly financed by the Federal Treasury has increased dramatically. In 1980, the vast majority of new road mileage was financed via the timber Purchaser Credit Program (9562 out of 10,485 total miles). But in fiscal year 1983, the Freddies built 7748.9 miles of road, with 5732.8 miles being financed by the Purchaser Credit Program, and a whopping 2016.1 miles directly financed by Congressionally appropriated funds. (More appropriated fund road miles—344.2—were built in Montana than in any other state.) The increase in the percentage of roads built via appropriated funds under the Reagan Administration is evidence of an actual conspiracy to road the last roadless areas, eliminating them from Wilderness consideration, so that timber can be extracted in the future when economic conditions (presumably) improve.

Evidence that the Forest Service is intentionally destroying wild country abounds. In fact, the first priority for Region 1 (Montana, northern Idaho) under its "capital investment program" as stated in the Forest Service Manual is:

> . . . provide new road and bridge access to commercial timber stands in RARE II and other unroaded areas released or available for development . . . (FSM 7710.33-R-1 Supplement 1981)

Also in fiscal year 1983, the average Forest road cost the American taxpayers about $120,000 per mile of construction, and the total cost to the American taxpayers was an astonishing 426 million dollars. In fiscal year 1984, Forest Service road-building rebounded to pre-recession levels, with 9700 miles of road construction and reconstruction, at a cost to Uncle Sam of over a half-billion dollars. As the remaining roadless areas are destroyed, the unit cost of road-building will continue to increase, due to the remoteness, ruggedness, instability, and correspondingly difficult and expensive construction techniques required to road these remaining wildlands.

The Forest Service has been building more miles of road each decade since World War II. The agency averaged 5200 miles of road per year in the 1960s, 8500 miles per year in the 1970s, and 9400 miles per year thus far in the '80s. The upward trend (with minor variations due primarily to economic conditions) has continued through both Democratic and Republican administrations and in spite of the passage of the National Environmental Policy Act, Endangered Species Act, and numerous Wilderness bills since the enactment of the Wilderness Act of 1964. Thus, the "victory" and "progress" claims of some environmental leaders, due to the passage of Wilderness bills, ring hollow. The road-building goes on, the destruction continues, and the overall quality of our National Forest System continues to decline.

The priorities of Max Peterson's Forest Service can also be illustrated by a look at the agency's 1983 accomplishments in comparison to congressional goals for that year, as expressed by the Forest and Rangeland Renewable Resources Planning Act (RPA):

Activity	Percent of RPA Target Accomplished
Roads (Appropriated Funds)	282%
Minerals (Applications Processed)	143%
Wilderness Maintenance	63%
Wildlife Habitat Improvement	51%
Soil & Water Improvement	30%
Trails	19%

In short, the Forest Service road-building binge continues to wipe out America's remaining unprotected wild lands, while costing the people of the United States hundreds of millions of dollars each year. This, in order to produce a mere quarter of this nation's annual timber supply!

Today, there are 32 million acres of designated Wilderness in our National Forests. Another 58 million acres remain roadless (in tracts of 5000 acres or more) and unprotected, while roughly 100 million acres are already laced with roads, clearcuts, ski resorts, mines, and other manifestations of multiple use forestry. Montana, one of our wildest states, has an estimated 30,000 miles of *existing* roads in its 16.7 million acres of National Forests. Nationally, there are nearly 350,000 miles of FS roads in our National Forests! (This does *not* include Federal, State and County rights-of-way.) The United States Forest Service manages more miles of road than any other government agency in the world.

Furthermore, Forest Service Chief Max Peterson estimates that during the next 15 years, the FS will wipe out between 1 and 2 million acres of roadless country per year. Thus by the end of the century, up to one-half of our remaining National Forest de facto wilderness could be gone.

Currently, about 1½% of the land area of the lower 48 states (32.3 million acres) is somewhat protected, via Wilderness designation, from road-building, logging, and other forms of industrialization. If all remaining publicly owned wild lands (Forest Service, BLM, Park Service, and Fish & Wildlife Service roadless lands) were protected immediately, less than a tenth the land area of the United States, outside of Alaska, would remain in a relatively natural condition. There is absolutely no rational excuse for *any* more road-building in our National Forests. By hook or crook, utilizing all available legal and extra-legal means, the Forest Service must be stopped!

What You Can Do

Urge your members of Congress to oppose all Congressional appropriations for Forest Service road-building. Urge them to support Wilderness designation for all remaining roadless areas, and urge them to develop and support legislation outlawing the timber "Purchaser Credit Program." (Write: House of Representatives, Washington, DC, 20515; United States Senate, Washington, DC, 20510.)

Also, hike along newly surveyed potential road corridors and proposed timber sale units after reading *Ecodefense.*

Sources for this article included Report of the Forest Service, Fiscal Years 1980–83; *telephone conversations with "Deep Root"; "Roads to Ruin" by Jeff Sher in* American Forests Magazine, April 1985; Earth First!; *and the author's files accumulated over the years.*

Editor's update: The Forest Service is continuing to build roads and cut trees at nearly record breaking levels. Legislation has been introduced the last few years to sharply cut the Forest Service's road-building budget, but it has been defeated each year so far. Public outcry against the forest destruction, combined with concerns about the huge federal budget deficit, appear likely to force the FS to reduce its road-building and its deficit timber sales soon. This will be a small step in the right direction.

CAROLE KING ON IDAHO WILDERNESS
Samhain 1985

Excerpts from Carole King Sorensen's testimony to the US Congress on the subject of wilderness in Idaho and Montana:

Members of Congress: I don't think most Americans are aware of how badly they're being taken advantage of by the Forest Service. If people are aware of the Forest Service at all, they usually think Smokey the Bear is in charge. We'd probably be better off if he were. Officials in charge of the Forest Service care less about the forest than they do about the large corporate interests who benefit from abuse of federal lands, as exemplified by strip mines used by big oil companies for tax write-offs; the continuing construction of unnecessary roads; and taxpayer-subsidized deficit logging projects.

Forest Service figures show approximately 55,000 miles of existing roads in Idaho's National Forests. Although some of the Forest plans have not yet been released to the public and projections vary, information provided by the FS indicates something like 11,000 additional miles planned for the next decade. (On October 31, 1984, the *New York Times* projected a cost of over $2 billion in the next 4 years for 21,000 miles of log haul roads in roadless areas in Idaho, Montana, and northern Wyoming.) At a cost of approximately $100,000 per mile, these roads will cost the federal government $1.1 billion in Idaho alone. Timber from those areas may yield $\frac{1}{10}$ that amount, at a loss to American taxpayers of over $890 million. That's without figuring in costs for management, reclamation, and other costs to the taxpayer "lost" in the FS shuffle.

Considering this Administration's veneer of concern over the national deficit, this is unjustifiable. We can't help family farmers, but the Forest Service is allowed to squander enormous amounts of money on federally funded corporate welfare, which they call "management." What they "manage" is to spend their entire allocation for the year so they can ask for more the next year, Pentagon-style. Why are we paying the timber industry to destroy our property?

I recommend the following:

First, consider the primary interest of Chief Forester Max Peterson. He's a specialist in road engineering. He's also head of an agency whose officials don't have to answer to anyone but themselves. Forest Service officials make decisions affecting all Americans and their property with no personal responsibility. If their actions are challenged by an individual, the resources of the entire US government are marshalled against that individual and paid for with her or his own tax money. I recommend Congress make these officials personally accountable. They should have to consider the consequences to themselves personally of any decision they make.

Second, I recommend designation of all remaining roadless areas in Idaho and Montana as Wilderness. The two states contain one contiguous ecosystem which should be protected.

Bob Marshall was a forester who worked during the 1920s and 30s to preserve wilderness. When asked, "How much wilderness do we need?" he replied, "How many Brahms symphonies do we need?" A similar question put to Ronald Reagan elicited the response, "When you've seen one redwood, you've seen 'em all."

At the very least, I recommend an immediate moratorium on roads in roadless areas. Don't give them the money.

Third: Road-building and trail construction/maintenance are part of the same item in the Forest Service budget, effectively hiding road costs. It's not uncommon for the FS to list items they want to hide under misleading or ambiguous designations in their budget. Therefore, I recommend that Congress withhold the allocation for items not clearly itemized. This could reduce the federal deficit substantially.

In the Forest Service budget for FY 1983, resource development items totaled about $600 million. On the other hand, resource stewardship programs totaled $170 million. Congress needs to redefine the mandate of the FS, placing a priority on the responsible guardianship of our National Forests. I recommend this be accomplished by legislation, and more immediately, by allocating federal funds only for programs necessary for stewardship and clearly itemized in the FS budget.

Fourth: In states like Idaho with much federal land, some elected officials are easily persuaded to be more responsive to the big oil and welfare timber corporations who contribute heavily to their campaigns than to the people they are supposed to represent. Some have deliberately misinformed their constituents about wilderness. Everyone should be made aware of the negative impact of corporate welfare on *all* Americans. City dwellers may not realize how building unnecessary roads in Idaho will cost them increased federal taxes or decreased federal services where they are actually needed. I recommend members of Congress keep their constituents informed and develop legislation to reorganize the Forest Service so its officials serve the forest and the American people instead of the highest bidder.

Editor's update: Idaho and Montana are the last states with sizable roadless acreage that have not passed Wilderness legislation. Wilderness bills for Idaho and for Montana have been introduced in Congress each year since the mid-1980s. The bills have been woefully inadequate, yet they've all been defeated. Strong conservationists are now uniting behind the Wild Rockies Land Conservation Act, a bill to protect all of Montana's 6 million and Idaho's 9 million unprotected roadless acres. Characteristically, mainstream conservationists are supporting inferior proposals, which would release to development most of the de facto wilderness in each state.

RANCHERS AND REFUGES: 3 CASE STUDIES
Mabon 1988
by George Wuerthner

In 1987, 460 Coyotes were killed on Malheur National Wildlife Refuge in eastern Oregon. Eighty percent were gunned down by hunters in airplanes with semi-automatic shotguns. The rest were trapped or were gassed while in their dens. Refuge personnel also poisoned 124 Common Ravens and shot 13 others. Their rationale for this control was that Ravens and Coyotes eat Greater Sandhill Cranes and this is inexcusable behavior at Malheur.

Malheur is not the only National Wildlife Refuge where "wildlife control actions" are commonly undertaken by the US Fish and Wildlife Service, the agency within the Department of Interior that manages the Refuges. At Idaho's Grays Lake National Wildlife Refuge, aerial gunners have killed Coyote and Red Fox. Grays Lake personnel also have used M-44 cyanide Coyote getters and trapping to keep the Refuge free of predators so that ducks and the Whooping Crane, an Endangered Species, would have higher survival rates. At Arapaho National Wildlife Refuge in Colorado, Beaver are trapped because their dams slow water on the Illinois River, allowing it to warm— which Refuge personnel feel threatens the river's trout fisheries. Although Coyotes are not on the Arapaho's present list of undesirable wildlife, adult Black-billed Magpies are regularly poisoned and shot, and baby magpies are destroyed whenever nests are found. Magpies eat duck eggs—an unacceptable diet at the Arapaho Refuge.

Besides outright killing of some wildlife species, many Refuges promote water development, including dredging and pond-building and the operation of elaborate ditch and irrigation systems. To keep these waterways free of vegetation, some Refuges use herbicides to kill marsh vegetation such as cattail and bullrushes. At some Refuges, Malheur again being an example, Beaver and Muskrats are trapped to prevent them from damming the canals and irrigation ditches. What place, if any, do poisons, herbicides, trapping, predator control and other ecological tampering have on the National Wildlife Refuges? This article will address that question, focusing largely on three particular Refuges—Malheur in eastern Oregon, Charles M. Russell in northeastern Montana, and Red Rock Lakes in southwestern Montana—but also drawing lessons from and for other Refuges.

Malheur NWR

Many US Fish and Wildlife Service officials think the purpose of our Refuge system is to churn out target animals such as ducks and geese. George Constantino, manager at Malheur, refers to the wildlife unit in his care as a "duck factory." To Constantino, we must manipulate the environment to maximize wildlife production because we have destroyed prime wildlife habitat elsewhere. In Constantino's view, if we are to have surplus ducks for hunting, we need to increase production at our Refuges above natural recruitment rates.

There is some merit to this argument. Malheur Refuge is only a small remnant of what was a huge marsh system lying at the base of Steens Mountain in eastern Oregon. Ranchers have drained wetlands and turned native meadows into hay fields, and their cattle have trampled the riparian zones, eliminating the most productive wildlife habitat in this arid region. Continued livestock grazing around and on the Refuge has further reduced the available habitat for wildlife. (The abuses resulting from livestock grazing on these public lands have been well documented in Denzel and Nancy Ferguson's book *Sacred Cows at the Public Trough*.)

In short, the area around Malheur may no longer be able to produce as many waterfowl and cranes as it did in pre-settlement times without intensive habitat manipulation and control of predation. Sadly, the wildlife habitat degradation at Malheur is minor compared to that in places along the Pacific flyway, such as the great marshlands that once covered much of California's Central Valley, now converted to rice, wheat and cotton fields.

Despite these habitat losses, we should still question the appropriateness of predator control at Malheur and other Refuges. Constantino says studies showed low recruitment in the Refuge's Sandhill Crane population, which, if not reversed, promised to extirpate the Refuge's entire breeding population. Many factors have contributed to crane population decline, including the loss of habitat when Malheur and Harney Lakes spread over surrounding lowlands several years ago following a number of wet years. Also adversely affecting the cranes is the antiquated irrigation system which makes it difficult to control water delivery to the Refuge meadows—crane habitat.

Malheur exemplifies a deep rooted problem with our present approach toward natural systems. Because of our static view of ecological relationships, we expect areas set aside as wildlife habitat to remain constant, and to fit neatly within the boundaries of our survey lines. We expect this land to produce the same number of animals year after year. We fail to designate areas large enough to sustain ecological change through time or to allow normal habitat quality fluctuations or changes in wildlife habitat use and distribution.

For the cranes at Malheur, predation losses were viewed as the only variable that could be controlled quickly and relatively inexpensively. Yet it is questionable whether predator control is really an important factor in crane and duck survival rates; and if it is, whether other management options could reduce crane and duck losses in a manner more appropriate to a Wildlife Refuge.

A review of past predator control actions gives some insight into this question. In the early 1970s, the poison 1080 was regularly used to control Coyotes on Malheur Refuge and surrounding lands. In addition, aerial hunting and trapping were part of normal Refuge operations. Despite this intensive predator control, the crane recruitment rate varied considerably from year to year. In 1970, the recruitment rate was 12.5%, in 1971 8.9%, and in 1972 only 8.3%. In the years 1973 and 1974 only 0.4% of Sandhills were fledged—even while predator control continued both on and off the Refuge.

Predator control was discontinued on the Refuge between 1977 and 1981. During this period, the recruitment rate was only slightly lower than during the years of heavy predator control. In 1977, 5.8 cranes per 100 were recruited, but it improved to 8.9 in 1978, 8.1 in 1979, 7.1 in 1980. In 1987, despite the killing of 460 Coyotes, the fledging success was 10.6%—only slightly better than years without any control at all! Thus, while recruitment rate is slightly lower without predator control, statistics indicate that factors other than predation exert greater influence over recruitment success.

No other experiments have been conducted to determine what these factors might be and if changes in them might increase Sandhill Crane recruitment without the need for predator control. One such factor not explored by Refuge personnel is the use of the Malheur Refuge for domestic livestock production. Ranching is the major economic use of lands surrounding Malheur. Many of the local ranchers graze their livestock on Refuge lands or obtain hay grown on the Refuge. In late winter, adjacent private lands are utilized as calving grounds and the abundance of afterbirth provides a rich food source for Coyotes and other scavengers which Refuge manager Constantino believes contributes to high predator populations.

If this theory is correct (it has not been scientifically tested), the Fish and Wildlife Service policy of allowing cattle grazing and forage production at Malheur may increase predator populations. Moreover, it is the inexpensive forage provided by public lands that enables many of these ranchers to survive economically. In short, the Refuge helps to maintain the cattle, which produce the afterbirth at calving time, which may contribute to higher predator populations, which *may* be a contributing factor in a crane population decline.

Even if it were found that livestock grazing had no influence on predator populations, there would be other justifications for eliminating livestock usage of Refuge lands. Research on the Refuge compared predation impacts between idle fields and those under livestock forage production (haying or grazing). The research found significantly higher nesting success in the idle fields, where cover is thick. Thus cranes are more vulnerable to predation in areas where livestock operations are conducted.

Despite the higher nesting success in the untouched meadows, Constantino asserts that crane chicks produced in manipulated environments have higher survival rates because they have more to eat in the mowed fields. Constantino feels livestock operations are necessary for the maintenance of crane populations.

Don Tyron of the Oregon Natural Resources Council believes "it's more than coincidental that the present grazing and haying system happens to be beneficial to livestock production." According to Tyron, methods not requiring livestock grazing for producing wildlife are not seriously considered at the Refuge due to the political pressure exerted by ranchers. This pressure goes all the way to Washington, D.C., since Oregon's eastern district Congressman, Bob Smith, is a rancher from Burns, Oregon, just north of the Malheur Refuge. Not surprisingly, then, the Refuge is presently considering an increase in grazing.

Of course, the political influence of livestock interests is not limited to Malheur. Nearly all large National Wildlife Refuges in the West are under some kind of grazing program, and in most of these, livestock grazing has significantly altered the native vegetative communities. However, this alteration is invisible to the average citizen except in the worst cases of range abuse. Unlike a clearcut forest, an overgrazed range may still be covered with a dense vegetative mat. Yet the species present are apt to be invaders, exotics, and opportunistic weeds. Few people know which plants are supposed to be present on a particular site, and grasses are particularly difficult to key out. The expertise is lacking even among Refuge personnel.

Complicating the identification process is the lack of controls. Very few areas of the West have not been damaged by livestock grazing and by disruption of natural ecological processes such as periodic wildfire. Professional range managers cannot properly assess damage if they have no idea of how undamaged rangelands appear.

In addition, unlike the abrupt change that accompanies the clearcutting of a forest, the degradation of most rangelands is a long-term gradual reduction in desirable plant cover. Overgrazing is a process so gradual that even individuals who frequently view the land, such as ranchers, may not notice the change.

Because of these problems, most Refuge managers, even where Refuges are severely overgrazed, are under little public pressure to reduce grazing. Some managers defend grazing as a useful vegetation manipulation tool. Managers at both the Malheur and Grays Lake National Wildlife Refuges told me that livestock grazing was necessary to open up dense marsh vegetation to provide foraging areas for ducks and cranes.

Many managers cite the widely held doctrine that unless plants are cropped, they become decadent due to litter build-up which prevents the establishment of new seedlings and limits effective leaf photosynthetic area on living plants due to shading by dead stems. But the terms "decadence," for grasses, and "overmature," for timber, are meaningful only from an economics perspective. They merely mean that the grasses or trees are not producing additional plant fiber at maximum efficiency. This is only of concern if one wants to maximize production of livestock or of wood fiber. To an ecologist, decadence does not exist [except in land management agencies]. Slow biological growth is natural in some ecosystems.

A healthy grasslands ecosystem is not necessarily one that maximizes grass production. The idea that stagnation results from a lack of grazing is firmly entrenched in range management textbooks and doctrine, yet (conveniently) little research has been done to document whether grazing is really necessary for the maintenance of healthy rangelands. Certainly this standard rhetoric is not supported by the high proportion of ungrazed grasslands where range plants appear to be extremely healthy and robust. The few unbiased studies conducted suggest that grazing is not essential in the arid West for maintaining good grass production. The Great Plains adapted to frequent and heavy trampling under the hooves of Bison and Pronghorn. In contrast, the arid West was not frequented by Bison, and Pronghorn were less common there than in the grasslands eastward.

Research conducted at Nichols Coulee on the Charles M. Russell National Wildlife Refuge in Montana, where grazing was excluded for 12 years, demonstrated "no range stagnation from nonuse." The research report stated, "the Nichols Coulee area had a higher productivity than similar sites which are grazed by livestock under a rest-rotation grazing system."

That grazing is essential to rangeland health is the central principle of the Holistic Resource Management program of range guru Allan Savory. But Savory and other researchers who support the idea that range quality declines through non-use by grazing animals do not account for another natural agent—fire. Under natural conditions, most lower elevation Western grasslands burned at periodic intervals of between 3 and 20 years. Natural fires prevented stagnation from litter build-up, even without grazing.

Unlike livestock, which are selective in the plants they choose to eat and hence leave the less palatable "weeds" behind, fire makes no distinctions. Thus while a grazed range can decline due to selective grazing pressure on the more desirable plants, fire is usually more benign insofar as all plants suffer an equal elimination of above ground parts. The desirable climax grass species usually rebound immediately after a burn, preventing weedy species from invading.

A cautionary note should be added here: Cheatgrass, an exotic, highly flammable annual which is taking over many Western rangelands, may actually increase the frequency of fires to the point that native perennial species cannot survive and cheatgrass may take over the site. It should also be noted that, even in areas formerly heavily grazed by large wild herbivores, domestic livestock's impact on grasses is, at least over the long-term, more severe than would be the native herbivores' impact. While both domestic and native grazers are selective in their eating habits, grazing patterns varied under natural conditions; plants received frequent respites. In contrast, under domestic livestock use, grasslands are subjected repeatedly and regularly to heavy grazing.

Fire releases nutrients bound up in dead litter, making them available for plant growth. Grazing proponents argue that manure left by livestock accomplishes this goal, but in the arid West, cow-pies remain intact for years, providing little more nutrient benefit than the unburned dead grasses.

Furthermore, there is a difference in the amount of time between cropping by fires and by grazing animals. Rangelands are often grazed while the grass is still growing. If cropped, the plant attempts to replace the lost photosynthetic surface by channeling more energy into the production of new leaves and stems. This energy might otherwise be used in building its root system as insurance against drought, or in seed production to ensure successive regeneration. Fire under natural conditions usually occurs in the dry season, after most range plants have become dormant, thus not draining their energy reserves.

Even though wildfires may be essential to the ecological health of grassland ecosystems, natural fires are usually controlled on our Refuges and other public lands. Part of the reason for control stems from present domestic forage use and consequent obligations of the managing agencies. A fire can temporarily reduce the available forage for livestock grazing, wreaking havoc on the forage allotment system in existing rest-rotation grazing programs. Ranchers are seldom willing to forego grazing their public land allotments because fire eliminated the year's forage production.

Some Refuge managers prefer grazing to fires because it allows specifically targeted cropping of vegetation. A marsh needing reduction of matted growth can be grazed without affecting adjacent lands which may not need cropping. Manipulation of fire is much more difficult and there is always the possibility that fires will burn out of control and char adjacent privately owned rangelands.

But even if one accepts that grazing can accomplish ecological goals in specific situations, it does not follow that grazing by domestic livestock is appropriate. Bison, for example, can fulfill the same ecological role and are aesthetically more appropriate to Wildlife Refuges.

Yet, for managers, reintroducing Bison would entail problems not presently associated with livestock. Refuge manager Barry Reiswig says he would like to see Bison again grazing at Red Rock Lakes NWR in Montana, but that the use of Bison might cost the financially strapped Refuge more than the present livestock grazing program. Several factors seem to suggest that his economic concerns are well-founded. For one, Buffalo would have to be confined to the Refuge all year, while domestic livestock only graze there during summer and are moved back to their home ranches during winter. Furthermore, on small Refuges, personnel would have to move the Bison frequently from pasture to pasture throughout the year to keep them from overgrazing any portion of the Refuge. On large Refuges a more natural approach would be possible but this would entail reestablishment of predators such as the Gray Wolf, a creature unpopular with ranchers.

Since it is unlikely at present that predators would be reintroduced with Buffalo, Refuge personnel would have to periodically cull excess animals to keep the shaggy beasts in balance with the finite amount of forage available on the Refuge. Again, the Refuge would need to artificially manipulate the environment because of past and current human disruptions of natural processes. Since no grazing receipts would be received, all Bison management costs would have to come from the Refuge's operating budget. Considering the ecological and aesthetic benefits of Buffalo grazing, such costs would be worthwhile, but in the present political atmosphere, Refuges are not given the opportunity to weigh the merits of Bison versus livestock.

Studies indicate that many negative impacts on wildlife are associated with high grazing intensity. For example, a study of passerine birds (perching birds, the largest order of birds) nesting in willow riparian habitat at Malheur NWR concluded "there was a significant negative correlation between the frequency of grazing in past years and the number of breeding passerines." Another study at Malheur demonstrated that habitat utilization by Marsh and Rough-legged Hawks was "disproportionately greater" on areas deferred from grazing compared to units grazed by livestock. A study of nesting ducks showed that "densities on plots idle (not grazed or hayed) for one season were more than 2.5 times greater than plots in other treatments." This is largely because livestock grazing reduces cover for the ducks.

Charles M. Russell NWR

In addition to eliminating cover for wildlife, livestock compete for forage with big-game species. At the Charles M. Russell National Wildlife Refuge (CMR) in Montana, more of the forage (64%) is presently allotted to livestock than is available for wildlife (36%). (If a grazing reduction plan is not blocked, this percentage will be reversed by 1992.) Most Refuges in the West maintain a similarly disproportionate breakdown of forage allotments. At the CMR in 1987, despite recent livestock grazing permit reductions, 9842 domestic animals utilized the Refuge, compared to an estimated 9000 big game animals.

In addition to consuming wildlife forage and cover, livestock grazing programs sap money away from wildlife needs. Though many Refuges break even, the CMR spends approximately $500,000 from its yearly budget to administer the livestock program, while collecting only $219,000 in grazing receipts.

Furthermore, Refuge managers are often forced to used funds from their general operating budgets to protect wildlife habitat from grazing impacts. On the CMR, cattle grazing has nearly eliminated young cottonwoods in riparian zones. Large old trees remain, but no young ones survive to replace these "historic" trees established last century prior to heavy cattle grazing here. The Refuge fenced off some cottonwood bottoms along the Musselshell River to keep out livestock and then had to drill two wells to provide cattle with a new water source. This cost the Refuge almost $30,000—which came from normal operating budgets, not from grazing receipts.

Even though many Refuges spend more money implementing their grazing programs than they receive in receipts, their managers actually fare better than land managers with the Bureau of Land Management (BLM) and the US Forest Service (FS) since they are allowed to charge higher prices per AUM (Animal Unit Month—a measure of the forage typically consumed by one cow per month) than these other federal land managers. For example, on the Arapaho Wildlife Refuge in Colorado, the present grazing fee is $5.40 per AUM, while on identical adjacent BLM land, a rancher would only pay $1.50 per AUM. (The federal government recently raised the standard fee for FS and BLM lands from $1.35 to $1.50.) Nonetheless, according to Arapaho manager Eugene Patton, "there are no complaints" about the higher price on NWRs since it is still a bargain compared to the price a rancher would pay to graze nearby private lands.

Unlike the BLM and Forest Service, the Fish & Wildlife Service has no set standard fee for AUMs on its lands, and the prices vary widely. At Malheur Refuge in Oregon, the price per AUM is set at $3.70 while at Red Rock Lakes Refuge in Montana, ranchers pay

$6.50 per AUM. Many Refuge managers maintain that the price paid by ranchers is a bargain. On the CMR, where the fair market value is estimated at $8.61 per AUM, and ranchers have been paying $7.61 per AUM, this past year, FWS Director Frank Dunkle ordered the management to reduce CMR's grazing fee to $3 per AUM. Dunkle's rationale was to provide an "incentive for ranchers to cooperate with refuge management goals."

Many Refuges are managed with an eye toward providing forage for domestic animals. Management techniques and range evaluation tools used by Refuge personnel reflect this goal. One standard measurement technique widely used on public lands evaluates "range condition." To assess range condition, the manager looks at the vegetation growing within random plots. The plants present are compared to the theoretical climax for the site.

This method has many problems. It uses key indicator plants and most indicator species selected are those utilized by livestock (according to Dennis Macomber at the CMR). Thus some plant species that benefit wildlife are not considered, or are considered indicators of poor range condition. An abundance of sagebrush may not be good for cattle production, hence may result in a lower range condition rating, but it is absolutely necessary for Sage Grouse.

In addition, this method only requires visual estimates of the percentage of plant species found on each plot; variation occurs between observers. If certain plants are flowering or prominent, they may be overestimated, while less noticeable plants may be underestimated.

Worse, built into the range evaluation system is a bias toward acceptance of poor ecological health. For example, range estimated to be in "fair" condition may have as little as 26% of the expected plant species for that particular site. Range rated as "fair" often shows excessive soil erosion and other problems the range condition technique fails to consider.

Another problem with this system is that it averages the condition of an entire allotment into one figure. Thus, when a particular allotment is rated as being in "good" condition, portions, such as steep hillsides or areas far from water, may be untouched; while other parts, usually the riparian zones, wet meadows, aspen groves and other important wildlife habitat, may be severely damaged. By averaging together various areas within an allotment, the rating system can hide the real condition of key habitats.

Even if overall the allotment is in good range condition, it may fail to provide habitat for some important wildlife species. Dennis Macomber gives an example. Much of the CMR (74%) is considered to be in "good" range condition because the species composition is between 51% and 75% of the expected climax. Nevertheless, these same lands are cropped by cattle sufficiently to eliminate hiding cover for Sharptail Grouse, which require a minimum of 8–10 inches of residual cover. Over most of the grazed portions of the CMR, even those areas rated "excellent," less than 10 inches of residual grass remain after livestock grazing, hence most areas are of little value to Sharptails and other species dependent upon grass cover.

Red Rock Lakes NWR

The overriding presence of livestock on most Western Refuges has been mitigated somewhat recently by a general trend toward reduction in livestock numbers and use. The benefits have been substantial. Montana's Red Rock Lakes National Wildlife Refuge, where livestock grazing has been reduced 50% since 1974, provides an example. Refuge manager Reiswig says, "In the past cattle ate most of the young aspen and willow, so we had little regeneration, but since we've reduced grazing pressure, we're finding aspen suckers in groves that haven't had a sapling survive in 80 years. We're also seeing willow in places where they haven't been since the refuge was first established in the 1930s."

Another benefit of livestock reductions at Red Rock Lakes, Reiswig has noted, is the increased ability of Refuge lands to hold snow. Snow is trapped by the higher, denser cover of grasses and shrubs now growing on the Refuge, while it still blows away from the nearby heavily cropped private lands. The added snow accumulation results in greater water infiltration and hence soil moisture, which in turn results in greater plant productivity. Snow cover also provides insulation allowing higher below-snow rodent populations, which in turn provide an expanded winter prey base for predators like weasels, Red Fox and Coyote. In addition, Reiswig notes that recent studies have indicated that the resulting greater summer plant cover has contributed to a rise in ground nesting bird and rodent populations on the Refuge. This higher prey base has likewise led to larger hawk and falcon populations.

These encouraging trends show that in most instances management that most closely mimics natural ecological processes results in the most cost-effective wildlife benefits. Despite overwhelming evidence that the elimination of grazing on our western Wildlife Refuges would vastly improve their ability to sustain all native wildlife species, including target species like the Sandhill Crane, Refuge managers continue to accept grazing and its attendant impacts.

Great savings—both economic and ecological—would be won by eliminating livestock grazing from our Wildlife Refuges. On those Refuges where vegetation manipulation is essential due to outside or past human influences, managers may have to learn to utilize natural ecological forces such as fire, or import native grazing animals like Bison. Any higher costs associated with these methods would be negated by the aesthetic and ecological benefits of having native wildlife. Plus we could eliminate most or all range "improvements" such as cattle guards, water troughs, fences, hayfields and irrigation ditches.

Ultimately, it comes down to a question of why we have set up Refuges. Are they for cows; or for Elk, deer, ducks, cranes, Meadow Voles, and, yes, Coyotes too? For now, it may be necessary to occasionally manipulate the wildlife or environment on our Refuges to compensate for factors beyond their borders. Even if livestock grazing and haying operations were eliminated from the Malheur Wildlife Refuge, for instance, limited predator control might still be necessary because of conditions on adjacent private lands; but first, all other variables and possible impacts should be fully investigated. [Ideally, of course, the adjacent private lands should be purchased and added to the Refuge, thus eliminating the problems associated with livestock grazing. In these days of budget austerity, however, such purchases are highly unlikely.]

There is something fundamentally wrong with a refuge system when it is politically easier for the managers to shoot, poison or trap wildlife than it is for them to eliminate or reduce domestic livestock grazing on the refuges. This is the case for most of our National Wildlife Refuges in the West. Until this changes, our Wildlife Refuge system will not realize its potential or its philosophical mandate to provide a sanctuary for our nation's wildlife.

Vegetation, Fires, and Grazers at CMR, Malheur, & Red Rock Lakes

The vegetation at the different Refuges discussed in this article varies considerably, but vegetational patterns on each have been severely disrupted by livestock grazing and fire suppression. Most of the native species, however, do remain.

Charles M. Russell National Wildlife Refuge in Montana is short-grass prairie with cottonwood and Box Elder in the riparian zones. Ponderosa Pine and Limber Pine inhabit some Missouri River "breaks." Other common species include Silver Sage, Big Sagebrush, Greasewood, Shadscale, Douglas-fir, juniper, Buffaloberry, Wild Rose, Snowberry, and Rabbitbrush. Grasses include Western Wheatgrass, Bluebunch Wheatgrass, Blue Grama, Needle and Thread Grass, and Little Bluestem.

Plants on the Malheur NWR in Oregon include juniper, willows, Bluebunch Wheatgrass, Greasewood, cottonwood, bullrush, Shadscale, Big Sagebrush, and Great Basin Wild Rye. Cheatgrass is invading the area.

Vegetation at Red Rock Lakes NWR in Montana consists of Quaking Aspen, Douglas-fir, Subalpine Fir, and various grasses. The many shrubs include willow, and Cinquefoil.

Knowledge of natural fire patterns on these Refuges is even more limited than knowledge of pre-disturbance vegetational patterns. What follows is admittedly speculative, but it is safe to assume that fire played a major role in each of these ecosystems.

The CMR, as a grassland ecosystem, probably had fires quite regularly—likely at 1–10 year intervals. Indians often set them, as did lightning. The rougher land in the Missouri breaks was covered with Ponderosa Pine and other trees because the bare rock did not provide fuel to support fires.

At Malheur, fires likely burned periodically through the region. In dry years, even the bullrushes burned out.

Knowledge of native grazers prior to disturbance is also incomplete. Early explorers' accounts and current faunal patterns provide many clues, however.

Malheur probably did not have many large grazers prior to the white man and cattle. A Bison skull was found in the lake during the 1930s drought, which suggests that this may have been the western edge of the Bison's distributional range, but they were not numerous here if they existed here in breeding numbers at all. The only other large grazers at Malheur were Pronghorn, Mule Deer, and Bighorn Sheep in the mountains near what is now the Refuge.

Lewis and Clark came through the CMR [long before CMR] and marveled at the abundance of wildlife, including Bison, Elk, Bighorn Sheep, Pronghorn, Mule Deer, Gray Wolves, and Grizzlies. Bison at times overgrazed portions of their range. Terracing and trailing, such as major trails to the river for water, were noted. However, wolves, Indians, and hard winters periodically thinned the herds, preventing widespread overgrazing.

At Red Rock Lakes, Bison, Elk, Mule Deer, and Pronghorn, along with Grizzlies and Gray Wolves were present. Old Bison trails can still be traced in the valley. Here too, some local overgrazing did occur, but again vegetation recovered whenever predators, fire, or Indians reduced Bison numbers.

In areas with heavy grazing, the fuel loading would be reduced, and with it the ability of the rangeland to carry a fire. But the biological productivity would then decline, so grazing animals would go elsewhere to graze since no fences confined them. They probably tended toward areas that had burned several years ago, as the new growth would be succulent and thick. This would relieve grazing pressure on the heavily used areas and eventually enough fuel would accumulate so fires could burn these areas. The grazing pressure would shift back to these areas and the cycle would continue.

NATIONAL WILDLIFE REFUGES OF THE WEST: A PRIMER
Mabon 1988

by Mollie Matteson

Teddy Roosevelt set aside the first National Wildlife Refuge by executive order in 1903. During his administration, 52 more Refuges followed Florida's five acre Pelican Island, and by the time he left office, Roosevelt had secured the National Wildlife Refuge System as an American institution. Today it encompasses approximately 90 million acres.

There are approximately 230 National Wildlife Refuges in the western half of the system (all states west of the Mississippi River, excepting Alaska but including Hawaii and some Pacific Islands).

Stump Lake Refuge in North Dakota and Wichita Mountains Refuge in Oklahoma were among the earliest created in the West; both were set aside in 1905. Among the largest are Montana's Charles M. Russell (898,250 acres), and Arizona's Cabeza Prieta (860,000) and Kofa (660,000). By comparison, the largest Refuge in the eastern US is Florida's Arthur R. Marshall Loxahatchee (145,635 acres). Most of Alaska's Refuges are over a million acres in size and the two largest, Arctic and Yukon Delta, both exceed 19 million acres.

Refuges are still being created. One of the largest NWRs in the West, Buenos Aires in Arizona (111,506 acfes), was established in 1985, and Midway Atoll (90,097) was declared in April of this year.

Many Refuges in the West provide forage for livestock, despite this conflicting with the use of Refuge lands by wildlife. Of 109 Refuges in Region 6 (Montana, Wyoming, Colorado, Kansas, South Dakota, North Dakota, Nebraska, and Utah), all but six currently have livestock grazing. Grazing occurs on about half of the 32 Refuges in Region 2 (Arizona, New Mexico Texas, and Oklahoma), and 37 out of 227 Refuges in Region 1 (California, Hawaii, Idaho, Nevada, Oregon, Washington, and Pacific Islands).

Each Refuge sets its own grazing fees, which usually range between $4 and $8 per AUM. Buffalo Lake NWR in Texas charges $13 per AUM, probably the highest public lands grazing fee in the country. Detailed information on whether the costs of grazing programs are covered by the fees is not readily available, but according to one official in Region 2, "grazing is used strictly as a management tool," and is thus seen as bringing returns beyond the merely monetary.

There are five ways in which a NWR may be established. Teddy Roosevelt used executive withdrawal during his administration. Refuges created to perpetuate Endangered Species, and lands acquired for recreation and other purposes, can be financed by the Land and Water Conservation Fund. This money comes from off-shore oil and gas leasing revenues. The Migratory Bird Conservation Account provides monies for the creation of Refuges for migratory birds. The sale of duck stamps provides the revenues for this fund. Refuges that are not designed primarily to protect migratory birds or Endangered Species can be established through an act of-Congress. Finally, the Secretary of Interior may accept donations of land for Refuge purposes.

Editor's update: The US Fish and Wildlife Service last year reviewed the management of the National Wildlife Refuge system and sought comments from the public. A series of public hearings is scheduled for 1991, but so far there has been little indication that the FWS will make serious attempts to end the abuses on the Refuges. The degree and types of exploitation vary from Refuge to Refuge but may include livestock grazing, off-road vehicle driving, hunting, trapping, mining, and timber cutting. A bill was introduced in 1990, and will be reintroduced in 1991, that would curtail uses of the Refuges not compatible with their overall purpose of providing sanctuaries for wildlife. The "Big 10" environmental groups (Sierra Club, The Wilderness Society, National Wildlife Federation, etc.) are not publicizing this strong legislation, the Wildlife Refuge Reform Act, and instead are supporting a much weaker Refuge reform bill.

DEVELOPERS TAKE THE LEAD IN THE NORTHEAST 10 MILLION
Eostar 1989

by Jamie Sayen

A once in a lifetime opportunity to convert upward of 10 million acres of privately owned forests in the Northeast to public lands is being squandered. The Diamond land sale of one million acres (*EF!*, May 1988) in Maine, New Hampshire, Vermont and New York, has presented an historic chance to restore vast tracts of the Northeast to ecological health. Unless defenders of biodiversity act now, business and politics will squelch this opportunity.

Currently, Maine, New Hampshire, and Vermont—an area of 33.5 million acres—have only a little over one million acres of public land. More than 80% of Maine (a state with 22 million acres) is privately owned commercial forest. The largest contiguous tract in the Lower 48 with no year-round inhabitants is in Maine, yet only 110,000 acres in Maine are federally owned.

Last year's Diamond sale is only the beginning. Even industry supporters acknowledge that the long-term industry strategy is to sell as much as 10 million acres by the end of the century. Aside from the timber firms themselves, only developers and the federal government can afford to buy the lands. The story is still unfolding. It could have a happy ending, if the public demands an appropriate answer to the questions "what are the needs of the land?" and "how can we restore the biodiversity of the Northeast?"

Industry Exodus

Why was Diamond International (DI) selling its land? Those familiar with Maxxam's takeover of Pacific Lumber, and its liquidation of the remaining fragments of privately-owned Coast Redwoods in California to pay off junk bonds, will recognize a pattern here.

In 1982 British corporate raider "Sir" James Goldsmith purchased DI for $240 million in a leveraged buyout. He probably only had to pay one-tenth of the sale price, while banks and investment firms loaned the rest.

What made this deal possible was that the book value of DI's assets was $315 million, and by selling the assets, Goldsmith was able to pay off his creditors and turn a 200% profit within two years. After selling DI's paper mills and corporate headquarters, he transferred its 1.5 million acres of timberland to a Cayman Islands holding company, which General Occidentale, France's privately owned water utility, purchased in 1987. Goldsmith then put one million acres in the Northeast on the market.

In the Winter 1989 *Amicus Journal*, Robert Anderberg writes: "Paper companies may be avoiding the purchase of timberland since a large investment in a low-yield, long-term commodity may lower their price/earnings ratio [which determines a stock's price] and makes them, too, a more likely candidate for takeover and dismemberment."

Foreign competition, intense stockholder pressure to have timberlands show a profit, corporate raids, aging technology of mills in the Northeast, increased competition from more efficient and modern mills in the South and Midwest, and a corporate view of land as nothing but an "asset" to be turned into cash are the major pressures on industry to sell. Another factor is the declining health of the forests after centuries of abusive logging. Foresters project a shortage of spruce and fir in Maine in the early 21st century.

The development boom of the past decade has caused the price of land to skyrocket in the region. Industry is finding that the value of land for development (especially in choice spots such as lakefronts) surpasses the land's value as a timber holding. Many companies, especially in Maine, are identifying the so-called highest and best use (HBU) lands and putting them on the market.

In May 1988, the *Maine Times* reported that 223,000 acres owned by Boise-Cascade, Georgia-Pacific, and the Penobscot Indian Nation were for sale. Two tracts (of 350,000 and 187,000 acres) belonging to International Paper were available. The J. M. Huber Company indicated that an offer "well beyond" what it was realizing in timber sales would induce it to sell 450,000 acres. Champion International was making an inventory of valuable portions of its 760,000 acres in Maine for possible sale to developers. Meanwhile, Maine's largest landowner, Great Northern, with 2.1 million acres, was struggling financially.

In Vermont and New Hampshire, Champion attests that it is "not actively engaged in land sales." But you can bet it would sell its 300,000 acres in these two states for the right price, and already it is peddling 2000 acres in Canaan, Vermont.

NH Diamond Land Sale

Late in February 1988, news of the Diamond land sales shocked the public. In New Hampshire, 67,000 acres were for sale, including about 40,000 acres in the Nash Stream Watershed (NSW) which lies in the townships of Stratford, Stark, Odell, and Northumberland. The NSW is one of the few undeveloped watersheds in the East, and it contains seven lakes, numerous streams, and the east side of Mt. Sugarloaf (el. 3701') and the Percy Peaks (3418' and 3200'). The Diamond holding included the entire drainage. Moose have returned there. Cougars have been spotted. It is ideal habitat for the rare (or extirpated) Lynx.

Environmentalists, politicians and North Country residents agreed that the Nash Stream Watershed deserved protection from development. The first step was a meeting in Concord, NH, on March 10. There Earth First! and Preserve Appalachian Wilderness (PAW) urged that the federal government buy all Diamond holdings. Federal and state politicians told us there was virtually no money in either budget to buy DI's 90,000 acres in NH and VT for $19 million. Later, we were warned that calls for wilderness would cost us our "credibility."

On May 23, at a second meeting in Concord, we were chastised by "environmentalist" Paul Bofinger as "selfish." Bofinger, president of the Society for the Protection of NH Forest(er)s, fought to prevent wilderness additions to the White Mountain National Forest in 1986.

He told us there was no way of getting funding from Congress to create "just another wilderness."

Before the week was out, the region was stunned by the news that NH developer Claude Rancourt had bought Diamond's New Hampshire and Vermont holdings. Public outrage was so great that politicians who had told us earlier there was little public money now jumped into action.

New Hampshire's US senators Gordon Humphrey and Warren Rudman vowed to scuttle the deal if the NSW was not protected from development. They asked for federal money and spoke of using "eminent domain" if necessary.

At the end of July, then-NH governor John Sununu announced that a deal with Rancourt had been struck to save the NSW and several thousand acres of inholdings in the White Mountain National Forest (WMNF). Approximately, 45,000 acres would be purchased for $12.75 million in state and federal funds. The NH Nature Conservancy agreed to supply a "bridge loan" until federal funding could be arranged. The state of NH would own the NSW outright.

Many environmentalists now feel that the state, the federal government, the Forest Society and The Nature Conservancy (TNC) were too anxious to strike a deal. Rancourt might well have defaulted on its $1 million downpayment had not the state and federal governments agreed to buy the NSW. Instead, Rancourt was bailed out. Laughing all the way to the bank, Rancourt sold the NSW for $283 per acre a couple months after paying only $211. Yet the press has portrayed Rancourt as the White Knight of the story for selling the NSW to "environmentalists."

Instead of buying 89,500 acres for $19 million ($211 per acre), 45,000 acres were purchased for $12.75 million ($283 per acre). Later, the VT Nature Conservancy loaned the state of Vermont $1.9 million to buy five tracts in the Victory Bog (another 7600 acres). New Hampshire, through its Land Conservation Investment Program (LCIP), paid $7.65 million and the US government paid another $5.1 million. As of this writing, $4 million of the federal money has not been released, and TNC, which loaned this money, will have to start paying interest on the loan in June if it is not released.

Rancourt auctioned off 15,000 acres on September 10; another 15,000 acres are still for sale. As an example of the skyrocketing price of land, in September Rancourt sold one 90-acre tract in auction for $322 per acre. At the time Diamond put its lands on the market, timber land was valued at $150 an acre. The speculator who bought it then sold it to a southern NH greedhead for $422 an acre. Now the land is heavily mortgaged and is being clearcut to pay the banks.

The Sununu deal was finalized in October only after Governor Sununu stepped in again and negotiated directly with the US Department of Agriculture (the department with jurisdiction over the Forest Service). The deal was hailed as a great "conservation victory," but was it?

The state will recoup much of its investment through the sale of timber rights to private companies ($3.2 million), and Rancourt retained the mineral rights to the first five million cubic yards of gravel along the Nash Stream access road. Thereafter, Rancourt and the state will evenly split the revenue from additional mining on the 100 acre gravel deposit. Also, Rancourt received significant federal and state tax advantages.

The mining will take place about 100 yards from Nash Stream. Damage to the watershed will be severe, though Sununu stated that sand and gravel mining "is consistent with the environmental concerns that we have."

Sununuke has waged a successful war to keep the Seabrook Nuclear Facility alive. Now he is George Bush's Chief of Staff. A powerful man, he has made numerous enemies along the way. His high-handedness may yet cause the deal to collapse.

Sununu's Role

Paul Bofinger likes to remind those who don't share his pro-timber bias that "We have a history of working together in New Hampshire [on environmental issues]." This helps explain why New Hampshire has such an abysmal environmental record: the only state in New England with no bottle bill; no meaningful regulations for timber harvesting; opposition to wilderness in the WMNF; traditional statewide hostility to public lands; and liquidation clearcutting and whole-tree chipping in the northern counties.

But Bofinger and the Forest Society didn't live by this solidarity theme during the Diamond land negotiations. After the March 10 meeting in Concord, PAW and EF! were deleted from the mailing list while the old "consensus" line was being peddled to the media. After Rancourt bought the lands, the Forest Society and TNC excluded other environmental groups, including the Sierra Club and The Wilderness Society.

When Sununu entered the picture, he made deals directly with Rancourt in July and the Agriculture Department in October. The NH congressional delegation, the Forest Society and TNC were kept informed. The public and other environmental groups and key members of the House of Representatives were not.

Sununu's arm-twisting got results, but it also polarized the issue. The US Forest Service feels it got the shaft because the state of New Hampshire will own and manage the Nash Stream Watershed, while the FS will have the thankless task of monitoring the state's performance. Southern NH feels money set aside in the LCIP fund for conservation in the southern part of the state was used to keep a working forest in the north, rather than conserve vanishing undeveloped lands in the south.

But the real blunder was to antagonize Representative Bruce Vento (D-MN), chairman of the National Parks and Public Lands Subcommittee of the Interior and Insular Affairs Committee; Harold Volkmer (D-MO), chairman of the Forests, Family Farms and Energy Subcommittee of the Agriculture Committee; and Sidney Yates (D-IL), chairman of the House Interior Appropriations Subcommittee. These three representatives were told that they were appropriating $5.1 million to purchase additions to the White Mountain National Forest. When they learned that only about 5000 acres of WMNF inholdings would be owned by the feds, while the other 40,000 acres in the NSW would be owned by the state, they blew a fuse.

They were not mollified by the explanation that the federal share of the Nash Stream sale ($4 million) was to purchase an easement (the terms of which have not yet been made public) from the state. Allegedly, this easement would assure that the state does not develop or sell the NSW and that public access is maintained.

There is a rule that the federal government cannot buy state lands or interest in state lands without going back to both House and Senate appropriation committees for approval. Representative Yates has invoked the rule, so the Forest Service cannot legally spend the $4 million until it returns to Yates's subcommittee. It is not clear yet if

Bush and Sununu will order the Forest Service to ignore Yates and pay
the money to the state. If this happens, hell will break loose on
Capitol Hill.

Early in December, Representatives Vento and Volkmer released a
letter they had sent to the Secretary of Agriculture on November 22.
It said the easement was valueless because the state had already
declared its intent to preserve the land.

"The state is attempting to take dollars from the national taxpayer
without giving that taxpayer anything of substance or value in return,"
the congressmen wrote. "This scheme was developed behind closed
doors without consulting any of the members of the House of
Representatives who had supported the appropriation."

Vento and Volkmer feel the agreement violated the intent of
Congress, and they believe the federal government ought to buy as
much land as possible and take the rest by eminent domain, as the law
allows. They called for incorporating it into the White Mountain
National Forest because it is adjacent to the Forest and because that
was the intent of the appropriation. Off the record, there is strong
feeling that Bofinger and Sununu deceived the House during the
appropriations process.

For the time being, Representatives Vento, Volkmer and Yates
would like to see joint ownership of the Nash Stream Watershed by
the state and federal governments. Once the $4 million is properly
spent, they would like to appropriate enough money to buy out the
state so that the NSW could become a part of the WMNF. But until
this "dirty deal" is resolved, there will be no further federal money
available to New England for land purchase.

The time is ripe to buy out the state of New Hampshire. When
Sununu left office, he boasted of a budget surplus of $13 million. His
successor is discovering that actually there is a $24 million dollar deficit.

Of primary concern is whether New Hampshire would manage the
Nash Stream Watershed by US Forest Service or state regulations—the
latter of which are a public joke in the North Woods. The state has neither the ability nor the will to manage a treasure like the NSW. It can't
even enforce the few toothless forestry regulations it has on the books.

Congressmen Vento, Volkmer and Yates smell the same rat PAW
and EF! have been smelling for a year. Efforts to "save" the NSW were
really designed to save a cheap source of wood for local mills. The

well-meaning Nature Conservancy was used by the timber interests, and it was all dressed up as an environmental victory.

PAW and EF! agree with the representatives: The Sununu deal must be defeated. In its stead, Congress should: 1) appropriate $7.65 million to buy out NH's interest in the Nash Stream Watershed; 2) appropriate $1.6 million to buy over 7000 acres in the Stratford Bog adjacent to the NSW; and 3) prohibit sand and gravel mining in the watershed.

Informed sources say that TNC and even the Forest Society opposed the mining. But the Forest Society, being above all else "pragmatic," gave in to Sununu, who insisted on the $1 million mining clause as a prerequisite for state participation. TNC, sincere in its desire to save a few endangered species, also chose not to rock the boat.

The Nature Conservancy does important work, but its limited funding restricts it to preserving small, often isolated tracts. It simply cannot purchase the millions of acres we need to begin restoring biodiversity.

The Nature Conservancy's main failure is its aversion to controversy, which, at times, seems to take precedence over the defense of biodiversity. On the NSW sale, a few plots with endangered plant species have been saved, but Cougar and Lynx habitat has been sacrificed to economic interests.

The Forest Society deserves to be roundly thumped. It is an industry lackey. It has set the agenda of the NH "environmental community" for too long.

The price for not rocking the boat may be high for The Nature Conservancy. If federal funding is delayed past June, TNC will have to start paying interest on its loan. This would be the fruit of pragmatism, compromise, secretiveness, and lack of courage to stand up for what they believe in. If the Forest Society and TNC had included the public and other environmental groups with Washington connections and savvy, they probably would have avoided the wrath of the House leaders.

One of the most dangerous long-term consequences of the Nash Stream sale is the precedent set by this hodge-podge state/federal/private transaction. If the Sununu deal goes through, one of two scenarios is likely. Either it will be very difficult to get any more emergency funding in the future from the angry House (as is currently the case), or a new version of pork-barrel politics will emerge.

Of course, the welfare timber industry likes the idea of the federal government paying the state to buy lands for the benefit of industry. The industry aims sophisticated disinformation campaigns against "government interference," even while demanding greater subsidies. From industry's vantage point, the Sununu deal saves the forest for their mills while everyone celebrates an environmental victory. This is a public relations coup of the highest magnitude. Using "environmentalism" to secure industry subsidies will also appeal to congresspersons wary of taking heat for overt pork-barreling.

The Maine Woods

The situation is even more dire in Maine. Development pressures; liquidation cutting; and industry woes tied to aging mills, out of region competition, and centuries of abusive logging are resulting in land sales and massive overcutting.

The so-called highest and best use lands (HBU) on lake and river fronts are being sold to developers at a record pace. Maine's lack of zoning and planning regulations in the unincorporated townships, which cover 10 million acres, facilitates unregulated development.

Diamond sold 800,000 acres in Maine last year. Canada's Fraser Paper Company bought 207,000 acres in June for $33.5 million. In September, the James River Corporation (JR) bought a 23% interest in Diamond Occidentale, including 560,000 acres of Diamond's Maine holdings, for $223 million. JR cited a need to assure a reliable wood supply for its north country mills. Of this purchase, 65,000 acres are considered HBU and will probably be sold to developers.

The JR purchase should not be interpreted to mean that the industry plans to remain in the Northeast. As one Maine forester-economist said, "Possibly the price [about $200/acre] was too good to pass up."

Well over a million acres of Maine forests remain on the market, including three miles of shorefront along Mooselookmeguntic Lake in the Rangeley Lakes region. T-M Corporation, a land speculator and developer in Greenville (on the southern shore of Moosehead Lake), is purchasing 106,000 acres in western Maine from Boise-Cascade. That land was recently subjected to "salvage" logging in the wake of the latest spruce budworm outbreak. Consequently, timber owners did not want it.

The fortunes of the Maine timber industry have declined markedly in recent years, allegedly due to forces "beyond their control." One such force is the spruce budworm epidemic of the 1970s. It is now blamed for an assured shortfall of spruce and fir in the early 21st century.

The spruce budworm crisis resulted from generations of mismanagement. Budworm outbreaks are periodic, natural disturbances, which, in the 19th century uneven-aged, mixed species forests, were infrequent and isolated. But abusive logging practices, with more and more even-aged monocultures of spruce and fir, created conditions conducive to widespread budworm outbreaks. Successive outbreaks in 1910, 1940, and 1970 covered 10, 25, and 55 million hectares respectively in the northeastern US and Canada. Plantations were especially susceptible to budworm. Nonetheless, industry has accelerated the even-aged (clearcut) approach through pesticide applications and "salvage" and "pre-salvage" clearcuts.

Studies have shown that about 2% of the mortality in tracts managed for uneven-aged stands with mixed species was due to budworm. In even-aged monocultures, budworm caused 99% of the mortality. The mixed stands also produced 55% higher yields than the even-aged stands.

Pre-settlement forests of Maine were remarkably stable. Major fire disturbance cycles were probably greater than 800 years. Poplar, an indicator of disturbance, constituted only 2.3% of the presettlement forest. Today it is the second most numerous hardwood species in Maine, and is increasing rapidly. This is good only for whole-tree wood chippers, who now have markets (wood burning electricity generating plants) for formerly "worthless" species like "popple."

A 1987 survey showed that Maine will face a shortage of spruce-fir in the early 21st century because there are not enough young trees growing. Another report revealed that industry harvests 7.8 million cords of spruce and fir a year despite annual growth of only 2.7 million cords. Current estimates are that hardwood pulp demand will increase 25%, and biomass demand 75% by the year 2000!

In 1987 about half of the 301,277 acres harvested in Maine were clearcut. A land use manager with Great Northern says the clearcuts will continue for the next decade: "We're dealing with a single age forest ranging from 60–90 years. That leaves us with few harvesting options . . ."

On November 8, the *Christian Science Monitor* reported: "Every lake [in the Maine woods] is edged by a logging road. Great swaths of woodland . . . have been denuded by chainsaws." The reporter noted that nearing Chesuncook Lake (due west of Baxter State Park) from the air, "hundreds of acres of treeless 'clear cut' parcels seem to out-number the wooded areas."

Ten thousand miles of logging roads have been built in Maine since river drives were halted for environmental reasons in 1974. Great Northern has over 3000 miles of roads. The Paper Industry Information office boasts that no place is more than two miles from a road.

Until about a decade ago, 2,4-D and 2,4,5-T, which contain diox-ins and are known carcinogens, were sprayed in Maine to suppress weed species (hardwoods like alder, maple, birch, cherry and poplar) so that spruce-fir would grow without competition. The practice con-tinues in New Brunswick. Although alder is economically "worthless," this nitrogen-fixer appears to combat acid deposition by increasing the alkalinity of the soil.

The federal government ought to institute immediate condemna-tion proceedings against industrial landowners in Maine. Eminent domain has been used ruthlessly to build our highway system. It is time to use it to preserve biodiversity.

Sometime this spring, The Wilderness Society (TWS) will unveil plans for a 2.7 million acre Maine Woods Reserve which would con-tain public and private lands. The reserve outlines are not yet known, but it will probably encompass the final 120 miles of the Appalachian Trail, all of Moosehead Lake but the overdeveloped southwestern shore, the West Branch and East Branch Penobscot regions, Baxter State Park, and the Aroostock River region.

Coming from a mainstream environmental group, the plan deserves support from the region's timid environmental community. Unfortunately, well-financed disinformation campaigns are succeeding in scaring Mainers into thinking creation of the reserve would drive them from the woods.

Earth First!, however, holds that The Wilderness Society's plan should be viewed as only a first step toward a large regional preserve including several million more acres in northern and western Maine, northern New Hampshire and 'Vermont. TWS's plan focuses on only a small portion of the entire area in which the large land sales are occurring. If we follow its strategy, we will lose millions of acres. The use of ecosystems rather than political lines to define boundaries is important. Due to the random manner large holdings are entering the market, however, a flexible strategy is needed. All industrial timberlands should be purchased by the federal government as they come on the market.

New York

Diamond's 96,000 acres in New York's Adirondack region were sold in September to Lassiter Properties, Inc., a land speculator from Atlanta, for $17 million ($177/acre). New York state, The Nature Conservancy and the Adirondack Council have purchased 15,000 acres outright and conservation easements for about 40,000 acres from Lassiter for $10.8 million.

Paper companies still own a million acres within Adirondack Park, and the Park's future will be jeopardized if developers are able to profit as middlemen between the timber companies and the public. The profits of the Lassiter sales, as well as the Rancourt sales in New Hampshire and Vermont, should be taxed 100% and that money should be applied to future land purchases. Eminent domain should be used to confiscate land from developers.

Shifting Attitudes Toward Public Land

A little over a year ago, you risked life and limb if you suggested to North Country residents that we need more public lands. The traditional hostility has been a product of Yankee independence from federal government bureaucracy, a fear that public lands would mean restrictions on land use, and timber industry propaganda. Local governments preferred that the public view land in this way, as it assured their tax base and kept open the option of future development.

When PAW and EF! called for the federal purchase of the Diamond lands last year, we were told by politicians and "environmentalists" alike that there was no support for public lands in New England. The Forest Society was especially pernicious in this respect. In April, even as the Society denied that there was support for federal ownership, a survey in Vermont's Northeast Kingdom showed 56% of 48 polled favoring a Northeast Kingdom National Park.

After Rancourt bought the Diamond lands in NH and VT, the public outcry proved to the NH congressional delegation that strong support exists for keeping the land wild. The public now realizes that undeveloped private lands are being fragmented by such developers as Patten Corporation to satisfy the second home market (in a society overrun by homeless). People now realize that as long as forests remain in private hands, they are vulnerable. As state bond issues are incapable of dealing with the crisis, the federal government is the only hope.

On July 12, the *Concord Monitor* endorsed George Wuerthner's proposal (in *Wilderness*, summer 1988) to create giant National Parks and National Forests in northern New England. On July 30, the *Boston Globe* quoted Michael Deland, head of EPA's Boston office: "Buying land is a significant step, but there also are areas that are so valuable they must be preserved by government fiat."

In December, the Committee of the Environment of the New England Governor's Conference issued a report that stated, "A formal process should be created by which the Governors can work together with the entire New England congressional delegation to obtain federal funds for land acquisition in the region." The report called for the establishment of "a new federal land preservation program focusing on rivers," and proposed an "emergency revolving loan fund" to save endangered land.

The growing support for public land in the Northeast can no longer be excused by the timber industry and its well-behaved "environmentalists" as the idea of radical environmentalists. The tide has turned, and the availability of millions of acres of Northeastern forests is now a national issue.

A Vision of Healthy North Woods

If we wish to free ourselves from the failures of business as usual, we must change our way of doing business. "Unless we change our direction," Confucius warns us, "we will end up where we are headed." We need a populace and politicians who recognize that all decisions have a biological component.

The health of an ecosystem is measured by its biodiversity. Coe writes in *Conservation Biology* (ed. by Soulé and Wilcox, p.286), "Any natural habitat will continue to function only if all the trophic levels from primary producers to decomposers fulfill their independent and interdependent roles."

As Euroamericans settled the Northeast, they destroyed massive old-growth forests and many of the forests' inhabitants, including Gray

Wolves, Cougars, Wolverines, Lynx and Pine Martens. These species need inviolate tracts of millions of acres of wilderness. TNC-style fragments will never support viable populations of these natives, let alone the processes of adaptation and speciation.

In addition to size, several other biological considerations are critical to designing preserves. Of special concern are the needs of migratory species, species that require a variety of successional stages during their life cycles, and species patchily distributed. Preserves should encompass ecosystems representing all vertical (altitudinal) and horizontal (forest, valley, wetlands, etc.) components of the bioregion. The poor soils of the Northeast require greater areas to support viable populations than do areas with nutrient-rich soils.

As we confront the consequences of the greenhouse effect and ozone depletion, we must develop a strategy to deal with shifting climate zones and increased ultraviolet radiation penetration. Shifting climate zones associated with natural glacial-interglacial cycles must also be considered. Normally, as climate zones shift, the associated biota also shift. But insular regions [e.g., preserves surrounded by developed lands] typically do not span a sufficient latitude to provide refugia for species ill-adapted to climatic shifts, especially shifts accelerated by humans.

If we are to preserve biodiversity, we must preserve all available land, whether or not it meets TNC's criteria for ecological uniqueness. Conservation biologist Robin Foster writes, "It seems entirely reasonable to take large areas of cheap land that are currently of no biological significance and set them aside as reserves which, after succession with some manipulation, will eventually harbor a rough approximation of the original community" (Soulé and Wilcox, p.89).

Presettlement forests of the Northeast, with their rich array of species and communities, enjoyed remarkable stability. Diversity leads to stability; stability leads to diversity. To restore biodiversity, we must protect the natural disturbance and succession regimes, and safeguard the adaptive and evolutionary options of species and communities.

In the Northeast, this means the creation of a biological preserve of at least 10 million acres, with large core Wilderness Areas and Wilderness Recovery Areas. Surrounding the cores would be buffer zones, with acceptable levels of human reinhabitation increasing toward the periphery.

The North Woods Preserve should include northern and western Maine, New Hampshire north of Route 110, and the Northeast Kingdom of Vermont. Areas in southern and central NH and VT should ultimately be incorporated into the network along the lines advanced by PAW's vision for the Appalachian Trail (*EF!*, 5–87). Adirondack Park should be expanded. The preserve needs wild river corridors to the ocean. The Allagash, St. John, Penobscot, Androscoggin, and Connecticut Rivers and their watersheds should be restored, along with wetlands, estuaries, and coastal areas.

Only then will Cougars, Gray Wolves, Wolverines, Atlantic Salmon, sturgeon, Peregrine Falcons, and healthy soil microbes and mycorrhizal fungi flourish. This vision requires a national, not merely regional, long-term strategy structured to anticipate future sales.

The current Northern Forest Lands Study (NFLS) offers a glimmer of hope. Massive public support for the federal purchase of timberlands could overcome the pro-timber industry bias of the NFLS.

Senators Rudman and Humphrey demonstrated, belatedly, that federal funding can be secured on short notice if political leadership is shown. We need a Northeastern Trust Fund of $3 billion dollars. Even at the inflated price of $300/acre, $3 billion could buy 10 million acres!

The Land and Water Conservation Fund, with assets of over $6 billion, is being used not to purchase public lands, but rather to make Reagan's budget deficit appear $6 billion smaller. Environmentalists should storm the Capitol and refuse to leave until that money is liberated.

Eminent domain should be used in a carrot and stick manner. If timber companies want to sell moderately healthy forests, they should receive a fair market price (frozen at 1988 regional land prices). If they plan liquidation cuts and selling of HBU lands to developers, confiscation is appropriate.

A once in a lifetime opportunity is at hand in the Northeast. The choice is ours: Do we want to perpetuate the loss of biodiversity associated with business as usual? Or do we want the progeny of all native species to live in a healthy, biologically diverse bioregion?

Outlaw Clearcuts

It took several years before the "civilized" world awoke to the Nazi slaughter of millions of innocent Jews, Gypsies, dissidents and other "undesirable" members of one unhappy species. It is time "civilized" people wake up to a more heinous holocaust: the slaughter—for profit—of thousands of innocent species by the timber industry Nazis. New England EF! groups are working to outlaw clearcuts on public and private lands. The following facts are from a flier PAW passed out at a rally in Concord, NH, on February 3:

> Today New Hampshire is 89% forested as compared with 15% at the turn of the century. As the land regenerates, many extirpated species return. Clearcutting ends this process. The regenerative process after a clearcut is not comparable to the regeneration of farmland to forest. Abandoned farms provide habitat for weed species like Woodcock, grouse, deer, fox, and cottontail rabbit. Farms grow back with a variety of plant species of many age groups, providing niches for many wild species. In contrast, the plants that reinhabit a clearcut are generally of very few species and of the same age, leaving very few niches.

> Clearcutting severely disturbs the soil. Forest duff is exposed to the sun and baked. This kills soil microbes and mycorrhizal fungi. The death of these organisms delays the reconstruction of the healthy soil needed for reforestation.

> Deforestation through clearcutting upsets the hydrologic cycle of the forest ecosystem. It eliminates ephemeral streams and ponds, which are important habitat for amphibians, and disturbs the nutrient distribution in the forest. Clearcutting leads to increased flooding downstream.

Editor's update: New Hampshire officials have appointed a committee to develop a plan for the management of the Nash Stream Watershed. Predictably, they have staffed the committee with persons averse to habitat preservation. A plan is due out in 1991.

Meanwhile, forest lands in northern New England and northern New York are enjoying something of a respite from the onslaught of developers due to the economic downturn in the region. Unfortunately, however, federal officials have shown no inclination to use this opportunity to buy and save lands. New York voters narrowly rejected a bond measure that would have provided funds to the state to purchase private lands within Adirondack Park for preservation. Ironically, the recession in the Northeast seems to be slowing development even as it precludes federal or state purchase and protection of undeveloped lands.

OLD GROWTH VS. OLD MINDSETS
Beltane 1989
by Mitch Freedman

The Pacific Northwest is now embroiled in perhaps the greatest environmental controversy in its history. The rich biological value of old growth (ancient) forest, and the Northern Spotted Owl's connection to the forests, were generally not appreciated until the mid 1970s. Since then, efforts to protect the ancient forests have been largely unsuccessful.

The Oregon and Washington Wilderness Bills of 1984 failed to protect much ancient forest. The Forest Service (FS) and Bureau of Land Management (BLM) have shown their intentions by logging some 8 square miles of old growth each month in Oregon alone. Therefore, the battle has been fought in the woods. Earth First!ers, seeing the futility of timber sale appeals, have put their bodies down in the Kalmiopsis, Middle Santiam, Swauk Meadow, Illabot Creek, Breitenbush and other threatened areas. At the same time, tree spiking has become increasingly frequent. Some estimate that as many as 30 FS timber sales in Washington alone have been spiked in the last two years.

Meanwhile, the national groups postponed petitioning the US Fish and Wildlife Service (FWS) to list the Spotted Owl as Endangered (a small New England group, Greenworld, finally petitioned in late 1986), or suing the FS for failure to meet viable population requirements of the National Forest Management Act (NFMA). The groups feared political backlash from Oregon's powerful and diabolical congressional delegation.

But now—as the lawsuits have been filed, restraining orders have been granted, the industry has been embarrassed by its exports of unprocessed logs to Asia amidst cries of US jobs, and the national media has begun following the whole issue—it seems something is about to give. For better or for worse, ancient forest legislation will happen soon.

How Much Remains?

Ironically, even with all the lead time to the present old growth frenzy, we still don't know how much remains or where it stands. For years, environmentalists have been requesting that the Forest Service inventory old growth on National Forests. With their own interests at heart (what good is an informed public?), the FS never performed the inventory.

Admittedly, 'old growth' is a troublesome term. Rarely is it clear to what people are referring when they say "old growth," or worse, and more recently, "ancient forest." The Forest Service set up an "old growth definition task force" to finally define it. The task force published its findings in 1986, yet the FS, even in forest plans released after that year, failed to use its definition. The FS instead left each National Forest to provide its own meaning, generally based on timber inventory data, such as "largesaw timber" (greater than 21 inch diameter at breast height [dbh]). Moreover, there has been no formal effort to define 'old growth' for forests in the eastern two-thirds of Washington and Oregon.

This isn't just a matter of semantics. It's the difference between millions of acres of natural growth (never logged, though perhaps otherwise disturbed), and about 350,000 acres of classic old growth (contains several trees over 40" dbh per acre). A recent report published by The Wilderness Society found that the Forest Service had, through inconsistent definitions and old data (disregarding recent logging), overestimated existing old growth by as much as 125%. Furthermore, most of what's left is high elevation and/or heavily fragmented. The Wilderness Society report estimated a total of 1.2 million acres of old growth on the 6 National Forests in the Pacific Northwest that contain the bulk of the remaining stands. Most of this is fragmented beyond usefulness as old growth habitat.

In a 1988 appropriations bill, Congress instructed the Forest Service to find its old growth. But we won't have the benefit of that information for a couple years, and our protection efforts must happen now. To maintain a viable ancient forest ecosystem will require more than just saving the majestic big trees; we must save all unfragmented mature stands, and restore those degraded, to achieve a matrix of habitat capable of supporting populations of old growth dependent species in perpetuity. This will be difficult, not knowing where the forest stands are.

The Lawyers Take Over

A turning point in the old growth struggle was when the Sierra Club Legal Defense Fund (SCLDF) opened a Seattle office in 1987. Volumes could be written on recent effective litigation, but I'll describe only those suits now pending.

When the Fish and Wildlife Service refused to list the Spotted Owl as Threatened or Endangered, two things happened: SCLDF filed suit against the FWS; and Congress's General Accounting Office (GAO), at the request of a House committee, opened an investigation of the agency.

In November of 1988, Judge Thomas Zilly, a Reagan appointee to the Seattle Circuit Court, ruled that the FWS had been "arbitrary and capricious" in their decision to not list the species. No biologist— including the agency's own experts—had agreed with the decision to not list. The FWS has until May to reconsider.

In February of this year, the GAO issued its report. It found that high level officials within the agency and Department of Interior had interfered with the listing process for the owl. [Ed. note: The FWS is within the Interior Dept.] The GAO also found that, in conflict with the Endangered Species Act, nonbiological considerations (read "political/economic") had factored into the decision to not list. This report contributed to the removal of Frank Dunkle, Fish & Wildlife Service Director, in March. Ominously, James Cason, Bush's recent appointment to Assistant Secretary of Agriculture (overseeing the Forest Service), has been fingered by Rolf Wallenstrom—then-Regional Director of FWS—as one of the high Interior officials who applied pressure to not list the owl.

It is now likely that the Spotted Owl will, come May, be listed at least as Threatened throughout its range, and Endangered in parts. Unfortunately, an actual recovery plan, which would protect habitat, is a long way off.

Lawyers Part II: Taking Candy from a Baby

Back in 1984, National Wildlife Federation appealed the Forest Service Regional Guide for Region 6. The appeal went all the way to then-Assistant Secretary of Agriculture Douglas McCleary (timber beast), who decided that the agency would have to do an environmental impact statement on the Spotted Owl, but that all other points in the appeal would be dropped. From that day on, the owl has taken all the heat for the old growth issue.

In December of 1988, the FS Chief finally signed a Record of Decision on the Spotted Owl EIS. Immediately, everyone and their lawyer appealed the plan. (Appellants included the state of Washington; but in the political heat after the state's appeal, Governor Booth Gardner—a Weyerhaeuser heir—changed his tune to pro-jobs, and the state never filed suit to follow-up their appeal.)

The Assistant Secretary of Agriculture denied all appeals—in effect, forcing the owl issue into the courts. So, the industry filed suit in Portland—saying that the plan will have too big an economic impact and is based on insufficient understanding of the owl's biology. SCLDF filed in Seattle, primarily basing its claims on NFMA violations—the plan would not provide for a viable population of owls. On February 17 in Seattle, Justice William Dwyer heard motions for injunctions from both sides.

Dwyer rejected the industry's arguments that the plan should not be put into effect. The conservationists asked for an injunction against the FS selling any more sales in Spotted Owl habitat until the suit could be resolved. Dwyer said he needed site-specific information, and wouldn't make a blanket ruling.

Within a week, SCLDF presented the judge with some 140 sales in owl habitat. Dwyer issued a Temporary Restraining Order removing all these sales from the agency's timber program until the case is heard in June.

SCLDF and others also have a suit against the BLM in Oregon, where that agency is destroying vast amounts of Spotted Owl habitat on revested O&C Railroad grant lands. This suit is based on restrictions in the Migratory Bird Act under which the owl is protected.

These legal actions, coupled with the massive log exodus to Asia (discussed below), have shocked old growth dependent mills—many of which were already fated to suffer timber shortages sooner than they'll admit. Timber prices are now being bid up faster than in the late 1970s market boom. From mid March to mid April, log prices have nearly doubled.

The State Level

While all the above is occurring in the federal arena, the states also own and log forests, partially supporting school construction with the revenue. In Washington this has led to some interesting political dances.

About 5% of Washington's owl habitat is on state (Department of Natural Resources [DNR]) land. A crucial chunk of this amount is on the state's Hoh-Clearwater Block on the west side of the Olympic Peninsula. This area, ravaged by past decades of logging, is a critical habitat link between Olympic National Forest old growth to the north and south.

The Washington Department of Wildlife has been in a trench war with the DNR over timber sales in owl habitat in this 270,000-acre fragmented forest. The WDW Nongame Division is excellent on this issue; but the DNR, with its devious Commissioner, Brian Boyle, holds the cards. Even though Washington lists the species as endangered, the state has no endangered species act to give that designation teeth.

Undoubtedly, before the battle is resolved, some politicians on the national level will pose as old growth champions—and become popular doing so. The state governments of Washington and Oregon, however, being tied to the industry, will probably remain against the owl.

Indeed, in March, the Washington Senate considered a bill that would force the DNR to immediately log all its old growth. This is, of course, logistically impossible, but a watered-down version of the bill did pass. State representatives sent mailings to their constituents pitting "owls against kids." These mailings actually publicized a demonstration by loggers (which occurred in Olympia, and was countered by EF!ers and others).

The WDNR is dominated by timber beasts. Several DNR employees entered an anti-owl float in the July 4th parade last summer in Forks, the so-called "logging capital of the world." Washington EF! has protested the DNR several times.

In Oregon, the state legislature has passed a ban on all whole log exports from state land. However, as trade is a constitutional issue, the US Congress must act to give the state authority to do this. Such an action has been initiated (see below).

Mounting Tension

Amidst this fury, some have taken a pragmatic approach to stopping the logging holocaust. Spiking is rampant, but what is infuriating the loggers more is the equipment damage. In Whatcom

County (west side of the North Cascades), several hundred thousand dollars of damage has occurred (several incidents) in recent months. Plum Creek (Burlington Northern) suffered considerable damage, supposedly near and on the weekend of the Washington Earth First! spring gathering. Most of the damage has been at prime target federal timber sales. Yet much has also occurred on private lands, second growth operations, even gypo log shows. The latter is the sort of non-strategic "vandalism" that Ecodefense warns against; it comes with a cost.

Washington loggers are livid. Loggers have begun to organize here, as they had already in Montana and Oregon. In early April, 300 log trucks and several ranchers paraded through Omak (near last year's Round River Rendezvous site) against a lawsuit that has bound up most of the Okanogan National Forest cut and against monkey-wrenching. The sheriff of Okanogan County, Jim Weed, appears to be using fear-of-EF! for his own political ends.

Enforcement efforts have been redoubled, if press statements are to be believed. A vigilante trend is running through the logging community now. Bald Mountain sage Lou Gold, in a recent appearance in Gifford Pinchot National Forest country, was greeted by scores of boisterous men in suspenders!

Loggers attended a recent talk I gave to the Audubon Society in Bellingham. Coincidentally, an article about the recent flurry of equipment damage ran in our local paper the day of my talk. I was quoted therein saying that monkeywrenchers aren't born, they are created by situations. The loggers didn't appreciate me blaming their forestry practices for the ecotage.

Communication between loggers and environmentalists has broken down in the past month. Even people like Robert Pyle, author of the excellent book Wintergreen, accustomed to good relations with neighbors in his small logging hometown in southwest Washington's Willapa Hills, have lately noticed relationships chilling. The sources of the tension are concerns about jobs, owls, spiking, and money, and loggers' fear that they face hard times.

The timber industry is eagerly aggravating this situation with propaganda campaigns in small communities. By directing their workers' eyes toward Spotted Owls and insensitive environmentalists, they're able to continue sneaking the last logs onto Asian ships.

On a recent radio broadcast, a logger said, "The people at Hanford (a nuclear plant now being shut down) are engineers—they can be retrained. Loggers can't do anything else." This is a real problem, and one that the corporations have no interest in resolving. If we are not sensitive to it, any protection for old growth will be short-lived.

Legislative Threats

Though our eventual hope for saving the remaining ancient forest is through the US Congress, there also lies our greatest danger. The faster the Northwest pot boils, the more likely it is that Oregon's Senator Hatfield will cook up some law to exempt the Spotted Owl from the ESA, or circumvent NFMA or NEPA (National Environmental Policy Act).

Even if Hatfield does not enact some such diabolical scheme, and even if favorable protection legislation passes, areas not contained in the bill will probably be destined for the mill. Unlike the Wilderness bills, in which we've succeeded in getting "soft release" of areas not included (meaning that these places don't necessarily get cut; they must still be considered for wildlife and recreation value), a bill intended to finally put to rest the ancient forest issue will almost certainly contain "hard release" (read "clearcut") language.

The best way to combat both these threats (note that both come from the Northwest delegation) is to expand support for ancient forests nationally—even internationally. Already it's a national issue, with coverage in *Time*, the *New York Times*, TV news, etc.; but this support must be solidified on the grassroots level. We need a national network of people ready to demand from their elected representatives the support for or squashing of ancient forest legislation.

That is the purpose of the Ancient Forest Rescue Expedition. [Ed. note: This expedition involved speakers and musicians touring the country with a truck bearing an old-growth log, publicizing the plight of the ancient forests.] Our networking of informed grassroots people, coupled with similar work by Lou Gold and others, will help us control the meddling of hostile politicians.

International Issue

Ancient forest is implicitly an international issue for two reasons. One is that Canada is destroying its old growth even faster than the

US. The other is the exports issue.

In British Columbia, Canada, because of the absence of environ-mental laws and the industry bias of the present provincial government (the Forest Minister is from an industry coalition), the situation is bleak. The issue revolves around "hotspots," specific places where environmentalists, such as Western Canada Wilderness Committee, can focus public education efforts.

Each of these places, including the Stein watershed, Carmanah Creek, Meares Island and Shelter Inlet (the latter two in Vancouver Island's Clayoquot Sound), is a story in itself. Most of them involve native land claims, because the laws relating to Indians are far stronger than those on environment. Though we can be optimistic about these specific battles, we're losing the general war in BC.

In that province, 95% of the land is "Crown land"—meaning it is owned by the provincial government. Those lands that are forested are granted to huge corporations in open-ended contracts called "tree farm licenses" (TFLs). The corporations, including MacMillan-Bloedel and New Zealand's massive Fletcher Challenger, then control the land, free. They cut the trees, then—in the few areas actually replanted—the province generally pays for replanting. In BC forests, there is a fine line between subsidization and corporate ownership of state.

Presently, about 1/5 of the province is in TFLs. The Forest Mini-ster is now trying to get the balance divided. A recent article in the *Financial Times of Canada*, the nation's largest financial paper, said the industry is finally getting tough with tree huggers. This means multi-million-dollar ad campaigns, and rampant government graft. It seems the industry fears changing times and attitudes and is trying to get its take before the reckoning.

Both Canada and the US export whole (unprocessed) logs, but the Northwest US exports a far higher proportion of its timber. Having a law limiting timber exports to surplus—beyond mill capac-ity—timber, only about 3% of BC's cut goes abroad; and in early April the provincial government slapped a 100% tax on any whole log exports. In contrast, the Northwest US exports some 7 billion board feet annually, much of it unprocessed. No other country in the world trades this way.

Washington state is the leader in wood exports. Some 40% of our cut goes to Asia. Timber exports are now a matter of much debate in Northwest politics.

In 1988, Oregon Representative Peter DeFazio and Washington Representative Don Bonker introduced legislation in the US House that would have allowed states to regulate exports. The bill didn't even get out of the committee that Bonker himself chaired. Moreover, Bonker lost a bid for the Senate, and now is gone. Yet between last year and this, the issue has so intensified that legislation is likely to pass soon.

Such export restrictions, some say, would put more trees into American mills, reducing the jobs impact of old growth protection. Whether the common ground represented by export restrictions is real or imagined, it may allow some interesting alliances to form.

April 10 will be the West Coast-wide day of action against log exports. In Olympia, Washington, not only are Audubon Society members expected to take to the streets, but so too are millworkers and construction unions.

A major coalition was being built in Olympia, involving even the Pulp and Paper Millworkers Union. But last week, apparently, copies of falsified "minutes," from a meeting of environmentalists that never happened, were mailed to the industry-type groups of this coalition. The minutes allegedly mentioned planned sabotage. As of this writing, some of the groups are withdrawing from the coalition—the industry's paper monkeywrenching has worked.

Conclusion

Everything is happening so fast that the outcome remains unclear. It seems certain, however, that something big will happen by the end of this summer. The economy of the Northwest will be affected by changes in timber base and export policies, and some people—probably not the real villains, though—will suffer. In those areas that don't gain protection, nifty tricks will be needed to keep the forest standing.

Editor's update: The fate of the remaining natural forests in the Northwest has still not been determined. The Northern Spotted Owl was listed as Threatened, and an inter-agency committee produced a report that recommended saving many large tracts of forest land—much to the consternation of Congress. Whether the agencies will abide by the recommendations of the committee's report remains to be seen. Surprisingly, the Forest Service has shown some willingness to do so.

Federal timber export legislation did finally pass. The economic recession has slowed the cutting somewhat. Environmentalists managed to defeat the nomination of James Cason as Assistant Secretary of Agriculture. Instead, a pig farmer was chosen to oversee the Forest Service.

The "Big 10" environmental groups are supporting the Ancient Forest Protection Act (AFPA). Less compromising conservationists are supporting the Native Forest Protection Act (NFPA). AFPA was introduced in Congress in 1990 and gained considerable support. It will be reintroduced in 1991. NFPA supporters are seeking sponsors in Congress to introduce that much stronger proposal.

OF POLITICS, EXTINCTIONS, AND ECOLOGICAL COLLAPSE
Samhain 1989
by Jasper Carlton

At a time when almost every magazine and TV station in the country is touting a new "environmental awareness," our laws and regulations related to the preservation of natural diversity are being thrown to the wind. America is dying biologically and we are allowing the "destroyers" to either limit confrontations to debates over small biotic fragments or to eliminate citizen challenges altogether. While newspapers are filled with details about the destruction of tropical rainforests, little is said about the decline of natural diversity in the US.

Over 6000 species are biologically threatened in the United States! This estimate is of species either critically imperiled because of extreme rarity or very rare as a result of habitat destruction, and includes native vertebrate, invertebrate, and plant species. At best, 20% of these species are presently receiving adequate protection.

Rights of Nature and Citizens Under Fire

In October Congress passed a bill, HR 2788, making appropriations for the Department of Interior and related agencies for fiscal year 1990. Riders on the bill brought by Oregon's and Montana's political leaders allow clearcut logging in the essential habitats of the Northern Spotted Owl, the Grizzly Bear and several other Threatened and Endangered species.

Congress and the American public have failed to realize that such legislative maneuvers are a veiled attempt to circumvent the democratic and legal process. They attach major legislation to an unrelated bill so as to avoid debate or a meaningful vote on the floor of either house of Congress. They bypass the congressional committees charged with handling Forest Service matters. As these amendments become law, the recommendations of field researchers will be thrown aside, management plans ignored, formal appeals made moot, and decisions by federal judges rendered meaningless.

The mutual favor political tactics of the 60s are back again! Shades of the Tennessee Valley Authority (TVA) dam building era, but whereas before it was the destruction of the last free flowing rivers in the Tennessee Valley and the existence of small unknown fish (Snail Darter), now it is annihilation of this country's last ancient forests and of relic Pleistocene spruce-fir forest. The stakes are even greater now. Bioprostitution and political trickery are laying waste to North America's last natural diverse ecosystems.

Congressional maneuvers around US environmental law have aided various economic interests over the years. Corporations facing project delays or cancellation have on a number of occasions lobbied Congress for waivers of NEPA (National Environmental Policy Act). It occurred in 1972 with nuclear power plant licensing after the Calvert Cliffs decision, in 1973 with the Alaska Pipeline, and in 1975 with a freeway case in the Northeast. Some senators and representatives, particularly a few from Arizona, Utah, Wyoming, Idaho and Montana, seem obsessed with flogging NEPA and the Endangered Species Act (ESA). Their flogging is hastening the extinction of many plant and animal species. The nation should rebel!

Due to the machinations of Senator Mark Hatfield (R-OR), the ancient forests of Oregon have taken the worst beating in recent years. Hatfield has attached to appropriations legislation riders exempting destructive timber harvesting from existing conservation laws. The 1985 Senate Interior Supplemental Appropriations Bill included a rider that authorized what would otherwise have been illegal timber sales on Oregon's Siuslaw National Forest. Timber sales had been enjoined by a federal court for NEPA violations; the rider, in effect, overrode the court decision. A rider on the 1988 Senate Interior Appropriations Bill exempted Bureau of Land Management and Forest Service plans in Oregon from judicial challenge. Despite a heroic effort by grassroots activists, the 1989 Senate Interior Appropriations

Bill included a rider that barred court challenges to salvage timber sales in the Silver Fire burn area of Oregon's North Kalmiopsis Roadless Area. As a result, an area that should have been added to the Kalmiopsis Wilderness was logged.

Agencies Above the Law

Predating the latest round of exemptions from environmental law, a similar case demonstrating agency complicity in the subversion of the Endangered Species Act was the proposal for the Stacy Dam on the Concho River in west Texas—now under construction. Pursuant to Section 7 of the ESA, the US Fish and Wildlife Service (FWS) is charged with the responsibility of issuing a Biological Opinion for projects that involve federal funds or lands and that may affect a federally listed Threatened or Endangered species. Under the Act, it is illegal for political or economic considerations to influence the preparation of a Biological Opinion. Though biological data showed that the Stacy Dam would destroy essential habitat of the Concho Water Snake, a Threatened species, FWS released a no jeopardy decision, allowing development to proceed.

Like the National Park Service (whose negligence is most apparent in its mismanagement of Grizzly Bears in Yellowstone National Park), the Fish and Wildlife Service has a better reputation among conservationists than it deserves. The Park Service and Fish and Wildlife Service are thwarting environmental regulations almost as egregiously as are the notorious Forest Service and Bureau of Land Management. What makes the latest series of exemptions particularly dismaying is to see Congress aiding these agencies in the subversion of environmental law.

Biological diversity has also been impacted by such political tactics in the Southwest. In 1988, the University of Arizona engineered a high priced lobbying campaign that convinced the entire Arizona congressional delegation to support a rider approving an astrophysical observatory atop the unique Mt. Graham Sky Island Spruce-Fir Ecosystem, within southern Arizona's Coronado National Forest. Attached to an unrelated bill [which included some environmentally benign measures, thus making it hard for environmentalists to effectively oppose], the rider passed through Congress without debate. It exempted the project from NEPA and NFMA (National Forest Management Act) and seriously weakened already watered down US Fish and Wildlife Service mitigation measures. The federal agencies that allowed this political contrivance may have doomed one of the most critically endangered mammals in North America, the Mt. Graham Red Squirrel.

Whether the Arizona rider functionally exempted the project from all provisions of the Endangered Species Act is now being decided by the Ninth Circuit Court of Appeals, in response to a suit filed by Wayne Woods, the Sierra Club Legal Defend Fund and other co-plaintiffs. Despite the suit, bulldozers are even now scraping a road up the mountain.

The Forest Service and University of Arizona knew that an astrophysical development on Mt. Graham would probably not be allowed if the issue was resolved in the federal courts, pursuant to the mandates of the Endangered Species Act, National Environmental Policy Act and National Forest Management Act. To win an exemption from judicial review in Congress, they needed the support of the Fish and Wildlife Service—ostensibly the lead federal agency in the conservation of the nation's Endangered species—and they apparently got it. Ignoring the preponderance of biological data indicating the squirrel was nearing extinction and its habitat was in decline, the FWS Southwest Regional Director concocted a series of cosmetic mitigation guidelines that allowed the astrophysical development to proceed. The Biological Opinion, upon which the congressional action (exemption) was based, was skewed by political considerations, even as the Stacy Dam decision had been.

The Fish & Wildlife Service similarly abrogated its responsibilities under the ESA in the Upper Yaak Road case in the Kootenai National Forest of northwest Montana. FWS's after-the-fact Biological Opinion [necessitated by the presence of the Grizzly, a Threatened species, and Woodland Caribou, an Endangered species] allowed road construction and timber harvest to continue. In this case, an Environmental Impact Statement—as is required under NEPA for all major federal projects—is the main document of contention.

Montana grassroots activists recently sued under NEPA and won a decision in the Ninth Circuit Court of Appeals that has stopped most logging in the Upper Yaak. The rider in HR 2788, reopening the Yaak to exploitation, was in response to this legal action. The timber to be cut in the Upper Yaak area of the Cabinet/Yaak

Ecosystem would be sold for some of the lowest prices of any standing timber in the country. Using "pine beetle infestation" as a justification, the Forest Service (FS) is planning what amounts to a Lodgepole annihilation program, so that they can replant with fast growing pines for later timber harvests. The sales would lose money; i.e., they would cost the US taxpayer.

The ultimate cost of the cutting, however, may be the elimination of the area as a Grizzly Bear, Gray Wolf, and Woodland Caribou recovery area. Combined with the road-building plan under the Kootenai National Forest Plan and the FS's and FWS's likely approval of two huge new silver mines in the heart of Grizzly Bear habitat, the cutting may spell the biological death of the Cabinet/Yaak Ecosystem. Environmentalists now plan to sue again, despite the rider, over the agencies' failure to consider the cumulative impact of timber and mining development in the Cabinet/Yaak Ecosystem. [The agencies are treating timber cutting and mining in separate EISs, and ignoring overall impacts.]

Meanwhile in the Northwest, the Fish and Wildlife Service failed to propose ESA listing for the biologically endangered Northern Spotted Owl until it was forced to do so through the federal courts. This battle, the most widely publicized of the three main conflicts at present over endangered species and exemptions, also rages on, with the recently passed riders ensuring further felling of the Ancient Forests of Oregon and Washington.

To summarize the foregoing, it appears that much of the administrative and legal system for protecting rare and endangered species has broken down under the Reagan and Bush administrations. Whenever economics comes into conflict with ecology, economics wins. And would the "Environmental President" veto a destructive bill such as HR 2788? As well ask: does James Watt defecate in a composting toilet?

Congress may have been seriously misled by the US Forest Service into believing that roads and clearcuts in the Upper Yaak area of Montana would not jeopardize the Grizzly Bear or that a huge astrophysical development on Mt. Graham would not harm the Mt. Graham Red Squirrel. Congress trusted FWS conclusions. Again, however, Congress too is at fault, as is most evident in the Northwest, where timber sales that threaten listed species are being allowed because of riders approved by Congress. Moreover, congresspersons from the Northwest, Northern Rockies and Southwest have applied pressure on the Secretaries of Agriculture (which department has jurisdiction over the FS) and Interior (which has jurisdiction over FWS, BLM, and NPS) to ensure that management plans for Endangered species do not stand in the way of economic development.

Conservationists need to realize that these riders, which preclude judicial review (citizen legal challenges) of Forest Service and BLM management plans, were not initiated solely by the timber industry. The agencies themselves requested many of the exemptions. Tragically, they come at a time when we should be *strengthening* NEPA and ESA.

Loss of Species

Under the present administrative system, there is a major difference between *biologically* threatened or endangered species, and *legislatively* Threatened or Endangered species. In the legislative sense, only those species that are formally listed by state or federal agencies are Threatened or Endangered. However, thousands of species in the United States are now at risk but have not been placed on either state or federal endangered species lists. If they are not cute and cuddly charismatic mammals, they typically receive little attention and less protection. How many of us are defending rare plants, bugs and slugs, bats and rats?

The number of species being placed at greater risk by Forest Service management and the recent legislative moves is disconcerting. In Montana's Cabinet/Yaak Ecosystem, the Northern Bald Eagle, Peregrine Falcon, Gray Wolf, Grizzly Bear, Western Big-eared Bat, Wolverine, Coeur d'Alene Salamander, Common Loon, Harlequin Duck, Boreal Owl, Woodland Caribou, and many sensitive plant and fish species are in serious trouble or already extirpated.

In Arizona's Mt. Graham Ecosystem, the Apache Trout, Twin-spotted Rattlesnake, Mexican Garter Snake, Peregrine Falcon, Mexican Spotted Owl, Apache Goshawk, Black Bear, Coues' White-tailed Deer, Mt. Graham Pocket Gopher, Long-tailed Vole, Mountain Lion, Pinaleno Monkey Grasshopper, *Erigeron pringlei*, *Dodecatheon ellisae*, *Corralorhiza maculata*, *Habernia hyperborea*, *Primula rusbyi*, and *Veratrum lanatum* are all in trouble. Some of these are subspecies found nowhere else.

Within the Northwest's Ancient Forest Ecosystems, the Clouded Salamander, Foothill Yellow-legged Frog, Northern Flying Squirrel,

Pine Marten, Long-eared Myotis, Northern Spotted Owl, Bald Eagle, Marbled Murrelet, and some hawks, ducks, and wrens are threatened by old growth forest destruction. Scientists are unsure how many plant and animal species are associated with or dependent upon old growth.

Owls, Squirrels, Bears and the ESA

The legislation surfacing all over the West in the past few years not only exempts timber sales and other development activities from judicial review, it also preempts the mandate of the Endangered Species Act, arguably the strongest environmental legislation ever passed in this country. We should consider how this environmental law has broken down.

One factor is that congressional mandates and court precedents, even at the Supreme Court level, are often ignored by the timber industry, Forest Service and some congresspersons. The FS, BLM, FWS and the U of A have all conveniently ignored or forgotten the Supreme Court decision in the infamous Snail Darter Case (TVA v. Hill). The words of Chief Justice Burger, in his majority opinion for the Court, still ring beautifully in my ears:

> One would be hard pressed to find a statutory provision whose terms were any plainer than those in Section 7 of the Endangered Species Act. Its very words affirmatively command all federal agencies "to insure that actions authorized, funded, or carried out by them do not jeopardize the continued existence" of an endangered species or "result in the destruction or modification of habitat of such species . . . " This language admits of no exception . . . (437 US:174)

The Supreme Court held that Section 7 of the ESA barred the completion of federal projects in conflict with Endangered species, and that in enacting the ESA, "Congress intended endangered species to be afforded the highest of priorities," even over the "primary missions" of federal agencies. George Bush, Manuel Lujan [Interior Secretary], John Turner [FWS Director], Dale Robertson [FS Chief] . . . are you listening?

In response to the Supreme Court Decision in TVA v. Hill, Congress within a few months introduced an element of "flexibility" into the ESA by passing new amendments, one of which allowed for possible exemption from the Act for some federal projects. The exemption process established by this amendment now merits special scrutiny in light of the plight of the Mt. Graham Red Squirrel, Grizzly Bear, Northern Spotted Owl, and the recently emergency-listed Desert Tortoise.

One aspect of the new flexibility was the creation of the so-called God Committee (or "God Squad"), empowered to exempt projects from ESA under special circumstances. This committee was and is composed of such political appointees as the Secretaries of Agriculture, Interior, and Commerce. Little has ever been heard of the God Committee because it has rarely been used.

Indeed, the passage by Congress of an ESA exemption process has not proven as disastrous as initially it appeared. In only a few cases has the exemption process even been attempted. Many environmentalists don't realize that when the Snail Darter issue reached the God Committee under the new exemption process, its exemption was denied. It was the US Congress, acting later as an even higher but less moral god, that exempted the Tellico Dam from the ESA, by passing special legislation. Without the powerful pork-barrel tactics of Tennessee's congressional delegation and the fact that the dam was 90% complete, the project might have been defeated even in the halls of Congress.

The proper ESA exemption process has not proven as dangerous as feared because it entails public scrutiny before exemptions may be granted. Now, however, exemptions from judicial review in the form of riders in agency appropriation bills are functioning as *de facto* ESA exemptions, without full congressional and public scrutiny. The Forest Service and timber industry and the University of Arizona all realize that they risk being perceived as hostile to Endangered species preservation if they request an exemption through the proper ESA process. They also are cognizant of the complex procedures they would face in the exemption process itself. Most important, they know that they would probably fail in that effort since most of the public and members of Congress support the preservation of Endangered species.

In short, if any federal agency, state governors, or industry permittees affected by the Endangered Species Act are so inclined, they are entitled to seek an exemption under existing provisions of the Act. If they are honest enough not to employ the surreptitious tactics and collusion characteristic of recent ESA *de facto* exemptions, they will do so in full public view.

Congress has long recognized the need for citizen monitoring and enforcement of environmental laws and regulations. Without citizen challenges, enforcement of laws would be minimal under such administrations as Bush's. To remove the right of citizens to challenge illegal and destructive government actions not only undermines the principles of our democratic form of government, it invites more radical and revolutionary intervention strategies.

In the long run, these undemocratic political maneuvers will result in a greater number of legal actions since their implementation is increasing endangerment of hundreds of species. The population levels of many less known and little studied species will drop so low that recovery efforts in the wild will become exceedingly costly. The programs for the California Condor and Black-footed Ferret [both now apparently extinct from the wild] should have taught us that habitat protection and restoration measures must be taken in advance, while species populations are sufficiently healthy to allow for recovery in the wild.

Local Economic vs. Global Concerns

Perennial critics of the Endangered Species Act, such as the timber, energy, cattle, off-road vehicle, and power boat lobbies, argue that the preservation of "obscure" species should not stand in the way of economic development. A double standard exists in this country where enforcement of conservation law is concerned. If enforcement is popular due to economic benefits derived, or a cute and charismatic mammal is involved, local and regional protection may be possible. Of all rare and endangered plants and animals, however, 90% do not fit these requirements. Consequently, thousands of species are falling through the cracks of environmental planning in the US.

Local economic interests argue, in effect, that Las Vegas should be allowed to devastate the Desert Tortoise in order to sustain its housing boom; that the Anastasia Island Beach Mouse should be sacrificed for more condominiums on Florida's Anastasia Island; and that the Forest Service should be allowed to continue promoting logging, road-building and energy development in the Northern Rockies, to the detriment of the Grizzly Bear. These are merely three of many examples of species ostensibly protected under the ESA but in fact continuing to lose their habitats to development.

Unfortunately, in our society at present, thinking globally and acting locally will not suffice to prevent extinctions. Many towns throughout the country, if permitted, will willingly sacrifice native species in the name of economic progress. If it were up to Libby or Troy, Montana, there would be no Grizzlies in the Cabinet/Yaak Ecosystem; if it were up to Bonners Ferry, Idaho, there would be no Woodland Caribou in the Selkirk Ecosystem; if it were up to Reserve, New Mexico, there would be no Mexican Spotted Owls in the Gila/Aldo Leopold Wilderness complex; if it were up to Innokalee, Florida, there would be no Florida Panthers in the Everglades; if it were up to Cedar Key, Florida, there would be no Manatees in the Suwanee Sound; if it were up to Cheat Neck, West Virginia, there would be no Flat-spired Three-toothed Land Snails in the Cheat River Gorge. . . .

As habitat is altered and destroyed, extirpations—local and regional extinctions—result. These extirpations are leading to the ecological collapse of this country's last natural, diverse ancient forest, wetland hardwood, desert, and tallgrass prairie ecosystems.

In most North American ecosystems now supporting multiple rare and endangered species, no mitigation measures could render proposed economic developments environmentally acceptable. A moratorium on development in biologically sensitive areas should be imposed, but local governments are unwilling to take such a step.

If we leave decisions to local political and economic planning, thousands of species will be lost in this country. Local extinctions that society accepts in order to accommodate development will eventually result in global extinctions. Yes, education and organizing are essential, but even if local cooperation cannot be gained, we should not accept the loss of natural diversity at the local level.

Those who espouse an economic remedy to forest mismanagement may deserve part of the blame for the economics vs. ecology predicament. By declaring that an economically well run forest will produce an ecologically sound forest, they encourage a continuing emphasis on economics and jobs at the expense of natural systems. Jobs are not the major issue. Loggers can be retrained and reemployed in ecologically benign jobs.

Dire Implications

Citizens must obey the law or go to prison, but federal agencies that supposedly operate in the "public interest" are being allowed to violate the law. The Forest Service, to name perhaps the worst offender, not only subsidizes the timber industry, it also supports the industry through its management plans and its thwarting of environmental laws. If Congress does not reject these underhanded political tactics, if Congress does not uphold citizens' rights to appeal, what will be the next liberties we lose?

These tactics demonstrate that exploitive industries are unwilling to pay the price of doing business on the public lands. That price is full compliance with US laws and regulations. The response of citizens and Congress should be quick and decisive: individuals and companies that destroy biotic systems should be barred from conducting business on our public lands!

What to Do with the Forest Service

If the GAO (General Accounting Office) were to publish annual statistics on the cumulative adverse environmental impact of the projects of the US Forest Service, Congress and the American people would see that this agency should be dismantled. The Forest Service cannot be reformed; no amount of economic mumbo-jumbo can correct its deficiencies.

The present controversies over our last ancient forests, the Grizzly in the Northern Rockies, and the Mt. Graham Red Squirrel bear stark testimony to the FS's abandonment of sound scientific principles. The constant seeking of exemptions from conservation laws constitutes an admission that even minimal standards of ecological protection are not being met.

Drastic changes in Forest Service programs would not solve the problem. Court challenges of FS actions could go on forever while agency mandates are ignored. Our entire system for protecting landscapes in this country must be overhauled. All biologically sensitive lands in the National Forest System should be removed from Forest Service jurisdiction and consolidated and protected as part of large, natural biological preserves under the umbrella of a Native Ecosystems Act.

No More Compromise

Ongoing negotiations in the Northwest and Northern Rockies do not reflect the severity of the situation. The old growth forests have been reduced to scattered remnants; there is nothing left to compromise. It is disturbing to witness the apparent rush by some so-called environmental groups to make compromises that further fragment Northwest Ancient Forest Ecosystems or "mitigate away" the last undisturbed Grizzly habitat in the Northern Rockies.

We must not limit our battle lines to small remaining groves of old growth trees or other small biotic fragments in the West. To do so would be to admit defeat. Has the demise of the Coast Redwoods in northern California and old growth hardwoods in the East taught us nothing? If lines are to be drawn, then they should be drawn generously to include entire ecosystems.

No compromise, no mitigation, no Habitat Conservation Plans are appropriate. All timber sales in Spotted Owl habitat in the Northwest should be stopped; the U of A should be banned from Mt. Graham; a permanent moratorium on logging, road-building and mining should be enacted for the Cabinet/Yaak Ecosystem.

As this issue goes to press, environmentalists are gathering the details of HR 2788 as it was finally passed by Congress. President Bush is expected to sign the bill without delay. According to the October 1 *New York Times*, the compromise approved by the House-Senate conference committee, later passed as part of HR 2788, includes the following provisions: 1) Federal sales of timber in the Northwest region would be reduced and the federal government could not sell timber from areas identified as Spotted Owl habitat. 2) Court challenges to individual timber sales would be allowed but would have to be filed within 15 days of the sale offering and the courts would have to decide within 45 days. 3) About half the timber now barred from sale by federal courts would be released. 4) The Senate would no longer insist on a 12 month ban on federal court orders blocking timber sales.

Details on the final form of the rider exempting projects in the Cabinet/Yaak Ecosystem from the ESA and NEPA are not yet known. In short, HR 2788 compromises away more of the Northwest Ancient Forest and Cabinet/Yaak Ecosystems.

What You Can Do

Write your senators (US Senate, Washington, DC 20510) and representative (House of Representatives, Washington, DC 20515) urging them
to oppose any future legislation that includes "riders" on agency appropriation bills designed to prevent administrative or judicial review of public
land management decisions. Ask them to initiate oversight hearings on
agency subversion of the Endangered Species Act. Urge them to support
the National Biological Diversity Conservation and Environmental
Research Act, which would establish a policy for the conservation of biodiversity in the US and would require agencies to fully disclose the impact
of all their activities on biodiversity. The EF! Biodiversity Project supports
this bill as a good first step toward preserving ecosystems.

*Editor's update: America has continued to die, subsequent to the above
events. The Northern Spotted Owl was listed as Threatened, yet cutting of
old-growth continues. The Mt. Graham Red Squirrel population dropped
sharply, yet clearing of the mountain top for the scopes proceeds. The
Grizzly Bear, Gray Wolf, and Woodland Caribou survive in perilously low
numbers in the Cabinet/Yaak Ecosystem, yet timber harvest levels on
National Forest there remain high. Moreover, the Montana Department of
Fish, Wildlife and Parks—perhaps with the support of federal agencies, certainly with the support of ranchers—is now trying to delist the Grizzly Bear
in the Northern Continental Divide Ecosystem, which would remove its
protection in Montana under the Endangered Species Act.*

*Bush Administration officials, including Interior Secretary Manuel
Lujan, are muttering about weakening the Endangered Species Act so that it
does not interfere with economic development; but Congress still appears to
support the ESA as is. The proposed Biological Diversity Act has been gaining support in Congress and will probably be reintroduced in 1991.*

LIVESTOCK GRAZING ON THE NATIONAL PARKS: A NATIONAL DISGRACE
December 1990
by Dale Turner and Lynn Jacobs

> *Grazing on park land is permitted where authorized by law or
> permitted for a term of years as a condition of land acquisition.*
>
> *Grazing and raising of livestock is also permitted in historic
> zones where desirable to perpetuate and interpret the historic scene.*
>
> —National Park Service Guideline NPS-53, Special Park Uses

America's National Parks are world-famous for their beauty and grandeur. Since the late 1800s Congress has been setting aside these lands as the most impressive examples of untrammeled Nature in this country. Today they comprise the most extraordinary system of natural preserves on Earth.

Naturally most Americans think their National Parks and Monuments are protected from commercial exploitation. And generally they are, outside certain heavily visited locations, where concessionaires are permitted to operate stores, gas stations, lodges, and other services deemed necessary for tourists. However, ranching is a glaring exception. A little history:

As with most Forest Service (FS), Bureau of Land Management (BLM), state, and other public lands, most lands in the West chosen for the National Park Service (NPS) system were, prior to designation, open to ranching. More than any other group, the stockmen holding permits to graze these lands, some of whom own strategic inholdings, influenced their fate.

In some cases, the federal government was able with generous offers to buy out grazing permits and base properties or make special deals with stockmen to establish ranching-free Parks. Many ranchers increased their wealth and power as a result; some left the livestock business, others expanded their ranching operations elsewhere.

In many instances, however, stockmen (supported by their elected representatives) refused to relinquish "their" grazing permits to the proposed National Park lands, even though usually most of their forage and browse needs were met by other lands. They forced the government into special agreements that allowed them to continue ranching the new Park lands in perpetuity or for a period of years. Consequently, some Parks (Sequoia, for example) have over the years paid off ranchers and phased out ranching, while others (such as Great Basin) plan to continue ranching indefinitely. Currently, a bill to expand southern Idaho's Craters of the Moon National Monument and turn it into a National Park contains wording mandating continued livestock grazing at near-traditional levels. A proposal by the Hell's Canyon Preservation Council to turn Hell's Canyon National Recreation Area (in Oregon and Idaho) into a National Park is likewise shackled with wording designed to continue ranching. New Mexico's newly designated El Mapais National Monument also plans to continue ranching.

Some stockmen owning base properties and/or other ranchland within proposed Park boundaries required that, as a condition of acquiring these private lands, the government allow them to continue traditional ranching on the new Park land. Others refused to yield their private lands and as a consequence some Parks, such as Zion in Utah and Black Canyon of the Gunnison in Colorado, still contain private ranches within their borders.

Some ranchers even convinced the government to allow them to maintain ranching operations in new Park units under guise of "preserving the historic Old West" for the benefit of tourists (Pipe Springs NM in northern Arizona is a disgraceful example). These and some other NPS units actively promote ranching. However, ranching in many Parks proceeds only under the ardent objections of Park supervisors and staff.

In the 11 Western states the National Park Service currently administers 23 National Parks; 47 National Monuments; 11 National Recreation Areas; and 17 National Memorials, Historic Sites, Historic Parks, Battlefield Parks, Seashores, and such. These 98 NPS units cover about 17 million acres, or 2.3% of the West. Close to 3 million acres of this land is open to commercial ranching, within 7 National Parks, 7 National Monuments, 5 National Recreation Areas, and 7 National Memorials, etc. Many NPS units outside the West also allow ranching, even Haleakala National Park in Hawaii.

Livestock production on National Park Service lands, mostly cattle ranching, is administered by the Park Service or, in several cases, adjacent federal land management agencies. Ranching impact on NPS lands generally is less severe than on any other public or private ranchlands in the West. However, some NPS units have serious problems and in most units historic ranching damage lingers (Yosemite, Canyonlands, and Petrified Forest, for example). Some ranchers with allotments on NPS lands—and even some without—are granted permission to trail livestock across NPS lands.

Most NPS stockmen pay the same micro-fee charged other federal permittees under the Public Rangelands Improvement Act formula— $1.81 in 1990, or about 1/5 fair market value. Also, as with BLM and FS permittees, the government sponsors nearly all of their range developments and guarantees construction and maintenance of any range "improvements" deemed necessary for continued ranching. Park

Service reports indicate that the agency spends millions of tax dollars each year on or because of ranching—at least several times what it takes in from grazing fees. Many of these reports complain of fiscal waste on ranching management, personnel tied up with ranching matters, overgrazing and structural damages to Parks, and cattle in campgrounds and other tourist areas.

> . . . there is no authorized cattle grazing in the park . . .
> There are inholdings of private land and many acres of private and public land along Zion's boundaries where grazing is permitted. Maintaining fence along the boundary is a large task. Although we have a very good fence crew, it needs to be bigger to completely exclude cattle. We also badly need additional managers to patrol for cattle trespass and other violations.

—Harold L. Grafe, Superintendent, Zion National Park, Utah, 8–18–89 letter

Rivaling and perhaps even surpassing permitted ranching as a problem on National Park Service lands is trespass grazing. The Parks' relatively lush vegetation is a magnet for nearby hungry livestock, which commonly break through fences or come through open gates, perhaps with a little help from their owners. Ranchlands border nearly all Parks in the West and the thousands of miles of protective fences in often rugged terrain are difficult and expensive for NPS to maintain. Thus, the job descriptions of many NPS employees, even in "ungrazed" Parks, include patrolling for trespassing livestock; closing gates; chasing cattle, sheep, and horses out of tourist areas; rounding up, moving, and caring for trespass animals; repairing developments and mitigating environmental impacts; dealing with permittees; and building and mending fence.

Most Parks in the West report problems from trespass livestock. A 1986 project statement by Kings Canyon National Park in California, for example, states that impacts from trespassing cattle include, "trampling of wetlands, conversion of grass to feces, formation of cattle trails, extra erosion, fecal deposition in streams, and destruction of sedges . . . " The statement requests "$300,000 for the first year and $20,000/yr thereafter for increased patrol and fence maintenance." A similar statement by Organ Pipe Cactus National Monument in southern Arizona requests $195,000 for fencing, patrolling, and other management due to "serious" trespass problems "which could multiply manifold" if protective measures are not taken. At Arizona's world-famous Grand Canyon National Park, officials state that trespass grazing has caused changes in soil, native wildlife, and vegetation; they likewise request more protective fencing. In northwestern California's Redwood National Park, 117 cattle and horses were reported to have trespassed 1170 acres in 1984 (the latest figures available); recently $22,000 was expended there to modify 4 miles of the boundary fence because Elk were dying on it. And so on.

Roughly *half* of all National Parks in the West are trespassed more or less regularly by livestock from adjacent public and private lands, or from NPS allotments themselves. The Rocky Mountain Region of NPS reports in its *Summary of Livestock Grazing for 1987* that livestock trespassed 11 of its 14 grazed units and ate 8% as much herbage as permitted animals. However, as with other federal lands, officially recorded amounts probably represent only a small fraction of actual trespass. I have several times witnessed trespassing cattle or sheep that were undiscovered or ignored or later chased out of Parks without official recognition.

> *Wyoming's U.S. Senator Clifford Hansen held, in the Tetons, the largest grazing permit in all the Park Service—for 569 cattle. The permit had originated as trespass grazing in clear violation of federal law years before. The record was clear—the Park Service would have to enforce its own laws and regulations and cancel Hansen's permit and others like it. . . . The chief ranger was a tall, experienced man who carefully read my memorandum before he called me into his office. He clapped a fatherly hand on my shoulder and looked both concerned and sympathetic. "Young man," he said, "I don't care what you find in those records; as long as Cliff Hansen sits on the Senate Interior Committee, we ain't going to fuck with his cows."*—Bernard Shanks, *This Land Is Your Land* (1984)

Here's the ranching situation on several NPS units:

In Wyoming's Grand Teton National Park 24,000 acres are grazed by 1600 cattle owned by 8 permittees. Most of this acreage is in the beautiful, grassy, and profitable Snake River Valley; political string pulling secured continued ranching here. Park visitors are encouraged to view the overgrazing cattle, fences, and other range developments as part of the natural scenery.

Southern Utah's Zion National Park, world-renowned for its spectacular canyons and colorful rock formations, hosts a private cattle ranch within its boundaries, with guaranteed access, though none of the Park is legally grazed. An adjacent permittee drives herds of cattle through part of the Park each spring. Reports show that in 1987, 200 trespassing cattle grazed 1200 AUMs on 5400 Park acres, upsetting fragile riparian corridors and desert ecology. Herds of sheep also trespass Zion's verdant high country, but little of this is officially recognized or challenged.

The recently created, largely overgrazed Great Basin National Park in east-central Nevada would have encompassed hundreds of thousands of acres of basin and range if it had been meant to truly represent the Basin and Range province. Under pressure from stockmen the proposed Park's size was reduced until all that remained was 77,100 acres—all in the steep mountains, with the least productive rangeland. Thus Great Basin National Park contains no basin! Language in the Park bill—without which the bill probably would not have passed—allows grazing to continue at more or less pre-existing levels indefinitely. A Park brochure assures tourists that "cattle grazing [is] an integral part of the Great Basin scene." It fails to say that visitors will see thousands of cattle en route to the Park and will hardly wish to see more, especially in the campgrounds, where they now graze. On the sides of the Park's 13,000-foot Wheeler Peak, you may (as I have) find cattle above 10,000 feet.

> *Throughout the grazing season, we assisted permittees with livestock management on the Park as often as possible. This fostered good working relations with the permittees.*—Resource Management Plan Updates, 1989, Great Basin National Park

Big Bend National Park in southwest Texas is a designated World Biosphere Reserve. Historic ranching there was so destructive that even now, several decades after the grazing was banned, much of the Park bears little resemblance to pre-livestock times. Although most of the Park is gradually recovering, trespassing livestock, mainly from Mexico, so heavily degrade the Rio Grande canyon that in many riparian areas cottonwood regeneration is virtually nonexistent.

Even Channel Islands National Park, off the southern California coast, has livestock problems. Ranching there is scheduled to be phased out over the next decade; however, officials report that largely from past and present overgrazing, all the islands have high rates of soil erosion. Livestock also cause vegetation destruction, disturbance of archeological sites, trail damage, and sloughing of sea cliffs.

Until a few years ago, 1800 to 2500 cattle grazed under BLM administration from October to May each year over most of southern Utah's fantastic Capitol Reef National Park—on 146,393 acres in 1987. A century of grazing had stripped off native vegetation, caused serious soil erosion, dried up springs and creeks, severely harmed the few remaining riparian areas, destroyed most of the cryptogamic layer, and helped extirpate Bighorn Sheep and other species. Cattle and ranching developments degraded the fragile desert scenery and disturbed Park visitors.

When the Park was created from Capitol Reef National Monument and surrounding public lands in 1971, the thirty-some permittees agreed to phase out grazing by 1982. That year, however, Utah Senator Jake Garn and other ranching advocate politicians introduced legislation to extend grazing in the Park for the lifetimes of the permittees and their heirs. Congress compromised by extending grazing until 1994. The Park supervisor recently attempted a buy-out of permits, but the politicos pushed through a provision extending grazing for permittees who don't want to sell, for their lifetimes and those of sons and daughters living in 1971. Today, negotiations and generous pay-offs have induced most stockmen to sell "their" permits, but several permittees still graze the Park.

Ranching in northwest Colorado's 200,000 acre Dinosaur National Monument has also been reduced in recent years, from about 120,000 acres on 22 allotments to about 80,000 acres on 11 allotments. A phase-out program similar to Capitol Reef's allows permittee family members to retain grazing privileges for their lifetimes or cash them in, whichever they desire. As in Capitol Reef, though ranching in the Monument is waning, its legacy will remain for decades or centuries—grasslands converted to sage and bare dirt, depleted soil and waters, ravaged riparian areas, worsened flooding (which damages the Monument's dinosaur fossil beds), road cuts, and devastated wildlife. Indeed, Bighorn Sheep were extirpated mostly due to ranching by the early 1950s.

Black Canyon of the Gunnison National Monument in west-central Colorado encompasses a 20-mile portion of the rugged Gunnison River gorge and some rangeland above it. Several permittees run nearly 1000 cattle on about 7000 acres (the remainder is inaccessible, much of it vertical). The owner of one ranch inholding has threatened to bulldoze an access road, clear brush, build stock ponds and ranch structures, harvest Christmas trees, and generally create as big an eyesore as possible if the Park Service doesn't make a lucrative offer for a scenic easement on his 600 acres, while he retains actual title. Another Monument rancher was recently paid 2.1 million dollars for his 4200 acre ranch inholding and given grazing privileges within the Monument for 20 years.

Glen Canyon National Recreation Area spreads across 1.25 million acres in southeastern Utah. Its infamous Glen Canyon Dam entombs some of the most wonderful river canyons on Earth under the dead waters of "Lake" Powell. Nearly one million fragile, arid to semi-arid NRA acres are included in 38 grazing allotments that could only support 554 cattle in 1987/88 (about 1800 acres per animal). Most of the remaining quarter million acres is under water. Several government agencies are presently conducting tax-sponsored studies for a Glen Canyon NRA long-term livestock grazing management plan.

The 1.5 million acre Lake Mead National Recreation Area of southernmost Nevada, northwest Arizona, and southwest Utah is host to the largest National Park Service ranching operation of all, covering about 1.1 million acres. Aside from the Colorado River and "Lake" Mead itself, the entire NRA is low-elevation, hot, arid, and relatively barren. An Eastern livestock producer might think it a cruel joke to turn cattle out on this burning desert. But the joke is once again on the public and its land, as well as the livestock. BLM resource area offices in Nevada, Arizona, and Utah provide ranching administration and assistance on the NRA for 20 permittees and their cattle. The huge bovines trample and erode the fragile desert soil, crush the cryptogams, and consume the scant greenery. They congregate around the area's few water sources and along the "Lake" Mead and Colorado River shorelines where they invade campgrounds and foul beaches. We pay to fence them out of the locations popular with tourists and a few of the most environmentally sensitive areas. Aside from the usual seasonal grazing, stockmen are allowed to bring their cattle into much of Lake Mead NRA whenever wet weather produces a "surplus" of forage or browse—what is termed "ephemeral grazing."

Point Reyes National Seashore north of San Francisco is largely a livestock operation. Eighteen permittees graze beef cattle, dairy cows, and sheep on about 25,000 acres and cultivate an additional 2000 acres for oats and rye—together, roughly 40% of the Seashore. This includes the most sensitive portion of the Seashore, with 23 rare plant species and 4 animal species targeted for protection (due partly to ranching impacts). Ranching roads, fences, and outbuildings displace wildlife. Overgrazing removes native vegetation, spreads "pest" species such as thistle and poison hemlock, and increases flooding. Herbicides, pesticides, and livestock wastes pollute fresh and salt water. These influences and increased soil erosion, calculated at 110,000 tons annually, threaten the health of the Drakes and Limantour Estuaries, the last two estuaries on the California coast in a semi-natural state. NPS is currently throwing hundreds of thousands of tax dollars at the problem, rather than halting livestock operations.

Several miles south, just across the bridge from San Francisco, commercial cattle and horses graze more than 2000 acres of Golden Gate NRA.

Through the years ranchers have been foremost among those working to prevent establishment of new National Parks. In some cases they halted them altogether, and often they were able to limit their size. At present, in California's Mojave Desert six permittees are fighting tooth and nail to prevent transformation of BLM's East Mojave Scenic Area into Mojave National Park. The ranchers graze only about 3000 cattle on the arid 1.6 million acre expanse—about *one cow per square mile*— but their opposition is a formidable barrier to Park designation.

On the 210 million acres in the Midwest that were tallgrass prairie, there are no National Parks or Monuments and less than 3% of the original grassland remains—in degraded condition. Ranchers there have thus far beat back serious attempts to establish a Tallgrass Prairie National Park, first in Kansas and then in Oklahoma.

And of course, many potential Parks will never be realized because stockmen own outright about a quarter of the rural West, including many locations that might otherwise have become Parks.

Nearly every NPS unit where ranching has been banned shows significant recovery—Grand Canyon, Petrified Forest, Rocky Mountain, Yellowstone, Yosemite, Sequoia/Kings Canyon, Canyonlands, Arches, Bryce, Natural Bridges, Wupatki, and many more. In 1978–79 livestock were removed from Arizona's Organ Pipe National Monument. Previously, most of the expansive 500 square mile Monument was desolate due to decades of ranching abuse. Today,

even this arid desert is relatively verdant. So the solution to the overgrazing problems on National Park Service lands is obvious: Remove
all livestock and ranching developments from all Park Service lands.

*Where grazing is permitted and its continuation is not in the
best interest of public use or maintenance of the park ecosystem, it
will be eliminated . . .*

—National Park Service (NPS) Guideline NPS-53, Special Park Uses

CHAPTER 3

Critiques of the Status Quo

ALONG WITH MILITARISM AND OVERCONSUMPTION, *the underlying causes of the global environmental crisis include technology, industrialism, and overpopulation. Partly because mainstream environmentalists have been loath to confront technology, industrialism, and overpopulation, Earth First! thinkers have devoted considerable attention to these subjects.*

Indeed, even as they have been developing a philosophical alternative to the techno-industrial paradigm, that alternative being deep ecology, or biocentrism,* these thinkers have attempted to subvert the dominant paradigm through analyses and critiques of its assumptions and its implications. The critiques presented in Earth First! Journal *by such writers as Christoph Manes and R.F. Mueller are uniquely radical indictments of techno-industrial society, daring to suggest that technology* per se *may be the problem, not simply inappropriate technology.*

Human overpopulation is perhaps the most intractable and inadequately addressed problem in the world today. Earth First! Journal *did not sufficiently address this overarching problem; yet it did so more than almost any other environmental periodical. If the following essays are on target, the reluctance of most people to confront the population problem is not surprising; ending the population explosion may require ending industrial society.*

---

*Many deep ecology theorists differentiate between deep ecology and biocentrism, considering the latter a tenet of the former. However, some opponents of anthropocentrism are not happy with the term 'deep ecology' and prefer to use the term 'biocentrism' for the worldview that united EF!ers. For the purposes of this book, it is easiest to set aside semantic differences and simply treat the two terms as roughly interchangeable.

TECHNOLOGY AND MOUNTAIN THINKING
Brigid 1986
by Christoph Manes

The question of technology lies at the heart of the environmental crisis. I say "question" because, far from being a self-evident issue, what technology is and how we should deal with it, is exactly what needs to be addressed if we want to start "thinking like a mountain"—to use Aldo Leopold's phrase for a clarity of vision and insight that took him beyond the anthropocentric delusions of our vainglorious culture. My point in considering the meaning of technology is not to float off into the philosophic ether; philosophy that corrupts action isn't worth an oyster, and probably isn't philosophy. We all know what needs to be done to an unattended bulldozer stumbled upon in an old growth forest. But larger, more complex environmental concerns are better approached with a view to the wider implications of the technological threat, which go beyond its ugly hardware.

You hear the following argument from all kinds of people, environmentalists included: Technology is a tool—admittedly it has gotten out of hand, but the problem is not with the tool, but how we use it. We have to learn to use "appropriate" technology. Sometimes environmentalists add the more insightful corollary that the problem lies mainly in who controls technology. The solution, then, is to decentralize, which would allow us to determine for ourselves how to use technology appropriately.

On the common-sense level all this is obviously true. Most decentralization is good, and who wouldn't prefer appropriate technology to the destructive technology now befouling our air, land, and water? Yet, it is the obvious things that should give us pause, because they sometimes conceal enigmas no longer questioned. We may be deluding ourselves in thinking we can have fluoride toothpaste without having nuclear warheads. It may be that we don't use technology at all, but that it uses us. Which is to say that its physical manifestations—the chainsaws and smokestacks we all deplore—result from a relationship between humanity and Earth which transcends our immediate power to control.

In *The Question Concerning Technology* Martin Heidegger comes to these perplexing conclusions. This is a work environmentalists should read, even if they disagree with Heidegger's views, because it upsets the usual assumptions about technology underlying modern ideologies of every type. In this it shows a kinship with some currents of deep ecology. Heidegger's argument implies that nuclear missiles (and deforestation and factories and bureaucratic minds) do, in a sense, come out of your tube of toothpaste. In other words, the institutions required to produce the technological advances we desire are the same that produce clearcuts and chemical wastes: an education system to develop and propagate techniques, centers of production, means of acquiring raw materials, transportation systems, distribution centers, currency, and other institutions all combining to make the modern industrial state. More importantly, the impulse toward an optimum humanistic existence insulated from the environment, even through the benign magic of "appropriate" technology, leads us back down the grievous path to environmental domination, whose ultimate form is total destruction.

I conclude from this that there is no "appropriate" technology. There are merely crafts, on the one hand, which tap into the abundant creativity of Earth; and on the other, technology, which always seeks to dominate it. Heidegger goes even beyond this conclusion. He argues that technology is not a tool at all, either for good or bad. Tools, like arts and rituals, play a part in the meaningfulness of the world. They engage us in the things of the world and insist on their independent existence by bringing forward their be-ing. Tools, rituals, arts let earthly things be meaningful things and manifest themselves as this particular stone to be cut or this plot of land to be hoed. At the same time, they confront us with the sheer intractable existence of things beyond any meaning we attribute to them. The two relationships belong together: both *what* something is and *that* it is.

Technology, on the other hand, effaces the things of the world, subordinating them to what Heidegger calls "the network" (Bezug) of production and consumption. Earth recedes into an amorphous "standing reserve" (Bestand), ready for use in some aspect of the network. A river becomes a hydro-electric plant; a forest becomes board feet. To use Heidegger's example, the airplane on the runway no longer even has the status of an independent, if highly artificial, thing. It is merely an arbitrary and replaceable unit of the tourist industry, which construes other lands and cultures as standing reserve to be consumed every summer, with the result that the tourists can be more efficient producers when they return to their own industries. Planes have become macroeconomic ciphers. And when terms are used like "recreation area" or "scenic wonder" or even "wilderness experience"—pleasant though these may be—isn't this also a technological representation of Earth as standing reserve?

This is a central point: technology is not an accumulation of machinery, but a relationship between humanity and Earth that challenges the existence of everything by forcing it into the production/consumption network. Everything. Including humanity. Indeed, Heidegger predicted in *The End of Philosophy* that technology must relegate humanity into standing reserve. This, he implies, is the impetus behind industrialization, whether capitalist or communist. And his prediction is coming true. The phrases "human resource" and "total mobilization of the nation" have become common, and we can only shudder at the fierce intrusion on human ecology that genetic engineering and in vitro fertilization represent. Deep ecology is not saving Earth from man; it is saving both Earth and humanity from complete effacement by technology.

This train of thought raises all kinds of questions. Good. Deep ecology is strong insofar as it refuses to accept any dogma. As Heidegger says at the end of *The Question Concerning Technology*, "Questioning is the piety of thought." But two questions about Heidegger's thought need to be addressed. First, whether Heidegger perhaps lets humanity off too easily concerning its responsibility for the environmental crisis; and second—just the opposite—whether perhaps he gives humanity special status as "meaning-giver" to Earth (a notion New-Agers are particularly fond of). The best way to answer these is to consider Heidegger's philosophy in relation to a central tenet of deep ecology: the "inherent value" of wilderness.

Reading Heidegger, especially his early works like *Being and Time*, it's easy to get the impression that he discounted any innate or inherent values or meanings outside humanity. Sartre came away from one of Heidegger's seminars with just such an opinion, and the illegitimate French children of Heidegger's thought brought forth existentialism and other self-absorbed, anthropocentric systems incompatible with deep ecology and a healthy planet. But this is a false impression, the result of over-sophisticated and insensitive minds. He does insist that value and meaning are human concepts, but he does not do this to thrust humanity into the center of existence—on the contrary, Heidegger wants to show how tenuous and derivational these concepts are. We evaluate; Earth doesn't require this. Earth simply is, and persists, beyond the dubious evaluations of humans. For Heidegger, to talk about the inherent value of Earth would be to anthropomorphize, and hence diminish Earth.

But this is merely a terminological disagreement, a question of emphasis. Some deep ecologists have quite rightly seen in Heidegger's thought a philosophic parallel to the sense behind the term "inherent value." Throughout his career, Heidegger was always concerned with the *Seinsfrage*, the question of what it means to exist. This type of inquiry usually becomes a swamp of abstractions, but Heidegger cultivates it in terms of our relationship with earthly things, of our dwelling here on Earth. He makes the startling claim that this relationship precedes the things related, that human existence and a meaningful world are dependent on the manifestation of things themselves, of the Be-ing of beings. In one fell swoop he topples the subjective and objective citadels of modern philosophy by pointing out that the world is never a barren accumulation of individual, unrelated objects to which an abstract subject assigns meaning. We are always *in* the world, inseparable from it.

This is a simple idea, and like many simple things, difficult to explain and grasp. Even if only humans articulate meaning through language, in the larger context, Be-ing itself (or, if you prefer, the inexplicable manifestation of Earth through earthly things) must determine our relationship with things, because we are subordinate to that relationship, with no more status than cabbages. We didn't "invent" meaning and value, nor is it in our control. In this sense, Earth and its Be-ing have a profound, unspoken, unspeakable meaning.

I'm condensing the ocean into a tea cup. Heidegger's point is to let a rose be as much as possible a rose, and not a representation of some idea. Or if we must make the rose a representation, at least we should concede that it is something other than our representation, whole and actual in itself.

In his later works, like *Building Dwelling Thinking* (Heidegger intentionally omitted the commas between the words in the title to suggest their unity), Heidegger leaps into the realm of poetry to get at this idea. Authentic human existence (as opposed to technological abstraction), he says, proceeds like a craftsman in his workshop. In making a chair or wood carving, the existence of the artisan and of his tools merge to create the meaning of the place where he dwells. His existence comes forward, as does the wood he smooths, as does the tree he felled, as does the horse that dragged it over a mountain path. This man doesn't diminish Earth; he takes part in its inevitable manifestation. "A shepherd of Being," as Heidegger says.

And thinking, too—real thinking—has this quality. Unlike the challenging-effacing of technological calculation, it attends to the clues sent from Be-ing through beings, a mode of thinking that is anything but passive. Heidegger doesn't absolve humans from the technological crisis to wallow in mystic impotence: authentic existence demands that we take responsibility for the past in order to strive to think like mountains again, knowing, however, that relationship is not a product of our will, but a blessing of Earth.

To think like a mountain—the phrase expresses a desire to go beyond the technological representation that afflicts Earth and darkens our dwelling here. I'm reminded of a few lines by the German mystic Johannes Schaffler which Heidegger liked to quote:

The rose is without a why,
it is because it is.

OF PIPEDREAMS, SCIENCE, AND WILDERNESS
Brigid 1987
by R. F. Mueller

They've done it again! The technocrats have a new plan to reprogram our world. Consider the age-old dream of our species, the dream of control over nature without any drawbacks. Well, they think they finally have it and it's called "nanotechnology."

This was revealed in an interview of MIT zealots on National Public Radio on June 24 of this year. The prefix 'nano' means "very small" and in this case refers to ordering manipulations on an atomic scale. They're not just talking about the natural and spontaneous ordering or disordering of atoms in crystals as a response to temperature and pressure changes (a field in which I once did research), which has numerous scientific and technological applications in its own right. What they mean is the deliberate multiscale ordering of the world from atoms on up!

But there is a catch, the same catch that has plagued all technological megaprojects, yet is almost never mentioned. The catch is that to achieve some megatechnological result, certain scientific principles must be ignored as assiduously as others are applied. It will come as no surprise that one body of these ignored principles is the science of ecology, but curiously, another is that brainchild of the industrial revolution itself, classical thermodynamics. Of course, thermodynamics is not ignored entirely, because no significant technological device or process can be achieved without taking it into account. The rub is that our technologically optimistic friends always stop with the technology as such and don't include the "externals" (read "environment") with which the technology necessarily interacts—environmental thermodynamics if you will.

Environmentalists are deeply suspicious of science. But whether science is ultimately good or disastrous for the planet (and I am strongly tempted to believe the latter) isn't a useful question here because science appears to be an inevitable product of a species that the planet is stuck with temporarily. So we might as well make the best of a bad situation by at least insuring that critical rules of the game like those of ecology and thermodynamics aren't disregarded.

Thermodynamics as represented by its first and second "laws" is the science of the possible and the impossible, a discipline that sets severe limits as well as serving indispensably in the development of technology. It is also well grounded in experience so that we know that no proposed industrial chemical reaction or physical process for which unfavorable thermodynamic numbers are obtained is possible unless it is driven by some external process; and these external processes are usually prohibitively costly in monetary and environmental terms. To illustrate, the frequently proposed use of water as a source of hydrogen chemical fuel would require a fearsome input of energy from another source, such as nuclear fission, to separate the hydrogen from oxygen—much more energy would be required than the hydrogen could ever yield.

Some will recall the first law as the rather prosaic statement that energy can't be created or destroyed as long as its equivalence to mass is recognized. The second law, which is more mysterious and pertinent to our problem, states that the disorder or "entropy" of any isolated system always spontaneously increases. In practical terms this means that although we can create technological order in local parts of the environment (e.g., an industrial site), a concomitant greater quantity of disorder will be created, inevitably not only at that site, but in external regions from which ordering elements such as energy and materials are drawn. This is a game that can't be won (as I have argued in past articles: *Thermodynamics of Environmental Degradation*, NASA document X-644-71-121, 1971; *Science* 196, 261, 1977, etc.).

Similar conclusions were reached by Nicholas Georgescu-Roegen with respect to economics (*The Entropy Law and the Economic Process*, Cambridge, MA, 1971, and other publications). However, the whole topic of environmental thermodynamics has been shunned by the technocrats because they consider it a "Bad News Science." From this we can infer that thermodynamics can be as powerful an ally for us as is ecology. It is, in fact, the purely physical basis for the so-called "laws of ecology" and is equally applicable to every aspect of society in which energy is involved.

In a not too remote tomorrow the dreamers of nanotechnology would attempt to order large segments of our world from the atomic level on up, to create unprecedented control of chemical, mechanical and biologic systems by fitting every individual atom into a predesignated framework to achieve a technological paradise. To get a feel for the magnitude of such a program, consider our everyday experiences, in which the same thermodynamic forces are at work. We all know how difficult it is to order our lives, simply to keep our dwellings neat, our personal effects in place. Note that we're talking here of our familiar macroscopic world. Imagine then trying to reduce the underlying microscopic world, vibrant and nascent, to this same brand of preconceived anthropocentric order!

We've seen that by the second law every ordered region we create calls into being an even greater region of disorder as a result of the increased energy flux. In environmental terms this technological energy, no matter how benign its origin, is synonymous with pollution. Even the most advanced microelectronic and solar energy systems, which were once regarded as "pollution free," are subject to the same energy degradation as are the crudest factories and mines except the degradation may take different forms (Mueller, *Environmental Action*

10, 15, 1978). If then by any chance—and this chance is small—the technocrats were able to order our entire planetary surface to create the wonder world of their dreams, the energy required and the resulting pollution might well be enough to disorder much of the solar system!

I won't tire you with the familiar and dreary litany of technological failures—all of them touted as examples of our "control" over nature—that are devastating this beautiful planet. However, it's useful to note in passing a few familiar cases that may not strike everyone as offensive.

Consider current attempts at super-control in the medical profession in which ever more "sophisticated technologies," such as organ transplants and complex life support systems, are being developed. Then be aware that burgeoning material requirements and costs of these technologies are driving the costs of ordinary health care beyond the range of those people (externals!) who will never need the new technology. Or consider the practice of "advanced societies" and particularly the US of keeping thousands of square miles of terrain in a technological straight jacket at enormous cost in labor, energy and materials. This applies not only to the monotonous monocultures of agribusiness, but particularly to the trimmed, herbicide and pesticide-saturated yards, roadsides and other artificially vegetated areas that are dedicated to nothing more than a perverted esthetic ideal willed to us by English lords. Add to these the inefficient estates of hobby agriculture that enslave more thousands of square miles as well as the large expanses of public land devoted to deficit timber, grazing and mining operations by the federal government. Finally, wonder that even the most nature-alienated MIT technocrat, confronted seasonally by his own crabgrass, could consider nanotechnology seriously.

What we have here is luxury feeding on necessity, the long-term consequences of which may be illustrated, according to Georgescu-Roegen, by the production of Cadillacs which will inevitably preclude the availability of plowshares to future generations (*Southern Economic Journal* 41, 347, 1975).

All this allows us to see wilderness in a new light. Wilderness, it appears, is the manifestation of harmony between order and disorder, both of which are necessary to maintain it. (Perhaps it is also nature's paradigm for the resolution of the contradiction between order and anarchy so frequently discussed in this journal!) The natural dispersal of seeds, for example, is a disordering process, as is the chemical diffusion of nutrients (positive change in entropy on mixing), but there is no better example of order than the adaptive survival of seedlings in specific sites.

In this scheme without a schemer, the life order created spontaneously through evolution as a response to geologic conditions and the solar flux is always exceeded by the sum of the disordering effects of decay, heat dissipation etc.; and it is this surplus disorder that drives the entire process. Part of this spontaneously expressed scheme, which is inherent in the chemistry of the system, is the enormous biologic diversity, the place-identity mosaic, which confers stability to the biosphere. However, this stability is threatened when any species becomes dominant and attempts to exert its own form of order, usurping the environmental mosaic and decreasing diversity. In the case of our species, this usurpation, acting through both excessive numbers and high energy technology, creates disorder of the type that clashes with natural order. Consequently the interaction of technology and nature is only a vulgar parody of the preexisting harmony.

It is obvious that pure wilderness terrain requires no inputs of technological energy or materials to maintain it. Using an analogy from physics, wilderness may be regarded as an energy "ground state." The technological energy required to deviate greatly from this state, even to accommodate existing human numbers under minimal living standards, let alone the flaunting of luxury, places in peril our long-term survival and that of all other species.

Modern cities and agriculture necessarily displaced wilderness to accommodate the needs of excess population. However, it is becoming increasingly apparent that large tracts of wilderness—larger than those presently existing—are themselves more necessary than ever as reservoirs of environmental amenities needed to support civilization's artifacts.

The foregoing is one of a number of possible "scientific" interpretations of the planetary dilemma, although one that is unlikely to be embraced by the scientific establishment with its demands for upbeat predictions of the conquest of nature. But at best science is only one facet of the real world—which is certainly mystical and poetic at its core. Yet given the inevitability of its presence in our lives, our efforts must be directed toward elevating science to a new analytical level, to a systems approach that recognizes the great panorama of biology, the limits set by thermodynamics and above all the unity and parity of all life forms.

At present wilderness is still regarded as basically inhospitable to the human intellect, the great chaos out of which we are elevating ourselves to unlimited heights of technological grandeur. Contrarily, central to the new level of scientific consciousness is the recognition of the wilderness source of our intellect and the continuing dependency of our intellect on wilderness, a dependency that all our high energy ordering schemes, our gleaming spaceships, cannot supplant. Finally, the new scientific consciousness also recognizes that wilderness is the life sustaining environment.

At this new level we give up the old pipedream of technological control over nature and see that what we now think of as control is only interaction and impact and that for each impact we direct at nature we are impacted in return. Only by accepting as our standard of reference the natural regimen of harmony between order and disorder—as best represented by the wilderness—can catastrophe be avoided.

OVERPOPULATION AND INDUSTRIALISM
Eostar 1987
by Miss Ann Thropy

In a recent meeting of the Common Market (European Economic Community), demographic experts, especially from France, expressed alarm at the decline in birth rates among some member nations. Part of this concern is cultural and ethnic: Because the politics of the postwar era have made it difficult for European nations to prevent immigration, a fall in birth rates may lead not to a fall in population, but an influx of immigrants, mostly from the Third World, where population is increasing due to the dispersion of medical and industrial technology that the Common Market encourages.

The main issue, however, was not national continuity but the continuation of *industrial economy*. Demographers pointed out that continuing decreased birth rates would produce a population graph in the shape of an inverted bell, top-heavy with elderly, "unproductive" citizens on a diminishing base of young, productive workers. The results would be disastrous to the social economy. The welfare and social security systems would lose their tax support. The accumulation of capital would shrink as total consumption fell. Agricultural prices would plunge. Soccer stadiums would be half empty. Almost every aspect of industrial society would be affected.

They are, of course, right. For that reason in itself, real population decline is desirable. But it indicates how deeply economic forces and the social power vested in them are involved in the population problem. For environmentalists, it's not simply a matter of convincing people of the soundness of population control—to do so confronts the very existence of industrial power (as indeed every deep ecological argument does).

We can take heart in the fact that industrial planners are not just being paranoid. Population decline can indeed undermine the way social power is organized and how it exploits Nature. (The axiom that large masses of people are easier to control than small ones is correct.) The demise of feudalism, for example, is directly attributable to the Black Plague, to which one-third of Europe succumbed. It became impossible for a landlord to keep his serfs on his fiefdom, despite passage of stringent laws, when serfs could sell their valuable labor in town or to property owners willing to pay for their services. As it turned out, the social economy that followed was probably worse than feudalism from an environmental point of view, but only after power reorganized itself into institutions that could exploit Nature, and only because a critique of feudalism had not been articulated in terms of its power relations.

What is happening now in Europe suggests that, government policies notwithstanding, populations naturally decline when they reach an unhealthy level. No doubt, there are biological constraints at work here, as scientific studies of animal populations indicate. The sheer stress of living in an unnatural, overcrowded, urban society must play a part in the declining birth rates of the West, though I'm not aware of any research concentrating on the physiological and psychological effects of overpopulation on human reproduction.

But this only underscores the necessity of seeing the population issue in the context of social power and its hierarchies. The problems of population, immigration and industrialism are interrelated to the extent that the power relations in our society cannot let this natural decline occur if they are to be maintained. No doubt, the tenants-inchiefs of feudal Europe would have used immigration to shore up their position, had the technology to move vast numbers of people been available. Modern Western technocracies certainly use immigration to propagate industrialism. Industrialism *requires* overpopulation: the concentration of power in government and corporate control implies a diffuse body of cheap labor from which that power can be organized. Whether technological societies get this through "incentives" for higher birth rates or through immigration makes little difference from an environmental perspective, although the subsequent rift between cultural and economic values entailed by immigration may be a point of access for a further critique of technological economy, assuming we understand "culture" in its proper, tribal, decentralized origins, and not as a product of the modern culture industry.

(It is interesting to note the problem of population maintenance in communist technocracies. These states haven't needed immigration and forbid it, since the concentration of power depends on a perennial, institutionalized source of cheap labor and this constitutes virtually the entire population of communist technocracies. At least this was true of communism in an undeveloped state like Bolshevik Russia. But the populations of some industrialized communist societies are now declining, probably due to the same biological causes as in the West, but also due to the availability of birth control techniques and the general suppression of sexuality as subversive. The recent move toward capitalism in communist Europe—such as the new Soviet law permitting family businesses—perhaps relates to government attempts to maintain overpopulation, though it wouldn't surprise me if the Soviet bloc countries eventually adopted a policy of large-scale immigration to sustain their languishing industrial economies.)

There is no way to dissociate the population issue from industrialism. To disregard their interconnections dooms any attempt to reduce population in the developed countries to an ecologically sane level, and ensures the sustained overpopulation of the Third World. Emigration from the Third World is a result of industrialization *and* an impetus for it. The importation of technology is at the root of population increases in undeveloped countries, since it is often based on "humanitarian" aims involving medical technology. The industrialization of the Third World cannot even sustain the expanding population in the short-run; the Western technocracies will not be able to do so in the long-run. The emigration resulting from the failure of industrialism to sustain the population that it promotes, encourages the global concentration of power in technocratic control by concealing the failure of industrialism. In contrast, traditional economies meet human needs within the bounds of natural cycles.

It should be clear from this that discussions of "social justice" taking immigration or economic inequality as their themes serve only to cloud the population debate, due to the simple fact that, in a technological context, there is no such thing as "justice," it being supplanted by a network of power relations that spread inevitably over every aspect of human and natural existence. Justice and freedom and all higher values are at home only in a decentralized, anarchistic setting, which presupposes Earth as wilderness. Ethical discourse in technological culture is merely the rattling of our ancestors' bones—unless it is directed against that culture in its totality. Otherwise a commitment to justice becomes just another way for technology to propagate its power relations (as I believe is the case on the overpopulation issue).

Whatever practical efforts we use to decrease population, they need to be based on undermining industrialism. Inevitably, this will involve controversial stands, since modern ethical discourse is bound up with industrial values. The loud criticism against Garrett Hardin and his call to end immigration brings this point home. But biocentric environmentalists must have the courage to take the population debate beyond economic and political calculations. Who else is there to do it?

SAPIENS AND SOURDOUGH SEQUEL: LIFECYCLE OF A DETRITOVORE
Eostar 1988
by Suslositna Eddy

Since the publication of "Sapiens and Sourdough" (Eostar 87), I have further reflected upon the similarities between the yeast in my sourdough crock and the human species of which I am a part. The most visible similarity between the two species is the fact that both depend upon "exhaustible accumulations of dead organic matter" for their sustenance. In the case of the yeast, flour is the energy source that is soon depleted as the yeast rapidly reproduces. Out of food and living in pollution, the yeast population crashes. Some yeast cells do survive, however, provided that new flour is added within a few days. The hardiest and most pollution resistant yeast cells then continue at a fairly steady state as their food source is regulated. This yeast population, living in a polluted environment after a massive population crash, can be compared to human survivors of industrial collapse.

The human race is currently involved in the same type of population growth pattern as the yeast. Our civilization and its teeming masses depend upon accumulations of dead organic matter—coal, oil, and natural gas—for their sustenance. The more industrialized nations, of course, are more dependent upon these fuels. The world's food supply depends on petroleum for fertilizers, pesticides and herbicides; and as fuel for trucks, trains, planes, and tractors.

I'll add a definition here from the glossary of the book *Overshoot: The Ecological Basis of Revolutionary Change*, by William R. Catton, Jr. (U of IL Press, Chicago, 1980).

> *Detritus: originally a geological term meaning fragments of rock or debris produced by disintegration and erosion; used by biologists to refer to the accumulated remains of organisms (e.g. humus in the soil, or decayed leaves in a pond); by extension, used in this book to refer to transformed remains of organisms that lived millions of years ago, such remains being useful as fossil fuels to organisms (humans) living today.* (p. 274)

It follows, then, that the human species is not a virus or a blight or even a cancer on this planet. We are merely technological detritovores blooming and crashing based on the availability of our fuel source. As Catton explains:

> *Detritus ecosystems are not uncommon. When nutrients from decaying autumn leaves on land are carried by runoff from melting snows into a pond, their consumption may be checked until springtime by the low temperatures that keep the algae from growing. When warm weather arrives, the inflow of nutrients may already be complete for the year. The algal population, unable to plan ahead, explodes in the halcyon days of spring in an irruption or bloom that soon exhausts the finite legacy of sustenance materials. This algal Age of Exuberance lasts only a few weeks. Long before the seasonal cycle can bring in more detritus, there is a massive*

*die-off of these innocently incautious and exuberant organisms.
Their "Age of Overpopulation" is very brief, and its sequel is swift
and inescapable.* (168)

Unless we humans cease to be detritovores and once again
become consumers of the annual solar income and reduce our numbers
to levels that are sustainable without the use of fossil fuels, our sequel
will likewise be "swift and inescapable."

Yet some survive! . . . The ones who survive are the ones who can
tolerate polluted conditions (alcohol smelling sourdough pot for yeast;
degraded environmental condition of planet Earth for humans). The
humans who will survive the coming population reduction are the
ones who have learned not to depend upon detritus (fossil fuels) for
their sustenance.

As a human with a conscience, I believe it is not only possible,
but inevitable that the human race will survive in symbiotic harmony with Earth. We may reach symbiosis through our conscious
efforts—population control, global wilderness designation and protection, replanting cut-over forests, revegetating strip mines and
empty lots, withdrawal from the use of fossil fuels with the ultimate
goal of meeting our needs with the annually occurring biological
surplus. If we do not consciously decide to live in harmony with
Earth, our global population debate will be solved by a massive die-
off due to starvation, pollution and disease. The remaining humans
will survive not on detritus, but on the annually produced plant and
animal material.

So what am I to do to ensure that I survive the population reduction? I must recognize that every action you and I take either increases
or decreases Earth's ability to support life. Every carbon monoxide
molecule you create when you turn the ignition key is one more than
ever existed in the atmosphere before man invented cars. Every time
you eat commercial, non-organically grown food you are paying to
have more oil drilled to make more fertilizer and pesticides. Each individual is responsible for her or his own actions.

Withdraw from the detritus system! Sell your car. Superinsulate
your home. Buy a solar panel.

Increasing our positive impacts is as important as reducing our
harmful impacts. Plant trees. Every tree you plant removes carbon
from the air and makes oxygen. It holds soil together, adds organic

matter, and provides habitat for innumerable life forms: insects, annelids, birds, mammals. The tree you plant adds to the planet's ability to support life. It may get cut in 60 years by a paper company or it may be worshipped by an earth tribe 1000 years from now. Defend the wilderness: Write letters; sing by a brook.

The "average" person might be surprised at the number of people approaching symbiotic living by withdrawing from the detritus economy. Nationwide, thousands of communities and millions of individuals practice non-fossil fuel consumptive ways of living. They walk, jog, bike; they heat their homes with the sun and renewable fuels. They produce as much of their own food as they can, and barter, or purchase goods manufactured with as little fossil fuel as possible. Crafters, gardeners, artists, and others are creating a growing economy that is separate from the "borrow, spend and tax" economy based on high consumption and endless economic expansion.

Let us be wise and humane, as our species' name implies we can be. Let us reduce population consciously and as fairly as possible. Every individual is vital in this endeavor. DO YOUR PART!

The solution to the population, pollution and environmental degradation problem is coming. Either we will make the changes within our own lives and societies (yes, that means *you* and *me* learning to live without fossil fuels) or we will die of starvation and disease "suffocating in our own slime."

THIS IS PRO-LIFE?
Beltane 1989
by R. Wills Flowers

Author's note: Florida A&M does not accept responsibility for the views expressed in the essay, which are those of the author and should not be attributed to any other member of the Florida university system.

"The Summer the Earth struck back" saw environmental problems make front page news. For the first time in almost two decades, the mainstream media are giving extensive coverage to ecological degradation. *Time* even named Earth "Planet of the Year." At the same time—and due in part to that same national media—we are on the brink of a great leap into accelerating eco-catastrophe. That increas-

ingly probable leap is the evisceration of *Roe v. Wade*—the famous
court decision that established women's right to legal abortions.

The furor over abortions in the United States may seem a distant
issue to some environmentalists. Since Roe v. Wade, birth rates have
been dropping, even in most of the Third World (though not as much
as needed); public support for abortion rights remains firm; and,
among the Earth First! tribe, some (e.g., Miss Ann Thropy in *EF!*,
11–86) believe that the "progressive" agenda of education, family
planning, and reproductive freedom for women is by itself not a
sufficient response to overpopulation. However, by the time George
"A Quail is not an Animal" Bush leaves office, the availability of abortion may be much more restricted than it is today. Does it really
matter? Yes, for two reasons.

The first (and lesser) is that abortion prevents 1.5 million extra
births in the US each year. Those 1.5 million fewer Americans are
equivalent to up to 150 million prevented births in the Third World
in terms of consumption of resources. That's more than the entire population of Brazil. Like others concerned with overpopulation, I agree it
would be better if abortion were never needed. I look forward to when
abortion as a medical procedure is as arcane and old-fashioned as
bleeding with leeches. Until other options of family planning are
widely used, freely available, and free of harassment, however, abortion will remain a necessary part of birth control.

This brings us to the second and far more important reason to support Roe v. Wade: abortion is not and never has been the true
objective of the religious/right-wing forces intent on sandbagging Roe
v. Wade. For them, outlawing abortion is just the thin edge of the
wedge to outlaw all forms of birth control. Today the clinic, tomorrow
the drugstore. Pronatalism is the real game and the abortion debate is
just the opening hand. The Vatican as ringleader of the pronatalists
has never hidden its desire to outlaw birth control; Protestant sects
have been more coy but over the years have regularly dropped hints
that they too intend to go beyond banning abortion. Since 1984 the
pronatalists, using abortion as an excuse, have tried to undermine family planning efforts and, with the connivance of the Reaganauts, have
had some success. If Roe v. Wade falls, the full well-heeled weight of
the pronatalist movement will fall on the right to choose any form of
birth control. In some respects, we are back where we were 20 years

ago when Paul Ehrlich wrote *The Population Bomb,* facing the same battles all over again.

One reason things have slipped is that pronatalists have played a sly public relations game. Take that best-known of pronatalist slogans: "right to life." Although they use rhetoric about "choosing life," being "pro-life," etc., Pope & Falwell Inc. express no concern for all the non-human life being exterminated by excessive human activity. Indeed, there has been only scant concern for the women, families and human communities forced to cope with children beyond their abilities to care for them. "Life" includes the whole biosphere with its 30 million or more species. Only those who subscribe to a biocentric world view are entitled to call themselves a "right to life" movement. Yet, by falsely claiming to be "pro-life," pronatalists have been able to move beyond their power base of right-wing fanatics and enlist a surprising number of liberals. The Marxist concept of Useful Idiot is a fitting description for the latter.

In recent years a parade of "pwogwessives" (of the Nat Hentoff ilk), "pro-life feminists" (whom other feminists have called the Feminist Fifth Column), and plain kooks with left-wing credentials (such as former California governor Jerry Brown) have seized the spotlight proclaiming their "uncomfortability" with abortion. They suspect that women may be using abortion as—gasp!—birth control, and that women have abortions for "frivolous" reasons (though providing no evidence for this sexist charge). While the polemics of the Useful Idiots lack the underlying misogyny of the fanatic Right, and are long on syrupy phrases like "life-affirming," they demonstrate no sympathy for non-human life nor even much awareness of the simplest principles of biological reality. There is also the "conservative-pronatalist" school that wants increased breeding to fulfill their geo-political fantasies. Ben (America-can-spawn-its-way-to-Greatness) Wattenberg has taken over Julian Simon's place as media darling of this group. Most of these recent converts loudly proclaim their devotion to freedom, tolerance and the liberal agenda even as they goose-step to the tunes called by Jerry Falwell and the Vatican autocrats. Pusillanimous lefties, Wattenbergites, and a great crowd of the ethically confused and biologically ignorant—they are the new Spawning Lobby.

Media hype has also played a significant part in the "New Civil War" (as *US News & World Report* calls the fight over reproductive free-

dom). Coverage of the recent "pro-life" traveling circus (soon to per-
form at a clinic near you) and other recent confrontations can be
excused as necessary news gathering. But the media have been egging
on the Zygotes-R-Us crowd in more subtle ways. In "new technology"
stories, for example, we get portrait shots of fetuses along with the
tedious pontifications about how the latest gizmo has really "blurred the
question of when life begins." Life began sometime in the Pre-
Cambrian; there is no evidence of repeat performances. Alert Ted
Koppel. Controllers of the mass media also seem fascinated by
fertility—the extremes to which some people go to have children make
good copy nowadays. Career women are now being urged to play Beat
the Biological Clock—drop everything and have that kid before it's too
late! This is not to suggest that the issues underlying some of these stories should be ignored; what's objectionable is the pronatalist spin put
on almost every story relating to human reproduction, with no mention
of the problems caused by too many people and by unwanted children.

To be sure, NOW, Planned Parenthood and many other liberals
have been working hard to thwart a pronatalist *putsch*. However, they
may have made a critical error in tactics: they have rested their entire
defense of legal abortion on the issue of a woman's right to choose—
"pro-choice." Granted, this is an important point—in fact, among
animals that care for their young, one sex usually provides most of the
care and that entails regulating the number of offspring in conformity
with the resources available for rearing them properly. Humans are
one of the few animals (maybe the only) where the sex that is largely
uninvolved in day-to-day rearing operations exercises dictatorial
power over the reproductive options of the rearing sex. At least, that
was the case until recently and that's what the pronatalists seek to
restore. However, as noted already, the Spawning Lobby has trivialized
the pro-choice argument with a devious campaign portraying any
woman who chooses an abortion as a frivolous bimbo. They have
managed to frame the issue as "freedom of choice" vs. "baby killing."
This has put pro-choice advocates on the defensive, endlessly apolo-
gizing for women's aspiration for something besides the "captive
breeding program" of patriarchal domesticity.

Planned Parenthood could hold the moral high ground more easily by adopting a broader, more ecological advocacy. To begin,
having that US baby will lower the living standards of 40–100 Third

World babies. Though there is no way to be precise about it, we can confidently predict that at least several of those babies will die each time a confused American teen-age girl is badgered into "choosing life." Among non-humans, of course, the death toll wrought by humanist "life-affirming" posturing is much higher. While the Zygotes-R-Us gang jabbers about a "holocaust of abortion," the real holocaust is what excess human breeding is doing to the rest of life.

It may be that a hyper-sensitivity over "coerciveness" and "elitism" has led defenders of Roe v. Wade to avoid mentioning over-population and chain themselves to their pro-choice positions. Unfortunately, there is still a tendency, even by people who should know better (like the staff of *Time*) to portray overpopulation as a Third World problem and birth control as something "they" need. Perhaps the best way for Planned Parenthood and its allies to protect women's freedom of choice is to stop defending choice and start attacking the holocaust of pronatalism and the immorality of our own contributions to overpopulation. Such a stance would not be so easy to dismiss with glib smear tactics.

Ironically, aside from the threat of pronatalists, the population situation is relatively promising. Everywhere that women are given even minimal control over their lives, birth rates are falling. In Africa (where everyone is supposed to want huge families), a recent AID (US Agency for International Development) survey found that women overwhelmingly want to either take longer intervals between child bearing or stop having them altogether. Far from falling in behind the Reagan pronatalist party line exhibited at the 1984 Mexico City population conference, and despite attempts at under-mining by the Reagan Administration, many countries have developed their own population control policies. At present the biggest obstacle to further progress in the battle against overpopula-tion is the US Spawning Lobby. Nullifying their hegemony over public policy should be a top priority for any environmental group, mainstream or radical.

We should lobby politicians against pronatalist laws as much as Zygotes-R-Us Inc. lobbies for them. The Hyde Amendment, and its numerous clones in both federal and state legal systems, forbids spending public funds for abortion but allows it for childbirths. The "pay the poor to have kids" legal system needs a legal abortion. It is

insane to spend taxpayers' dollars to subsidize breeding. Tell your
elected representatives that. Frequently.

Cowardly corporations also need attention from us. The recent
international flap over the firm Roussel-Uclaf and RU 486 shows how
far the pronatalists have penetrated. When a company has a socially
responsible product or program and shows signs of caving in to the
pronatalists, they need to hear from us that they will lose business by
pandering to the Spawning Lobby. The worst of the corporate panderers
are the major broadcasting companies. Everyone but the most fanatical
of the pronatalists agrees that birth control is superior to abortion. Yet
the broadcast media refuse to take advertisements for birth control. In
their own way, ABC, NBC, and CBS are as environmentally destructive
as Brazil and Maxxam. We need to harass these corporate unworthies,
particularly when they have to apply for license renewals.

In the judicial arena, pronatalists been creative in finding excuses
to obstruct reproductive freedom—"fetal rights," "daddy rights" and
the like. It is here they are looking for their biggest score: getting the
Supreme Court to backslide on Roe v. Wade. An ideal course for us
would be to somehow intervene (maybe even at the Supreme Court
level) on behalf of Earth and force judges to weigh environmental
issues in their decision. If that's not possible, let's at least bring
"national" issues to bear: security, economic health, resources—all
adversely impacted by extra consumers.

The coming months may decide whether Earth has a chance of
survival or whether it will eventually choke on human surplus. Will
the Lifelong Environmentalist continue to grovel before the pronatalists (as he has since the Republican convention) or will he think back
to his Langley days and recall that the National Security Council has
identified overpopulation as a threat to national security?

I conclude with a short parable for the well-meaning but ecologically confused in the pronatalist ranks. The Reagan Administration
has evidently convinced many that it is "pro-life" with attacks on
Planned Parenthood and legal abortion. Are the Reagan people blind
to the security threat of overpopulation? Not at all and they have a
plan to deal with it. The plan, to be administered by the Pentagon, is
called LIC—Low Intensity Conflict. LIC is now being tried in
Nicaragua, Angola and El Salvador, and plans are much more encompassing. In fact, LIC will become the mainstay of US policy for dealing

with Third World instability—an instability universally acknowledged to be aggravated by overpopulation. Thus, the Reagan Plan: make sure they get born, then kill 'em if necessary. It's a perfect paradigm of pronatalism—a contrived compassion that begins at conception and ends at birth.

WHITE HATS:
FIELD NOTES FROM A DEDICATED ENVIRONMENTAL ATTORNEY
Beltane 1989
by Cindy Ellen Hill

As a kid in the Long Island suburbs, I learned all the names of the plants of our disappearing pine barrens. I was active in scouts. By high school I became fascinated with the environmental issues around me: the Shoreham nuclear power plant, eroding shorelines, oil spills in the harbors. In college I was a political science/public policy major with a minor in environmental policy. I worked for a county legislator who was adamantly correct on environmental issues and led the way for the county government opposition to Shoreham.

It was through this county legislator's office that I came into contact with "environmental law" proper. I drafted legislation and dealt with administrative agencies. I began to notice that at public hearings, boards would sit up and take notice when an attorney addressed them. When everyone else seemed to be screaming that their kids wouldn't have a place to play, the attorneys would testify about some mystical set of regulations that was not being followed, and somehow their comments were the only ones that made sense to the hearing boards and would be acted on.

I became convinced that, although I would much rather be a forest ranger, becoming an attorney was the ultimate path to preserving the sanctity of Earth. I decided to go to law school, join EPA or a state agency, and save the world.

My experience at Vermont Law School was probably not that different from other starry-eyed "L" types. As classmates vied for law review spots and took unpaid internships with fancy city firms while living off their trust funds and taking Christmas breaks in St. Moritz, I waitressed and worked on political campaigns. After one semester of Environmental Law (and finding the *EF! Journal* and *Ecodefense* in the school library) I decided that working for a state agency or the EPA was *not a good thing*. Which was just as well since, in effect, the Reagan administration disbanded the EPA while I was in law school, and many states, overburdened with the constraints of the Reagan miracle economy were doing similar things to their own agencies.

Despite my abandonment of my original plan, I continued to sneer at classmates who were going to work for corporations, with visions of changing the system from within. I continued to sneer until I was forced to be unemployed for a few months while studying for the bar exam; and I discovered that I had about $30,000 worth of student loan debts, my applications for positions with environmental groups were being returned because I was "overqualified," and no one will hire an activist lawyer who refuses to work for bad guys and has a respectable but not notable academic record.

Being averse to starvation, I hung out a shingle. I had only a few simple rules: I don't do divorces, I don't do criminal law, I do as much environmental law as possible, and I DON'T WORK FOR BLACK HATS. I figured that developers and industries would come to me begging for advice on how to handle environmental regulations. I rehearsed countless "I don't serve your kind" speeches. I never had to use one.

Bit by bit, some folks in white hats did drift my way. It was then that reality reared its ugly head and I learned two lessons. First, the good guys are usually far more concerned about things like their pocketbooks, their property values and even keeping "them" out of the neighborhood, than they are about Earth. Environmental and land use laws are a convenient way for humble citizens to yell loud, make friends, meet the mayor, and influence people. Second, folks wearing White Hats have no money.

I had forgotten about a simple equation: Clients Broke=Lawyer Broke. I had set my rates at half the going attorney's charge, but every good guy that walked through the door said, "we're doing a good thing, why don't you work for us for free—you can write it off on your taxes, and we'll get you good publicity and lots of clients." At first I would fall for this line, but I soon learned that good guys don't know people with money so paying clients aren't waiting just over the horizon.

Most groups end up going to wealthy corporate lawyers who can spare a few hours of free time, even if they don't know anything about environmental law and also represent land rapers. My ethics and dedication mean nothing in the face of having to earn a little cash.

The battle stories are many, and they still evoke migraines. One group, which told me for six months that they were raising the money they owed me and would pay next week, now claims that I volunteered the thousands of dollars worth of hours I spent working night and day to help them block a development. I'm having to pay a mean business lawyer mean business rates to try to recoup at least the money that I spent out of my own pocket producing reports, interviewing experts long distance, buying supplies. . . . Other groups disbanded without telling me, while I was hard at work for them, and I didn't learn of it until I went to present them with my legal work and their bill. Time and again I get late night and early morning calls from people who are so glad I am not a "real" lawyer with a stuffy office so they feel free to call me whenever they want.

I'm broke and frustrated, but I will never break my last rule. I care too deeply about this Earth to work for her destroyers. But the other three rules will have to go. This has been a grand experiment, this attempt to practice ethical, independent environmental protection law. The end result of the experiment is that I know not many people are willing to pay a reasonable wage to a lawyer willing to zealously fight their environmental legal battles.

But there has been another end result as well. I came into all this thinking that THE LAW was THE WAY to protect the environment. Civil rights laws forced people to open their businesses to people of races other than Caucasian. But even today many people find subtle ways to cause as much damage as blatant segregation caused. Environmental law is the same. You can make a company write an environmental impact statement before they plow something down, but they will still plow it down. Many people are even more hateful of the environment because of this added layer of nonsense they must go through. Sure, many projects have been stopped—but only because the legal fights would have been too expensive and time consuming, not because any developer has ever realized: yes, after careful review I have found this meadow to be too ecologically beautiful to be a shopping mall. It is a long, slow, costly war, fighting one drawn out battle over one tiny piece of Earth at a time. Nearly every battle results in a "compromise," which means that Earth only gets raped a little instead of a lot.

I would much rather work toward solving unavoidable long-term problems than to apply myself to fighting each little new problem. It's no wonder that the massive world problems of energy supply, population, food, species extinction, and so on aren't being solved— all of us who care are too busy risking financial security to stop one small development.

There is no happy ending. I'm just a disillusioned environmental activist who foolishly thought she could make a living doing something she truly believed in. I've been applying for jobs for the last few months, and every week I've set my sights and my moral requirements for the jobs a bit lower. Anybody need a lawyer?

LOVE YOUR MOTHER— DON'T BECOME ONE
Lughnasadh 1989
by Leslie Lyon

A female acquaintance asked me recently if I could pick the happiest day of my life. It was a question that begged the usual answer of a wedding or an acquisition. The answer I gave shocked her. The best day of my life, I told her, was the day I decided never to have children.

My decision to forego parenthood was not easy. Like most women of the baby boom era, I grew up thinking that a woman's worth was measured by her skill as a mother. The suburban Utah street where I grew up was a representative slice of a state devoted to the cause of producing large numbers of children. From the time that first doll was placed in our eager hands, we girls were indoctrinated into the one certainty of our lives—that we would have many babies.

On our street, nary a house had less than four children. Our parents never noticed the price we paid for their fecundity. Classrooms of less than 40 children were rare. Only the children seemed dismayed about the endless construction of new houses, swarming up the mountainsides until we had no place left to play.

Never in that world of harried adults and neglected children did I hear a hint that unlimited parenthood might be inappropriate. No one thought of the problems our huge generation would create.

Not until I was in high school did I hatch the bold idea that I need not get married and pregnant immediately after graduation.

When it dawned on me that life might have more to offer than motherhood, I was racked with guilt.

And truly, a part of me wanted to be a mother. I loved kids, and I craved the immortality parenthood offers. I decided I'd have kids, but not very soon. I set my sights on 1980, ten years after I finished high school. That way, I'd have time for adventure before I settled down.

For the first few years, all went well. I assured my parents that I would do my duty, eventually. Like many young people of those days, I read Paul Ehrlich and celebrated Earth Day, and then decided to have only two children. I landed a boyfriend who looked likely to stick around.

As the appointed time approached, I felt the old dread again. It never occurred to me that I could reverse the decision, made in my foolish youth. Luckily, it did occur to my boyfriend. Perhaps, he said, it was even our duty NOT to have children. He had just read somewhere that when a wild species becomes too numerous, its members have smaller litters or no litters at all. Didn't it make sense for us to do the same?

That day, I knew what it was like to have a revelation. With a certainty that humbled me, I knew that the last thing the planet needed was my children. When the shock of this new conviction was over, I felt relieved, and only a little sad. Soon, I felt happier than ever before. I had not only rid myself of a compulsion society should never have forced on me, but I had done something noble for Mother Earth.

At first, my family and friends disapproved, of course, but in time, they came to respect and even envy my decision. My father took it surprisingly well when I told him somebody had to compensate for the fact that he'd had eight children. Now that some of my high school chums have unruly teenagers, they tell me how smart I was not to have kids. People usually assume that I passed up motherhood either because of a career or because I hate children. It's an eye-opener for them when they learn the truth.

Sadly, many parents I know admit that they jumped into parenthood with no planning. Prospective parents should always remember the impact they'll make if they bring a new consumer into the world. People have often accused me of being selfish for not having children, when it should be obvious to all that the opposite is true.

It's also true that in these days of right-to-lifers and slim birth control pickings, it can be very hard to keep from having children. As a female who was once atrociously fertile, I know this all too well. It takes considerable determination at times to avoid parenthood. The second happiest day of my life was the day I got fixed.

As for you men, it won't help much for you to decide you can do without fatherhood unless you do something to prevent it. It makes me furious to hear some guy put on airs about swearing off children, while insisting that birth control is the woman's responsibility. I have the greatest respect for a man who has the courage to take the ultimate step—a vasectomy.

Among the advantages of foregoing parenthood, the most important to me is the freedom I have to fight for the environment. With no children to occupy my time, I can devote myself to the defense of Mother Earth. Too many times, I've seen a dedicated activist lose interest in the cause when that bundle of joy comes along.

Some will claim that if too many environmentalists remain childless, we will doom ourselves to extinction. I would counter this claim by asking how many Earth First!ers were raised by environmentalists. Modern children learn as much from outside sources as they do from their parents. Also, just because I have no children, it does not follow that I can't influence youngsters. Most of us have nieces and nephews, and we can go to schools and teach kids to appreciate Nature. I present wildlife education programs to the 4th and 5th graders in my town.

Of course, this article is aimed more toward those who feel ambivalent about having a family. If you've already taken the plunge, or know you will, make it your duty to teach your children that parenthood is a privilege, not a right. Don't browbeat your children into providing you with grandchildren. And above all, don't criticize your childless friends. Our forbearance has made the future a little less bleak for your own offspring.

But what do you say, you ask, to people who point out that you might have spawned a Gandhi or an Einstein? All parents dream that their kids will grow up and save the world. But can such a tenuous hope really justify the cost of loading more burdens on an already staggering planet? Further, you definitely can help save the world by refusing to "be fruitful and multiply." Remaining childless is one of the noblest sacrifices we can make for Mother Earth. If wild animals can forego reproduction in an emergency, why can't we?

CHAPTER 4

Deep Ecology

IN A SENSE, THIS CHAPTER HEADING ENCOMPASSES all in this book, as deep ecology, or biocentrism as some people prefer to call it, became a guiding philosophy of the Earth First! movement and Earth First! Journal. However, we narrowed this chapter down to articles addressing philosophical matters from a deep ecology perspective. These articles explain the rudiments of the philosophy of deep ecology and some of its implications, and suggest further readings germane to deep ecology.

Along with the books and authors suggested in this chapter, also valuable from a deep ecology perspective are the growing number of Nature and natural history writings available in this country, as well as the many deep ecology books that have been published since these articles were written. Books describing Nature in a sympathetic manner, while avoiding the trappings of anthropomorphism and anthropocentrism, implicitly support deep ecology. One can scarcely read such books as Gathering the Desert (Gary Nabhan), Tropical Nature (Adrian Forsyth and Ken Miyata), Arctic Dreams (Barry Lopez), Grizzly Years (Doug Peacock), Conscience of a Conservationist (Michael Frome), and Sowing the Wind (Louise B. Young) without being moved toward a deeply ecological appreciation of Nature.

Among the important books related to deep ecology published most recently are Sacred Land Sacred Sex: Rapture of the Deep by Dolores LaChapelle; Thinking Like a Mountain: Towards a Council of All Beings by John Seed, Joanna Macy, Pat Fleming, & Arne Naess; The Practice of the Wild by Gary Snyder; Simple in Means, Rich in Ends by Bill Devall; The End of Nature by Bill McKibben; The Rights of Nature by Roderick Nash; Whatever Happened to Ecology? by Stephanie Mills; Ecology, Community, and Lifestyle by Arne Naess; Wilderness on the Rocks by Howie Wolke; and Confessions of an Ecowarrior by Dave Foreman. Of course, the best way to learn about deep ecology is to head for the hills; Nature untrammeled is the best teacher.

ABBEY ON BOOKS— AND GURUS
Samhain 1982

A reading list for Nature Lovers, resistance fighters, wild preservatives, deep ecologists and regular environmentalists—why not? The litera- ture is immense and old as civilization; I have read but a small part of it myself. One could range across the world, from ancient China—the writings of Lao-Tse and his disciple Chuang-Tse—to the surviving fragments of certain pre-Socratic philosophers—Democritus, Heraclitus, Diogenes—to the sermons of St. Francis, and such modern Europeans as the novelists Knut Hamsun and Jean Giono, the histo- rian Toynbee, the philosophers Spinoza (for his pantheism), Santayana, Heidegger, Naess. But for the sake of brevity I shall confine myself to American writers, some obvious, some little known:

Thoreau (of course); John Muir (dull but important); William Bartram; John C. VanDyke; Farley Mowat; Raymond Dasmann; Garrett Hardin; Barry Lopez; Murray Bookchin (see *Our Synthetic Environment,* which anticipated Rachel Carson by several years); Bernard DeVoto; William O. Douglas; Rene Dubos (but only in part, with major reservations); Loren Eisley; Paul Ehrlich; William Faulkner (in *The Big Woods, Go Down, Moses*); Colin Fletcher; Charles Bowden (*Killing the Hidden Waters*); the poets Walt Whitman, Robinson Jeffers, Robert Frost, Gary Snyder, Robert Bly, Wallace Stevens, James Dickey, Theodore Roethke, Jim Harrison, Peter Wild—to name but a few; Sigurd Olson; Wallace Stegner; Wendell Berry; Joseph Wood Krutch; Aldo Leopold (basic); Jack London (for his *Call of the Wild*); Annie Dillard; Ann Zwinger; Mary Austin; Rachel Carson; Paul Shepard; David Ehrenfeld (*The Arrogance of Humanism*); several oth- ers I'll think of too late; and Lewis Mumford who provided us, in such books as *The Myth of the Machine, The Pentagon of Power* and *The City in History,* with the best critique yet of our modern military-industrial culture—Mumford, in my opinion, is the one living American author who fully deserves the Nobel Prize for literature. No, two: Mumford and Stegner.

Ah well, many books. Of the making of books there is no end. I will close by reminding myself and others that writing, reading, think- ing are of value only when combined with effective action. Those I most admire in the conservation movement are those who act: such men as David Brower, Paul Watson, and the legendary Bulgarian brigand Georges Heiduk. Sentiment without action is the ruin of the soul. One brave deed is worth a hundred books, a thousand theories, a million words. Now as always we need heroes. And heroines!

Down with the passive and the limp. Avoid the Swami Moonbeams and the Roshi Bubbleheads and all other gurus whether native American or imported, that swarm of fakes and fakirs who pander to and fleece the foolish, the gullible, the sick, the desperate. Be your own guru. Little is gained by gaping at a blank wall in a stupor of meditation. If it's enlightenment you want, then seek the company of those who do real work in the real world—e.g., woodcutters; oldtime rangers and wildlife biologists; midwives, nurses and school teachers; farriers, bootmakers, gunsmiths, stone masons, veterinarians, carpenters, gardeners; astronomers and geologists; old soldiers and veteran seamen.

As my Aunt Minnie used to say, back in Stump Crick West Virginny, "*Too much* readin' rots the mind."

—Fraternally,
—Edward Abbey, Oracle, Arizona

THE BASIC PRINCIPLES OF DEEP ECOLOGY
Litha 1984
by George Sessions and Arne Naess

1) The well-being and flourishing of human and non-human Life on Earth have value in themselves (synonyms: intrinsic value, inherent value). These values are independent of the usefulness of the non-human world for human purposes.

2) Richness and diversity of life forms contribute to the realization of these values and are also values in themselves.

3) Humans have no right to reduce this richness and diversity except to satisfy *vital* needs.

4) The flourishing of human life and cultures is compatible with a substantial decrease of the human population. The flourishing of non-human life requires such a decrease.

5) Present human interference with the non-human world is excessive, and the situation is rapidly worsening.

6) Policies must therefore be changed. These policies affect basic

economic, technological, and ideological structures. The resulting state of affairs will be deeply different from the present.

7) The ideological change is mainly that of appreciating *life quality* (dwelling in situations of inherent value) rather than adhering to an increasingly high standard of living. There will be a profound awareness of the difference between big and great.

8) Those who subscribe to the foregoing points have an obligation directly or indirectly to try to implement the necessary changes.

Editor's note: George and Arne also formulated a list of comments on these basic principles which was published with this article when it appeared in Earth First! Journal. *These comments clarify some of the unavoidable ambiguities in their principles. The deep ecology platform and the comments appear in* Deep Ecology.

THE BOOKS OF DEEP ECOLOGY
Lughnasadh 1984
by Bill Devall and George Sessions

Editor's note: We've often asked Bill and George for a list of the most important books on deep ecology. They replied with this annotated bibliography.

Morris Berman, The Reenchantment of the World, *Ithaca: Cornell, 1981.*

In this study of the emergence of our modern scientific consciousness and challenge to its supremacy, Berman traces the rise of science as philosophy and political ideology. In his chapter on Isaac Newton he shows Newton to a be a transitional figure, part in the world of the participatory science of the Middle Ages, part mechanist. The concluding sections are devoted to "tomorrow's metaphysics" and the "politics of consciousness." Berman sees Gregory Bateson's epistemology as a possible alternative to mechanism. The subject-object merger, found in ecology, has some pitfalls, according to Berman, but is the most important vision for post-modern society.

Charles Birch and John B. Cobb, The Liberation of Life: From the Cell to the Community, *Cambridge: Cambridge University Press, 1983.*

This is a work of extraordinary breadth. The authors seek the liberation of life in both theory and practice: theory insofar as the authors invigorate the ways we think about life from the molecular to the cosmic level; and practice insofar as they call for a liberation of social structure and human behavior that would flow from and encourage such a changed way of thinking. They maintain a graded hierarchy of value, however, and base their position on Alfred North Whitehead's process philosophy. This graded hierarchy is a notion rejected by deep ecologists.

Murray Bookchin, The Ecology of Freedom: The Emergence and Dissolution of Hierarchy, Palo Alto, CA: Cheshire Books, 1982.

The most extensive statement by this seminal thinker on communalism and hierarchy, here Bookchin contrasts the outlook of organic society with that of mechanical societies. "The great project of our time," he writes, "must be to . . . heal and transcend the cleavage between humanity and nature that came with early wisdom." Bookchin's style of writing is turgid, but his analysis of communal traditions in the West shows cultural roots to which we can turn for cultural forms necessary for bioregional living.

Fritjof Capra, The Turning Point: Science, Society and the Rising Culture, New York: Simon and Schuster, 1982.

Capra is a physicist who challenged conventional wisdom in *The Tao of Physics* by demonstrating striking parallels between ancient mystical traditions and the discoveries of 20th century physics. In *The Turning Point*, he shows how the revolution in modern physics foreshadows an imminent revolution in all the sciences and a transformation of our worldview and values.

Rachel Carson, The Sea Around Us, New York: New American Library, 1961.

Rachel Carson's scientifically accurate and poetic book on ocean ecosystems and the human connection to them was first published in 1951, over a decade before her more famous book, *Silent Spring*. It shows a woman naturalist's deep ecology intuition.

William R. Catton Jr., Overshoot: The Ecological Basis of Revolutionary Change, *Urbana: U of Illinois Press, 1980.*

The only sociologist author on this list, although not a deep ecologist, Catton presents one of the clearest expositions in print of the meaning of "carrying capacity" as applied to human populations. Catton recounts the fate of other species and populations in circumstances that parallel our present crisis. His last chapter, "Facing the Future Wisely," presents no ecotopian vision but shows policy changes necessary to deal with catastrophe.

Michael Cohen, The Pathless Way, *Madison: U of Wisconsin Press, 1984.*

In this definitive study of John Muir as deep ecologist, Cohen's chapters on Muir's enlightenment and Muir's "stormy sermons" bring to life the founder of the American conservation/ecology movement.

Stanley Diamond, In Search of the Primitive: A Critique of Civilization, *New Brunswick, NJ: Transaction Books, 1974.*

Diamond demystifies civilization and explicates being in primitive society, thus writing a prolegomenon for a Marxist ethnology and an existential anthropology. The first chapter, "Civilization and Progress," is a fundamental critique of the dominant mode of thinking in modern societies.

David Ehrenfeld, The Arrogance of Humanism, *New York: Oxford, 1978.*

Humanism is the "religion of humanity," a supreme belief in our ability to rearrange the world of Nature and engineer our own future. Ehrenfeld, an ecologist, dissects the false assumptions of humanism. He calls for a union of emotion and reason and in his concluding chapter, "Beyond Humanism," makes tentative suggestions for "enduring somehow the unavoidable sadness."

Paul and Anne Ehrlich, Extinction: The Causes and Consequences of the Disappearance of Species, *New York: Ballantine, 1981.*

Paul Ehrlich is an ecologist and co-author of the textbook *Ecoscience.* In *Extinction*, the Ehrlichs describe the interplay of plants, animals, and lower organisms and dramatically illustrate the catastrophic consequences of humanity's interference in natural processes. They discuss the social and economic causes of the rising species extinction rate and strategies of conservation.

Stephen Fox, John Muir and His Legacy: The American Conservation Movement, Boston: Little, Brown, 1981.

The first part of this book is a biography of Muir in which Fox utilizes previously unavailable material to show Muir's deep ecology insights. Fox then chronicles the development of the major conservation groups, highlighting the careers of the "radical amateurs" who repeatedly revitalized the movement. His last chapter, "Lord Man: The Religion of Conservation," illustrates the continuing tensions between Christians and ecologists.

Elizabeth Dodson Gray, Green Paradise Lost, Wellesley, MA: Roundtable Press, 1982.

Gray is a feminist and Christian theologian who understands ecology. She provides an excellent explication of the impacts of patriarchal society and the domination of Nature. She calls for biocentric equality and deep ecology.

J. Donald Hughes, American Indian Ecology, El Paso: Texas Western Press, 1983.

Hughes's essay demonstrates the Native Americans' reverence for the land and animals and the kind of social structure that kept Native American societies in harmony with the rest of nature. Hughes implies that the cosmology of Native Americans has no racial or temporal bounds but beckons to us today and provides us with inspiration and ideas for a post-modern cosmology of the "future primal mind."

Dolores LaChapelle, Earth Wisdom, Silverton, CO: Way of the Mountain Center (first published by Guild of Tudor Press, 1978).

LaChapelle is a climber, skier, Tai Chi student, scholar and deep ecologist. Earth Wisdom, she says, is a beginning step toward restoring the lost communication with the earth that primal peoples knew for millennia. Part I includes experiences in the author's life that crystallized her feelings toward Earth and led to an intuitive understanding of the relationship of mountains and mind in the beginnings of modern religions. Part II investigates the nature and boundaries of mind in relation to Nature as a whole. Part III delineates the practical results of healing the split between human consciousness and Nature. Part IV helps those seeking to live as Nature intended us to live.

Aldo Leopold, Sand County Almanac, *New York: Oxford, 1968.*

This classic, first published in 1948, includes Leopold's essays on his own experiences in wilderness, and the importance of land health. In the foreword he wrote, "There are some who can live without wild things, and some who cannot. These essays are the delights and dilemmas of one who cannot." This book is required reading on the development of a biocentric "land ethic."

George Tyler Miller, Living in the Environment, Fifth Edition, *Belmont, CA: Wadsworth, 1987.*

This is a textbook with chapters on human overpopulation, resources, human impact on the earth, and economics. The concluding section, on ethics, includes a discussion of deep ecology, but Miller calls for a "balanced approach of resource use and preservation based on wise stewardship."

Roderick Nash, Wilderness and the American Mind, Third Edition, *New Haven: Yale U Press, 1982.*

This is the most thorough review of changing perceptions and understandings of ecological diversity and wilderness in the context of the European invasion of North America. This edition includes chapters on the philosophy of wilderness, the irony of victory in official Wilderness designation, and the international perspective. Nash does not articulate deep ecology in his chapter on philosophy, but it is there in the chapters on Muir, Thoreau and Leopold.

Theodore Roszak, Person/Planet: The Creative Disintegration of Industrial Society, *Garden City, NY: Anchor/Doubleday, 1979.*

Roszak asserts that "the needs of the person are the needs of the planet." He links the realization of personhood and saving ecological diversity to liberation from the large-scale bureaucracies that dominate our lives. He offers practical advice for home, school, work, religion, and farming. He especially addresses the responsibility of intellectuals and the politics of transforming large cities into places with economies of permanence.

Theodore Roszak, Where the Wasteland Ends: Politics and Transcendence in Postindustrial Society, *Anchor/Doubleday, 1973.*

Probably the most interesting book on the "single vision" of modern science and the uses and abuses of technology, Roszak's critique of the "citadel of expertise" is essential reading for those entering such professions as engineering. He concludes with chapters on the "rhapsodic intellect"—resonance and literalism in modern intellectual circles—and "the visionary commonwealth"—suggestions for ecotopia.

Paul Shepard, Nature and Madness, *San Francisco: Sierra Club Books, 1982.*

Shepard suggests we have overlooked something important in our analysis of the continuing crisis of the environment—the development of the human person. Utilizing a diverse body of literature, Shepard links the process of human development as genetically programmed with the changes in Western culture during the last 10,000 years. He reads the human development literature to mean that each human must go through a certain sequence of phases during the life cycle. Some cultures facilitate this process, some do not. Contemporary Western cultures leave most people stuck in early adolescence all their lives—a phase marked by intense emotion, "masculine" rather than "feminine" orientation, and rapid alternations between regressive infantile behavior and aggressive behavior that is pseudo-mature. Many environmental problems can be solved if we let people proceed through their natural ontogeny into maturity.

Paul Shepard, The Tender Carnivore and The Sacred Game, *New York: Scribners, 1973.*

Shepard discusses the gatherer/hunter traditions and the "ten thousand year environmental crisis." His provocative essay on ritual and the "karma of adolescence" foreshadows his more theoretical treatment in *Nature and Madness.* In the concluding section Shepard proposes a "cynergetic society" as his ecotopian vision.

Gary Snyder, Turtle Island, *New York: New Directions, 1974.*

Winner of the Pulitzer Prize for poetry, Snyder in this collection of poems and essays says Turtle Island is "the old/new name for the continent, based on many creation myths of the people who have been here for millennia, and reapplied by some of them to 'North America' in recent years." Snyder suggests a cross-fertilization of ecological thought with Buddhist ideas. Snyder concludes with his deep ecological manifesto written in 1969, "Four 'Changes.'"

Gary Snyder, The Old Ways, *San Francisco: City Lights Books, 1977.*

Dedicated to the memory of Alan Watts, this slim volume contains six essays including Snyder's statement on bioregional re-inhabitation and "the incredible survival of coyote."

THOUGHTS FROM THE ROUND RIVER RENDEZVOUS*
Brigid 1986
by Stephanie Mills

Public relations should be based on attraction rather than promotion, Alcoholics Anonymous holds. For a message to be sufficiently transforming, its bearer should evidence the message's positive effects. The message that Earth is alive and that the human species is of Earth—that what we do to her we do to ourselves—is not new. It was, very likely, the essential content of the religions of the Paleolithic era, an era which, from today's catastrophic vantage point, was incredibly stable and ecologically benign.

If Earth is alive, the implication, for those late 20th century humans alive enough to sense it, is that we must take personal responsibility for the fate of Earth. Earth's fate, Theodore Roszak eloquently argues in

Person/Planet, is, ultimately, the fate of the self. Thus ecodefense, the sort of nonviolent direct action practiced by members of the Earth First! movement, is simply a sophisticated form of self-defense, one that transformed the movement's founders from frustrated, politically adept Washington conservation lobbyists into fierce logging-road blockaders.

Earth First!ers and other humans who exercise themselves in response to the promptings of the planet embody and exemplify the joy of empowerment. Their activism, rooted in a personal identification with the planetary ecosystem, is simply human-species consciousness of the necessity to co-evolve with other life forms rather than destroy them. Such activism is the perfect antidote to the denaturing of Earth and of humanity that appears to be reaching its historical crescendo in our time. In attempting to satisfy narrowly-conceived individual needs at the expense of the ecosystem, man has homogenized, simplified, and sterilized both the planet and his psyche, debasing the biosphere that nurtured the evolution of everything that lives, including the human mind.

William James said, "Lives based on having are less free than lives based either on doing or being." It is the life based on having that our mass culture promotes and which is ultimately unsustainable. Consequently, human lives based on *being,* in the fullest biological sense, today virtually demand activism—*doing.* Thus the lives of ecodefenders are demonstrations of the vitalizing practice of courage; the sublimity of nonviolence; and the liberation of knowing that since none of us gets out of this one alive (in her or his accustomed form, anyhow), a futile clinging to life and comfort costs the very integrity that makes life worth living.

To return to the profound verity of that AA precept: in an era of decreasing literacy and increasing noninformation, individual flesh-and-blood human beings are the most compelling medium for the transmission of any radical message, including that of deep ecology—deep ecology being shorthand for a way of seeing and acting in the world wherein *Homo sapiens* is not regarded as over and above nature but as an integral, interdependent part of nature. This philosophy is explored by Bill Devall and George Sessions in their important book *Deep Ecology.*

Talk is cheap, but deeds are eloquent manifestoes in body language. An EF! action, such as camping 70 feet up in an old growth

Douglas-fir in the Willamette National Forest to impede logging, speaks revolutionary volumes. It burns in brilliant contrast to the dreary monoculture, the life of quiet desperation that is the culmination of the post-Paleolithic era. The lives of ecodefenders and other activists are like places of natural wildness; reservoirs of *elan vitale* and evidence of diversity relieving the sameness of an exhausted landscape.

It may be that deep ecology has an essential rightness to it not because it is a cause that serves something larger than self—many movements, secular and spiritual, which limit their concerns to human welfare, are so inspired—but because the larger-than-self something of deep ecology is not an abstraction like "justice," but a palpable reality. Robinson Jeffers called that reality "organic wholeness, the wholeness of life and things, the divine beauty of the universe." "Love that," he wrote, "not man apart from that." Ecodefense, then, is the expression of a love that transcends species identity. (The argument that it may also be the expression of a profound misanthropy is worth considering, but is the subject for another essay.)

Just as there are grave physical risks involved in acts of ecodefense (injury and incarceration the most common, though the bombing of the *Rainbow Warrior* marks a mortal escalation of hostility toward ecodefenders), there are great psychic risks in opening the heart to the insights of deep ecology. "One of the penalties of an ecological education," wrote Aldo Leopold, is realizing "that one lives alone in a world of wounds." Becoming vulnerable to and tender toward the planet's heartbreaking and beautiful truths of death, transformation, and regeneration; and of evolution's teaching of the inconsequence of the individual relative to the species, is a soul-cracking experience. Absolute compassion with Mother Earth—suffering her pangs of creation and destruction—demands inordinate strength of spirit, a strength nurtured by a sense of one's interpenetration with wild nature, a sense most often renewed in the very wilderness whose defense is being mounted.

Philosopher Leopold Kohr once said that you can't solve a problem at its own level. Neither can a problem be understood at its own level. Hence the need for a supra-rational, call it mystical, apprehension of the planetary ecosystem's functioning and possible destiny in order to begin to address the urgent problem of preserving the diversity of life on Earth. Such understanding is less often a product of the science of ecology than a result of an epiphany experienced in nature or distilled in poetry.

The workings of human ego, contaminated by the delusion of human superiority and so inexorably alienated from nature, have erected a damaging "civilization" that makes those epiphanies less and less available. So the ecodefender and deep ecologist need to share their insights with their fellow humans, particularly the humans committing the damage. It is tempting to dehumanize the perpetrators of wilderness destruction as evil murderers but kinder all around to offer them refuge in the insanity defense. Matricide is crazy, an abomination, and the extirpation of wilderness is a killing of the Mother. Perhaps it is an outcome of a lack of love, or the failure to perceive the overarching love that expresses itself in the glories, puzzles, and ingenuities of evolution. Accordingly, the ecodefender's vocation must come to include loving the matricides back to health and embodying the wilderness epiphany.

Earth First! founder Dave Foreman has characterized the fight for wilderness preservation as a losing battle and his comrade Howie Wolke bitterly despairs of communicating effectively with Forest Service and other government functionaries who capitulate to political and economic pressures to exploit publicly-owned wildlands for short-term industrial gain. It is not hard to sympathize with such pessimism. The only realized good of this cause may be the vitalization it affords—the solemn transport of the Ghost Shirt Dance. It may be that all we can accomplish in our lifetimes by the practice of ecotage, nonviolent direct action, and other more orthodox forms of ecological activism is a slight delay in the wholesale destruction of wilderness.

Be that as it may, in the geologically long run, Earth will abide. The life force seethes in her burning magmatic heart and is, finally, irrepressible. This (pen)ultimate consolation should be approached gingerly, since it may be misappropriated as an apology for a rapist approach to land use rather than as a cause for mystic faith in the potency of the planet. It also illustrates the paradox of attempting to transcend (unenlightened) species self-interest and to speak for the larger system that enfolds the planet. The risk is that those attempts may be a kind of psychological projection. Where one human is predisposed to see herself as but a part of an interconnected tissue of organisms—what Aldo Leopold called a "plain member and citizen" of the land-community—another, say James Watt, may see himself as an agent of a messianic apocalypse. Some say we are trapped in the solipsism of human consciousness and that there are no absolutes save those we choose. Yet the evidence of ecological destruction that mounts all around us suggests that we may not have infinite latitude for self-definition after all; that, in Paul Ehrlich's mordant phrase, "Nature bats last."

Whatever the true, unknowable reality, and whatever the out-come of our behavior as a species, it is clear that the most acute anguish for citizens and members of the land community is the near-term loss of friends and neighborhoods dear to us—the destruction of myriad species and sacred places. Compounding this anguish is the perception of the tragic blindness of our own species, that flaw in the human mind that sets humans over and against the rest of nature.

Whatever extraordinary fate is being worked out in these last days of the 20th century, we must do our utmost to reawaken in our fellow human beings an abiding compassion with all life on Earth. The strength and vision that result from making common cause with all life are gifts to share. The awareness of the countless evolutionary mir-acles unfolding in an acre of virgin forest or prairie is a precious gift to share, as is the wider knowledge of belonging to a living reality that transcends self and epoch.

Editor's note: The Round River Rendezvous is the annual national Earth First! gathering, held each summer, generally somewhere in the Rocky Mountains. The 1985 Rendezvous, during which Stephanie Mills gave a speech similar to this essay, was held on the Uncompahgre Plateau of south-western Colorado.

DEEP ECOLOGY AND CONSERVATION BIOLOGY
March 1990
by Arne Naess

In the late 1960s and early '70s many of us believed that most ecolo-gists would concentrate on research clearly related to the solution of the ecological crisis. But at the universities the atmosphere encouraged "pure" research—research without definite practical goals. And those who got jobs within the range of interest of big corporations work with goals in mind, but rarely focus on the crisis and rarely "go public."

Most high level papers in ecological journals are extremely specialized and only remotely relevant for critical issues. In the early '70s, those who focused on the general crisis warned supporters of the deep ecology movement not to expect much help from established researchers in scientific ecology.

Then came conservation biology! It started as scientists and managers from many quarters realized that they profited by working together to combine theory with practice in their effort to save the planet from further destruction. They were in a sense practitioners of ecology. They came from "biogeography, systematics, genetics, evolution, epidemiology, sociobiology, forestry, fisheries, wildlife biology, and the auxiliary sciences of agronomy, veterinary science, resource economics and policy, ethnobiology, and environmental ethics." (*Conservation Biology*, ed. Michael Soulé, p. 5)

Conservation biology is a movement. "The idea of conservation biology seems to convey several things at once, including scholarship, a common purpose, and the potential for making a significant personal contribution to the world. For students and established scientists alike, conservation biology seems to represent a community of commitment, and something of value to identify with." (Soulé, p. 5) "Consensus can also define a discipline. Disciplines are not logical constructs; they are social crystallizations which occur when a group of people agree that association and discourse serve their interests. Conservation biology began when a critical mass of people agreed that they were conservation biologists. There is something very social and very human about this realization." (p. 3)

Insofar as conservation biology is a scientific discipline, it is a crisis science like AIDS and cancer research. That is, it uses certain goals and values as axioms. The intrinsic value of diversity of life forms and the meaningfulness of a struggle to save life forms from extinction are taken for granted. Conservation biology is therefore not purely descriptive; it is "a prescriptive science." (Norton, p. 237) Consequently, it is activist-oriented and personal: "The planetary tragedy is also a personal tragedy to those scientists who feel compelled to devote themselves to the rescue effort." (Soulé, p. 11)

Despite conservation biologists' intense commitment to rescue the non-human world, they see the precarious situation of millions of people. "For example, the implementation of 'biosphere reserves' as sites for the harmonious coexistence for humans and nature (UNESCO-UNEP, 1984) depends on both a good grasp of the local biology and on the enthusiastic support of the indigenous peoples. In fact, the survival of many natural biological communities is going to require the creative cooperation of biologists, social scientists, and politicians, especially in the tropics. It won't be long before many conservation biologists are spending more time at community meetings than in the field or laboratory." (Soulé, p. 11)

From all this it is clear that members of the conservation biology community are supporters of the deep ecology movement—provided that movement is characterized along the lines of the 8 points of the Naess-Sessions platform. On the other hand very few deep ecology supporters can boast of being conservation biologists. Many supporters may be ignorant of conservation biology.

Some supporters of the deep ecology movement are active in the efforts to save the cultures of non-industrialized communities. The slogan "wilderness for the people" attests to the goal of letting people in who do not destroy or degrade wilderness and letting people who already are there remain. It is sad that some Third World authors feel "American deep ecology" threatens to save spectacular animals at the expense of humans. (Guha) It must be clearly stated that the average US lifestyle is such that wilderness and the US way of life are incompatible. The fight to save what remains of US wilderness does not teach anybody how to save Third World wilderness. Conservation biologists in the Third World try to preserve wilderness, but in cooperation with people who determine policies.

Conservation biologists "go public." That is, they try to make people aware of the perilous state of affairs. Here they part from the main body of Earth scientists, who tend to avoid propagating their strong views—if they have any—in public. Why do most scientists avoid voicing strong views? I have made a tentative list of reasons:

1. Time taken away from professional work.

2. Consequent adverse effects on promotion and status.

3. Feeling of insufficient competence outside their area of "expertise."

4. Lack of training in the use of mass media and in facing non-academic audiences.

5. Negative attitude toward expressing "subjective" opinions and valu-

ations, or violating norms of "objectivity"; reluctance to enter controversial issues.

6. Fear that colleagues or bosses think they dabble in irrelevant controversial fields and go public due to vainglory and publicity seeking.

7. Fear of fellow researchers, institution personnel or administrations;
fear of the stigma "unscientific." (Soulé, p. 513)

One of the dangers common to the two movements is elitism. It
"lurks whenever a field has a strong academic foothold. Whether the root
of elitism is arrogance from within the ivory tower or fear from without,
it is always a danger. There is no hiding the fact that much of the current
interest in conservation biology is occurring within academic circles . . . "
(Soulé, p. 5) The deep ecology movement faces a danger of being too
closely associated with the small group of deep ecology theorists, thus
obstructing the insight that the overwhelming mass of supporters do not
publish papers or speak over the radio. These supporters form the back-
bone of the movement. Their commitment manifests itself in the direct
actions going on all over the world. We need the activism of millions of
people with the basic attitude of supporters of the movement.

The two movements have another danger in common, "isolation—elitism's child." We should seek contact with groups competing
with us in making an impact on the public, avoiding false pretensions
and sectarianism. Some supporters of the deep ecology movement, like
myself, are professional philosophers and theoreticians. We ask about
the ultimate premises of sayings such as "every living creature has
intrinsic (or internal) value (or worth)." We may ask: Why is it so and
what exactly does it mean? What does it mean that we do something
for its own sake, and why should we do it? What is the relation of
Aldo Leopold's criterion in his *Land Ethics*—"A thing is right when it
tends to preserve the integrity, stability, and beauty of the biotic community . . . "—to general ethics, for instance dealing with friends stuck
in the mud or babies starving? Answers differ. According to supporters
who are not inclined to ask such questions, nothing much comes out
of philosophical speculation. But the less philosophically minded, as
much as the professors, somehow assume when acting in grave
conflicts their decisions are compatible with an ultimate basis,
whether religious or otherwise. We assume some kind of "ecosophy,"
some kind of wisdom, which we are able to verbalize only imperfectly

and fragmentarily. (A recent attempt to verbalize such wisdom is offered in Alan Drengson's book *Beyond Environmental Crisis*.)

Whatever happens in the years to come, one may expect conservation biology, as a distinguished "mission oriented crisis discipline," to inform us of great successes as well as great failures. Let us hope the former will color the news!

CHAPTER 5

Ecosystems and Their Members

THE ARTICLES IN EARTH FIRST! JOURNAL dealing explicitly with what we seek to preserve have been particularly important. Articles focusing on the natural history of, and attempts to recover, whole ecosystems have helped conservationists move beyond the habit of simply trying to save remnants of Nature and to realize that the preservation of biodiversity will require the restoration and preservation of whole landscapes and seascapes.

Studies in and applications of ecosystem restoration will be a growing concern of the environmental movement in future years. As several of the following articles show, it is becoming increasingly clear that ecosystem restoration will sometimes entail "hands-off management," or benign neglect. Nature is the best healer; and in many places, simply guarding against further intrusions will allow recovery. Indeed, a key lesson taught again and again by EF! writers through the years is that Nature knows best; human meddling usually damages ecosystem integrity.

This is not to say, however, that humans should never attempt to speed the restoration process. In places where native species have been extirpated and exotics introduced (almost everywhere in North America), some active restoration measures—e.g., predator reintroductions, eradication of Eurasian weeds, stabilization of devegetated stream banks—may be necessary to restore natural diversity. The articles in this chapter begin to sketch an outline of how to protect and restore natural diversity on this continent.

OF INDIVIDUAL SPECIES, ASSEMBLAGES AND BATS

Beltane 1984

by Reed Noss

Earth comes first! On a smaller scale, one we can deal with as activists, that means the natural community or ecosystem. We strive to maintain its integrity, structure (characteristic species composition and diversity), and function (nutrient cycling, energy flow, climatic regulation, etc.). By looking at the entire system, we can avoid the conflicts, narrowness and bias sometimes imposed by worrying about the fate of individual species.

On the other hand, the idea of a whole ecosystem is somewhat abstract. We could lose a lot of species and still have a functioning ecosystem. Some type of system, albeit an impoverished and unstable one, would continue to function if every bulldozer ran rampant over the earth, or even if we detonated all our nuclear warheads. If we value natural ecosystem integrity, we must complement the whole ecosystem approach with a focus on the individual species and assemblages of species that are most imperiled by human civilization.

The concept of indicator species can be used to target for conservation those creatures that are least tolerant of our disturbances. Some species, often characterized as "opportunistic" or "weedy," will prosper in a human-dominated landscape. Non-native (exotic) species frequently become pests in a new environment without their customary predators and competitors. But other kinds of organisms are able to persist only in the largest and most strictly protected wilderness areas. Large predators, ecological specialists, species dependent on patchy or unpredictable resources, and species with large home ranges or low reproductive potential are particularly vulnerable to extinction from human modifications of the landscape.

One group of organisms that has fared poorly since humans claimed the earth is the bats. Among mammals, the order *Chiroptera* is second only to *Rodentia* in number of species. Some 950 species, representing an amazing array of adaptations, have been described. Insects, fruit, pollen, nectar, flowers, leaves, blood, fish and other vertebrates are among the food items selected by different kinds of bats. In numbers of individuals, too, some species of bats are extraordinary. Sometimes they congregate in caves by the millions.

But these congregations are rapidly decreasing. People generally hate bats, perhaps even more than they hate spiders and snakes. Because bats have been so persecuted, they need protection above and beyond that of the particular ecosystems in which they function. The fact that they congregate in large numbers (in caves, trees, human structures, etc.) makes them especially vulnerable to persecution.

For example, 90% of the remaining Indiana Bats (*Myotis sodalis*, a federally listed Endangered species) hibernate in just nine caves. People have been known to destroy an entire colony in a cave just for the fun of it. In a study of the Gray Bat (*Myotis grisescens*, also Endangered) in Kentucky, a colleague and I found evidence of many former colonies that had been exterminated by man. Chiefly because of human persecution, the Kentucky population of Gray Bats had declined at least 89% from a past maximum.

People also make money killing bats. In the United States particularly, pest control companies sell a fraudulent remedy for poisoning colonies that occupy homes and other buildings. The virulent poisons used also menace human health, and new bats may come in after the others have been exterminated. Bat-proofing buildings (sealing openings) while the bats are away is obviously a better solution (although generally bats in a building do absolutely no harm), but the pest control bastards don't make as much money that way.

What can we do to save bats? Habitat protection and public education are essential. Both the foraging habitat, generally comprising extensive tracts of natural vegetation and unpolluted water, and the roosts (caves for many species, but also cliffs, large trees, and human structures in areas where natural ones have been eliminated) must be protected. But it is not enough to put a piece of land into public ownership. Even in a wilderness area, if people find a cave containing bats, the bats will likely be eliminated. Unfortunately, fences or properly designed gates may have to be placed around the entrances to those subterranean habitats. Particularly in maternity colonies and hibernacula, bats need to be left alone.

I know many so-called "conservationists" who are biased against bats, who flinch when one flies by. Hence the necessity of education. We have all been fed bullshit about bats. Do bats fly into your hair? Not if they can help it. Do bats commonly transmit rabies? No! This is one of the biggest fallacies, one willfully perpetuated by health authorities. A Florida county health official, who recently officiated the mass slaughter of several hundred bats harmlessly roosting in a junior high school gymnasium, claims that 20–40% of a bat colony typically harbors rabies. That is total nonsense! A correct figure, according to world bat authority Merlin Tuttle, is less than 0.5%. And neither healthy bats nor rabid bats attack people. They only bite in self-defense, and the teeth of many species are too small to break human skin (an exception is the vampire bat of the neotropics, which will feed on a sleeping human as readily as on a sleeping javelina).

We must explain that bats are tremendously important components of natural ecosystems, and directly help us by controlling insects, pollinating and dispersing food plants, producing guano for fertilizer, and a host of other functions. They are also amazing, beautiful and gentle creatures. Although some species have adapted to our modifications, others are critically endangered because of our ignorance, superstition, and cruelty. (For more information, contact Bat Conservation International, Inc., POB 162603, Austin, TX 78716; 512-327-9721.)

Bats are just one example of organisms that require special attention beyond that of ecosystem-level or wilderness preservation. Again, the holistic and indicator species approaches can be complementary. Ideally, we would concentrate on the most endangered elements at each level of biological organization, from genes, individuals, and species to ecosystems, landscapes and the biosphere.

Don't spend your time on puppy dogs, dandelions, or even baby seals. That is not to say the cute and cuddly are unimportant, or unworthy of our love. But other things, occasionally "ugly" to biased human eyes, are going faster toward oblivion. To preserve the integrity, structure and function of a natural Earth, we must concentrate on those forms that can least tolerate the cancer of humanity out of control.

ECOLOGICAL PRESERVES FOR THE EASTERN MOUNTAINS
Mabon 1985
by R. F. Mueller

During the past decade many millions of acres of public lands have been set aside in the West, and particularly in Alaska, for the express purpose of preserving whole ecosystems—and even many of these large preserves are clearly insufficient. Yet in the eastern United States only small fragments have been designated. Why? Is it that eastern ecosystems are less worthy of protection? To the contrary, eastern deciduous forests, with their floodplains and prairie openings, are recognized by biologists as some of the most diverse temperate ecosystems anywhere. Is it because such protection is precluded by the large private land holdings? No again, for this region contains 24 million acres of National Forest land alone. Despite this eligibility, the acreage devoted to ecosystem preservation is far less in the East than in the West even when the proportions of public lands in the two regions are compared. This situation became especially evident with the recent designation of eastern Wilderness Areas, which average less than 10,000 acres, while some western Wildernesses are in the range of a million contiguous acres. Clearly this order of magnitude imbalance is justified neither by geography nor biology.

We do of course have numerous public "playgrounds" in the East, including several National Parks and Recreation Areas as well as state parks, wildlife management areas, and other facilities. However, excepting perhaps the National Wildlife Refuges—which are largely confined to wetlands—these exist primarily to serve human needs, and in practice nature protection is only ancillary to them. As we shall see, even designated Wildernesses in the East are managed largely to satisfy human esthetic values rather than nature's requirements. The absence of an ecological perspective in the East has resulted in sundered ecosystems and degraded watershed integrity. It's time for a new initiative to revise and upgrade nature protection in the region.

In a stimulating article in *EF!* (5–83), Reed Noss proposed the creation of a deciduous forest ecological preserve in the Ohio Valley. It is logical to extend this idea to the eastern mountain forests, for these already have substantial tracts of National Forest. Also, these forests have a geographic coherence and unity imposed by the northeast-southwest trending ranges, and inter-mountain valley streams of a strong trellis drainage pattern, features that lend themselves to the establishment of natural preserve boundaries.

The US Forest Service's recently-proposed land and resource management plans for the National Forests again remind us of the abuse and exploitation to which these lands have long been subject and which their planners wish to continue in the future. As a consequence, there has been an outcry from citizens, particularly in the Appalachian regions, where most of the eastern National Forests are. Under these Forest plans, our most precious mountain landscapes would be sliced into ever smaller fragments by roads and powerlines, and devastated by clearcuts and mines. Wildlife would be rigidly managed as an adjunct to logging and common species such as White-tailed Deer and Turkey would be favored over wilderness species such as Black Bear, Eastern Cougar and the large raptors.

Furthermore, in this day of rapid advances in the earth sciences, the Forest Service plans fail even to acknowledge the importance of hydrologic and nutrient cycles or they selectively fix on certain aspects of these cycles to promote their nefarious ends. For example, one stated justification for clearcutting is that it would increase the water yield (read *run-off*) for a watershed since removing trees decreases evapotranspiration, which feeds moisture into the air. The FS does not acknowledge that this would also increase the fluctuation levels of streams, thereby intensifying drought, flooding and erosion, while the water-trapping and holding capacities of the landscape and the climate-moderating effects of evapotranspiration would be impaired. In short, the Forest Service ignores the criteria for poor watershed management most evident in the current rash of worldwide environmental catastrophes.

Closely related to these deceptive water management policies is the disregard of forest nutrient demands. The FS proposes expanded logging of marginal timber stands on steep terrain and dry, nutrient-poor soils, which, when bared by clearcutting, would rapidly lose their remaining nutrients through leaching and erosion. Detailed nutrient evaluation should precede *any* logging in these forests.

Even though the land currently being logged in the eastern mountain forests is generally the most accessible and productive in these forests, studies by Alaric Sample of The Wilderness Society (Issue Brief, 7–84) have shown that the timber sale return on management and road building is frequently 10 cents or less per dollar invested. Future returns from more leached, eroded and nutrient-poor soils would be even less.

Although a variety of habitats are included within the eastern National Forest proclamation boundaries, most actual public land holdings are confined to the highlands, and the designated Wilderness Areas lie in the most rugged cores of the ranges. The streams that drain these Wilderness Areas and nurture their wildlife are small secondary drainages. In the slightly metamorphosed rocks of the sharply folded Appalachians, these secondary streams lead into mainstems which form broad valleys with rich flood plains between and parallel to the ranges; but in the more massive and highly metamorphosed rocks of the Blue Ridge and elsewhere, the drainage is more complex. As might be expected, the small wilderness streams flow over the most resistant and nutrient-poor rocks. Fairly typical of Virginia wilderness is the St. Marys River with virtually the entire watershed in almost pure coarsely crystalline quartzite, a rock that contains only minute amounts of the important nutrients such as potassium, phosphorous, magnesium and calcium (nutrients which nourish rich forests which in turn attract the Forest Service and timber industry, thereby proving the forests' undoing).

Thus nature preserves in the eastern mountains are, by convention, confined to small watersheds, picturesque in terms of rapids, gorges and that favorite Forest Service category of "scenic vistas." While these streams are relatively sterile biologically, they flow into the larger intermountain streams whose floodplains are the repositories of the nutrients garnered and concentrated from diffuse mountain sources through flood deposition and subsurface flow. Unfortunately, although not heavily populated, the riparian zones of these intermountain valleys are usually in a degraded state due to a variety of human impacts including livestock grazing. It's not for naught that such streams in Virginia bear names like "Cowpasture," "Calfpasture," and "Bullpasture."

All of this brings us to the major problem. The designated Wilderness preserves are too biologically unproductive and isolated from the nutrient-rich and diverse riparian zones of the local mainstem valleys. They were designated merely to gratify narrow human esthetic tastes for "pretty scenery" and invigorating hiking.

In EF!, Beltane 1985, Noss discusses related problems in his review of a book by the ecologist Larry Harris (The Fragmented Forest). Isolated and confined preserves don't really safeguard the species they contain in the absence of sufficient communication with like areas through travel corridors and without adequate buffer zones to separate them from surrounding areas of intensive development.

Harris also stresses the importance of riparian strips. In the eastern mountains, the role of drainage networks is even more critical than in some other areas, since there are fewer mineral nutrient sources in their rocks as compared with the geologically young volcanic deposits on which many western forests are developed.

The eastern mountain forests present an opportunity to create a system of ecological preserves that could embrace areas of several hundreds of thousands of acres. These preserves could include the major ridges and certain of the major intermountain valleys and mainstem streams of the trellis pattern, particularly the valleys of which parts are already public land. The individual areas could be linked by communication corridors, including riparian zones whenever possible. This system would, of course, require the acquisition of some private land, mostly within National Forest proclamation boundaries. However, this land could be acquired with minimal impact over a considerable time period, with condemnation minimized. These preserves would require the closing of some Forest Service roads and secondary routes. The effects on local people of these closures could be mitigated by gradually limiting traffic to private inholders, while gradually acquiring private lands.

The mountain wilderness cores, with flanking and radiating riparian strips and communication corridors, could be surrounded by zones of greater access and more intensive human use. Although such zones would be devoted largely to recreational activity (hunting, fishing, camping, etc.), they might also include some timber production based on rotation periods long enough to justify economically productive selective logging. A major function of such zones would be to act as buffers between the Wilderness Preserves and outer zones in which more intensive recreation, logging and traditional firewood gathering would be permitted.

The integration of the intermountain mainstem rivers and communication corridors with the expanded mountain wilderness cores would make available to wildlife the nourishing floodplains and diverse riparian environments of these larger streams. Wilderness designation of these valleys would encourage reclamation of these riparian zones and consequent wildlife proliferation not seen in years.

While the concept of ecological preserves for the eastern mountains hasn't yet been presented for public approval, there is much support for wilderness in the region and this support favors ecological aspects rather than recreational opportunities, as was brought out in responses to Forest Service surveys (Draft EIS for Land and Resource Management Plan for the George Washington National Forest, 1985). The public also recognizes the relationship between forest degradation and road building, clearcutting with short rotation periods, and deficit timber sales. It is only a moderate step from this recognition to an appreciation of a need for reclamation of wilderness on the scale envisioned here.

The eastern National Forests that are the best candidates for conversion to ecological preserves are the Jefferson and George Washington in Virginia. Although these forests show a range of local climatic conditions, they lie in a general trough of low rainfall relative to surrounding areas. In addition, they occupy a belt of shallow soils consisting largely of imperfectly weathered rock fragments (Agriculture Handbook No. 271, Forest Service, 1965). These are the soils developed on rocks such as the quartzite previously discussed. As a result, trees grow relatively slowly; and while they form forests of picturesque beauty and good wildlife cover, timber quality is poor except in local coves and riparian zones which should never be logged anyway. Given these conditions and the short rotation periods employed by the Forest Service, the timber receipts to cost ratios (R/C) have been only 0.08 and 0.10 for the Jefferson and George Washington, respectively.

Other likely candidates for conversion to ecological preserves are the following National Forests, with their R/C numbers as given by The Wilderness Society: Daniel Boone of Kentucky (0.16), Cherokee of Tennessee (0.23), the Monongahela of West Virginia (0.30), and the North Carolina National Forests (0.31). The Jefferson-George Washington-Monongahela complex lies close to the major eastern population centers where water and air resources are under the greatest stress from a multitude of pollutants and where, consequently, the mitigating effects of significant wilderness are most needed.

It was the eastern wilderness forests, spreading over plains, riverbanks and mountain heights that, above and beyond all the mercenary instincts of European society, first imbued the American soul with its special love of freedom and independence. That wilderness deserves to live again, in a system of eastern ecological preserves.

SMOKEY THE BEAR'S LEGACY ON THE WEST

Brigid 1986

by George Wuerthner

No single human modification of the environment has had more pervasive and widespread negative consequences for the ecological integrity
of North America than the suppression of fire. Fire suppression has
destroyed the natural balance of the land even more than overgrazing,
logging, or the elimination of predators. One could easily build a case
that an environmental impact statement should be prepared prior to
any fire suppression activities by government agencies since control of
wildfires greatly alters the natural environment. Yet, most people are
oblivious to the long-term consequences of fire suppression.

Wandering through the Ponderosa Pine forests of northern
Arizona, the White Fir-Giant Sequoia forests of California, the
Douglas-fir forests of the Northern Rockies—everywhere throughout
the West—those who study fire ecology see dying ecosystems with
thick, overstocked stands. Looking at old photos of these places one is
stricken by how open and park-like these areas were. Even the rangelands are sick. Frequent fires favored grasses over cacti, shrubs and
trees. The beautiful waving grasslands seen by the early explorers are
gone as much because of fire suppression as overgrazing.

Some of the negative effects of fire suppression are less apparent.
Fire suppression may be a major force behind the decline in Grizzly
Bear numbers in Yellowstone National Park. Fires, prior to the advent
of white people, kept trees from invading meadows which are major
foraging areas for bears. Fires also stimulated the growth of Quaking
Aspen, which in turn attracted Beavers who built dams and created
wet meadow habitat, which provided forage for bears. With fire suppression, the aspen are declining, and with them the Beavers and their
meadows. Indirectly, we have eliminated food sources for bears.

Fires also kept the pine forests free of extensive pine beetle epidemics. As a result of fire suppression, pine beetles have been able to
invade the Whitebark Pine forests of sub-alpine areas, which, as far as
is known, never occurred before. Whitebark Pine nuts are a major
autumn food source for Grizzlies. Nearly 75% of a Grizzly's diet in the
Rockies consists of fire-dependent plant species. For the past 100
years, the Grizzly's food resources have declined within the Park and

the surrounding forests (now National Forests). However, because of the concentrated food sources at Park garbage dumps, the population did not decline; it may have even increased. With the closure of the dumps in the early 1970s, combined with increased unnatural mortality, and a decreased natural nutrient base due to loss of fire-dependent food items, the Grizzly's fate may have been sealed.

Poor nutrition means bears breed at a later age, breed less frequently, and fewer cubs survive to maturity. And while birth rates have declined, man-induced mortality has increased. Ironically, the National Park Service has killed more Grizzlies than poachers, ranchers, and hunters have killed. (The Park Service claims it is now following a policy of letting natural systems evolve without interference. This means they are opposed to any feeding of bears in Yellowstone Park, as this is unnatural. Yet, the high death rate is not natural, nor is the Park ecosystem any longer. There is nothing natural about Fishing Bridge or Grant Village and the killing of bears at these places.) But even if we stopped all conflicts and development in and around the Park, there may not be sufficient food resources left to support a viable Grizzly population over the long run. Although the Park Service has now adopted a policy of letting *some* fires burn, the amount of new habitat created each year is still far short of what was produced prior to the intervention of white men.

The present fire policies of most managing agencies not only discount the former role of natural fires, they also neglect the past effects of *human*-induced fires on the environment. Native Americans for countless centuries purposely set fires to clear away brush, attract wildlife to feed close to their villages, and perhaps to protect villages with a fire break from lightning-ignited fire. (I am not condoning arson, for in today's highly populated West such use of fires would be extremely dangerous.) In many areas of the country, particularly at lower elevations, human-set fires probably were at least as common as natural fires. In the Bitterroot Valley of Montana, for example, fire occurred on three to five year intervals and is attributed to Indian-ignited blazes. The resulting forests were open and park-like. Similarly, open slopes along the central California coast by Monterey were the result of fires ignited by Indians. Even in the eastern US, the forests were often open and one could ride a horse through them quite easily due to clearing effects of Indian fires.

The ecological benefits of frequent fires were many. Over much of the western US, the arid environment typical of the warmer months precludes rapid decomposition of litter. Usually, only during spring are the soils both moist enough and warm enough to provide decomposing organisms the proper environment for composting litter. Without fires, dead material accumulates and nutrients necessary for plant growth remain locked up. Fires release these nutrients.

The arid environment that favors grasses does little to promote nutrient recycling. Grasslands, even more than healthy forestlands, may depend upon fires for their existence. One frequently hears ranch-ers and range managers extoll grazing as a prerequisite for the ecological health of grasslands. Livestock, it is claimed, eat dead leaf matter and then release nutrients back onto the land thereby assisting nutrient recycling. While this is true to a certain extent, fires are much better for recycling range nutrients since they consume even the coarsest grass stems which cattle and sheep avoid. And they do so without the trampling, trailing, and streambank erosion that result from livestock use.

Much of the far North suffers from a similar shortage of available nutrients. In the boreal and arctic regions, decomposition is slowed by cold temperatures and acidic soil conditions. The results are the same. Nutrients remain in dead snags and rotting logs, and are unavailable to plants until released.

Fires are, then, analogous to river floods which each year provide a new layer of life-giving soil for plant growth. Stopping fires has the same consequences for nutrient cycling as damming the Nile had for soil building in Egypt. Indeed, fires even help to create soils. The rapid heating and cooling from fires breaks down rock and soil particles. No one knows what long-term effects fire suppression has had on soils.

Fires also cleanse forests. They directly reduce insects and diseases. In addition, many tree pathogens are killed just by the smoke. As a fire burns through a forest, especially if it is a cool, slow burning fire, it thins out the younger trees, and leaves behind the mature individuals, particularly those of species adapted to survive fires. Some species, such as Ponderosa Pine, Douglas-fir, Western Larch, Jeffrey Pine, and Giant Sequoia, have thick bark and tall limbless trunks that protect them from small, quick burns. The survivors of fires experience increased viability due to reduced competition for nutrients, light and water. Hence their ability to resist forest insects and disease is increased. The epidemics of pine beetles, Spruce Budworm, and other forest pathogens we see today are the direct result of fire suppression which has weakened the overall ability of forests to resist infestation.

The public pays three ways for this policy of fire suppression. First, we pay the high cost of fire fighting, which is frequently the highest budgetary expenditure of public land agencies. One big fire often costs five to ten million dollars for suppression. A 1450 acre fire just outside Missoula, Montana, this summer cost one million dollars to put out. The 65,300 acre Mortar Creek fire on Idaho's Challis National Forest several years ago cost five and a half million dollars to put out. How much better it would be to spend the millions of dollars it costs to suppress fires each summer on endangered species research or the acquisition of private lands with important wildlife habitat! Fire research has shown that, in addition to being expensive, fire fighting frequently has nothing to do with putting out the fire. Fires usually don't stop until the weather changes or the fire encounters another recent burn and runs out of fuel. In essence, we often throw money at fires just so we appear to be doing something.

Second, we pay for the below-cost sales that result when the agencies attempt to correct the imbalance they have created. For example the Forest Service plans to stimulate aspen production in Colorado by clearcutting. Since the timber cannot be profitably harvested, these will be deficit sales which cost taxpayers money. Simultaneously, the FS is spending our money to put out fires which naturally stimulate aspen regeneration!

Third, because many of these proposed logging sales are in presently roadless, wild areas, we lose wilderness. We do not need to cut down eight inch diameter Lodgepole Pine to save it from pine beetles. All we need to do is let fires burn. Much of the timber, range, and tundra that naturally burn have no commercial value. In Alaska, over half the acreage that naturally burns is treeless tundra where even the lame excuse of protection of timber resources cannot be used. Yet, even here the Bureau of Land Management has actively fought fires at great public expense. (Fortunately, the BLM in Alaska has changed its fire policy in the past few years, and is letting many large areas burn.)

Fire suppression also has negative effects on old growth forests and attendant wildlife species. In the past, frequent fires in drier forests kept fuel levels down. Fires swept through these forests quickly. Because of a lack of fuel, these fires seldom burned hot enough to invade moist, old growth timber stands. In the absence of large, hot, crown fires in adjacent drier forests, moist forests commonly developed old growth characteristics 400–500 years after the last major disturbance. Accordingly, our attempts to save species like the Woodland Caribou, which depends upon old growth timber, may be linked to our fire policies.

Although land management agencies are now experimenting with prescribed burns, their practices have several shortcomings. Most prescribed burns are too small. In the past the total acreage burned each summer in the western US was in the *millions* of acres. Even in the far North, extensive areas burned each summer. It is estimated that an average of one million acres of Interior Alaska burned every year prior to fire suppression.

In addition, most prescribed burns are set when the range or forests are moist, usually in the spring. Under natural conditions fires burn in the drier months. Small mammals, birds, etc., have usually completed breeding by the time natural fire seasons begin. Prescribed burns occur at a time when wildlife is less able to survive fire. Smokey lied. Studies have shown that under natural fire conditions, few wildlife species or individuals are hurt. They simply fly, walk or burrow away from the flames.

The problem with our fire policy is that we are not emulating natural systems. Fire suppression is analogous to cutting off a leg from a table and expecting it to remain upright. We must use energy now in the form of fire fighting, below-cost timber sales, etc., to hold up this table, or ecosystem. As litter accumulates, the load on the table becomes increasingly heavy and we must expend more and more energy to keep it from falling over.

The western US is sitting on a powder keg. One of these summers the West will burn down. Fuel loading is so high that a fire-storm of incredible proportions will overwhelm our suppression capabilities. We also face greater possibilities of loss of human life and property as people continue to build houses in forested areas. This is analogous to building on the flood plain of a river. Sooner or later you pay the consequences. Communities have not recognized this problem and thus have not faced it with zoning restrictions, as any observer of the southern California chaparral forest can attest.

What needs to be done? To begin, we must realize that fires are a needed part of our environment. Instead of spending money to put out all fires, we should build fire breaks around our communities, and scattered throughout commercial timberlands. Where fires have been suppressed for decades, it may be necessary to recreate wildlife habitat by frequent prescribed burning.

We need a massive public education program to promote the merits of fire. We should replace statements like "a forest fire DAMAGED 100 acres of land today" with statements like "a forest fire CREATED 100 acres of new wildlife habitat and fire break today." Fire fighters, instead of being viewed as heroes, should be called what they are: money grubbing mercenaries out to kill fires. [Fire fighters are forest fighters.] *Fires have as much right to exist as bears and wolves.* Just as predator control has upset natural balances, so too has fire control. Fire fighters are just as nasty as government trappers of lions, bears, and wolves.

If we can bring about this change in attitude, many of the land management policies environmentalists so detest may be brought under control. No longer will it be "necessary" to clearcut a forest to "save" it from Spruce Budworm or Southern Pine Beetle attacks. No longer will we have to tolerate chaining of rangelands to clear away juniper woodlands or spray to eliminate sagebrush. No longer will we have to tolerate new roads built to transport fire fighters to blazes or to provide access to "diseased timber."

Each year that we delay makes it that much harder to correct our past mistakes. Conservation organizations need to realize that many of the management policies they find unacceptable are related directly to fire suppression. If we truly wish to preserve wilderness and wildlife, we must preserve wildfires too.

HOW DEFORESTATION AND DESERTIFICATION AFFECT GENETIC RESOURCES
Eostar 1986
by Gary Nabhan

Both rainforest destruction and drought-related but man-made problems in dry lands are often in the news these days. While the biological depletion associated with tropical deforestation is implicit in most accounts, oftentimes soil erosion rather than genetic erosion is cited as the most significant long-term effect of desertification. The following commentary has been written toward remedying that oversight, comparing the deserts and moist tropics in terms of their plant resources.

The accelerating conversion of moist tropical forests is about the most alarming type of ecological destruction on Earth today. Not only do these ancient communities contain many undescribed plants that are threatened with extinction, but two to three dozen coevolved animal species may be endangered per plant when certain tropical trees are lost.

We are therefore witnessing the wasting away of more than just scattered plant species, for long-evolved ecological relationships are vulnerable as well. Entire genera and key links in particular food chains have been lost, as over half the land area once covered by moist tropical vegetation has been converted. Whether turned into cow pastures, lumber plantations or degraded second growth, it is a mere shadow of the former rainforest. The Global 2000 report suggested that a million kinds of moist tropical forest organisms will not last until the turn of the century if deforestation continues at its present rate.*

Conservationists have voiced several arguments against this devastation in their attempts to arouse the public on this issue. One is that this loss of biological diversity can be measured as a loss of the richest source of genetic resources useful for human welfare.

For instance, the International Institute for Environment and Development maintains that we must "put a value on forests." It suggests that the economic worth of genetic resources found within intact forests may be a measure that politicians and planners can be taught to understand. Following suit, admirable science writers such as Norman Myers and Catherine Caufield have stressed that tropical rainforests are "the [primary] source of undiscovered foods, medicines and materials" which, if destroyed, will drive society's agricultural economy toward "genetic bankruptcy." (Caufield)

Such reasons for protecting forest reserves have been raised by the many legal actions and economic boycotts that attempt to slow absentee-owned companies in their logging and grazing the life out of these habitats. But as a student of plants suitable for forms of sustainable agriculture far more "benevolent" than those from which most of us eat today, I feel queasy about emphasizing this "food and pharmaceutical storehouse" argument for saving rainforests. For one reason, the loss of genetic resources may be far more pervasive in intermediate arid lands than in moist tropical forests. By not challenging the truism that the rainforest's biological diversity will translate into the richest source of plant genetic diversity beneficial to modern society, we are selling the deserts short, and misunderstanding the rainforest at the same time.

Let's compare the moist tropical forests with drier lands. This is seldom done. Tropical forests are inevitably compared with temperate forests, I suppose for the benefit of those in Washington, Bonn and London. Global climatic classifications hierarchically sort out the temperate and tropical zones on the basis of temperature, arbitrarily dividing up a third of the world's land surface where moisture, not temperature, is most limiting to life. Deserts which cohesively extend from cool temperate to hot tropical climes get lost in the statistical shuffle.

Estimates vary, but one reliable source suggests that true tropical rainforest covers 17 million square kilometers, while desert scrub (including intermediate desert and degraded semi-desert) covers 18 million square kilometers. Another 7.5 million square kilometers lies in tropical drought-deciduous forest, but extreme dry desert covers even more—an additional 8.5 million square kilometers. Plant communities adapted to dry climates clearly cover more of the global land surface than do those adapted to hot moist climates.

Of course, areal extent is not the best indicator of importance. Net primary plant productivity of a hectare of rainforest is roughly four times that of a hectare covered by desert scrub. Many rainforests house 50 to 200 species of trees, vines and epiphytes per hectare, with exceptional stands peaking at 750 species of plants. In desert scrub, finding 30 to 50 plant species per hectare is rare but possible during a wildflower bloom in an exceptionally rainy season. When soil moisture is more limited, 10 to 15 species of shrubs and succulents may be the only cover apparent over many kilometers of desert. Another 20 to 30 ephemeral herbs may still be in reserve in the soil during droughts, for unlike moist tropical floras, desert plants invest in seed dormancy.

Despite these differences, there are some similarities between rainforest and desert. There is high endemism in both. Additional species may be found over a wide geographic range, but in minuscule patches within this range. They may depend on coevolved pollinators, seed dispersers or fruit detoxifiers that are tightly specialized on one or two plant species.

But what about characteristics that relate more directly to plant genetic resources and their presumed vulnerability? One of the most striking differences between these two biomes is in their lifeform diversity. Ecologists R. M. May and T. Givnish have demonstrated that desert vegetation is the most diverse and rainforests the least diverse in Raunkiaer lifeforms or plant architectural strategies for reproduction. Nearly all moist tropical forest species are woody-trunked plants which place their fruits or seeds high above the ground before letting them loose for dispersal. Desert lifeforms range from deep-rooted trees to columnar cacti, dwarf shrubs and rhizomatously-propagating yuccas, through tuber-bearing herbs and vines, to root parasites, short-lived bellyflowers and rock-mimicking succulents.

Whereas the tropical agroforester has few growthforms but many tree species from which to choose, desert agroecologists are actively investigating the genetic resources of water-efficient cacti, drought-evading annuals, drought-escaping perennial tubers and salt-tolerant shrubs. Of this latter category alone, hundreds of species of halophytes from coastal deserts are now being evaluated as new crops, while the moist tropical coastlines of the world have hardly contributed any crop candidates for saline agriculture. Since salt build-up on farmlands has become a problem of global magnitude, even a few successful candidates could salvage the productivity of millions of hectares of degraded fields, rather than forcing the cultivation of additional wildlands.

Yet can such plants contribute to the world food supply? Desert floras seem particularly well-endowed with non-toxic seeds rich in oil, protein, and hygroscopic fibers. The Sonoran Desert of Mexico and the US harbors 450 edible plant species, 20% of its flora. Particular moist tropical floras are also high in the number of edible plants, but perhaps their percent contribution is relatively lower.

My own research has shown that intermediate arid lands are the homes of many crop wild relatives. In the arid Americas, we find that wild beans, sunflowers, amaranths, potatoes, maniocs, gourds, prickly pears and agaves are sources of genes for resistance to drought, heat, pests and diseases. The Old World deserts have contributed wild wheats, barleys, melons, watermelons, millets, sorghums and many pulses. In fact, desert fringes appear to be the cradles of seed agriculture in part because of their diversity of species of economic annuals. Evolutionary ecologists have long recognized that the transition from true desert to semi-arid lands is intrinsically diverse. There are greater numbers of species per genus, and more complex variation within species found in this transition zone than in either wetter or drier adjacent areas.

As genetic conservationist Jose Esquinas-Alcazar has observed, "The arid intermediate regions are the laboratories in which many new adaptive complexes of plant groups are produced, while the arid extreme regions become the museums in which . . . relictual species are preserved."

Tragically, this diverse transition zone is exactly where desertification is taking its greatest toll, as poor management diminishes the soil moisture-holding capacity and plant productivity, creating a more arid landscape. The United Nations Environment Program estimates that 6 million hectares of semi-arid or subhumid land is annually reduced to desert-like conditions. Within true, hot deserts, another 21 million hectares is annually reduced to minimal cover, or to sweeping sands. As a result, we are seeing the genetic wipeout of populations, and in some cases, entire species of agaves, barleys, sunflowers, prickly pears, millets, beans, potatoes, and wheats.

The extent of disturbance in the moist tropics is roughly the same, and no less tragic. About 5.6 million hectares of rainforest and drought-deciduous forest is being completely eliminated every year. Another 20 million hectares of moist tropics is annually being degraded.

Most rainforest and desert countries currently suffer from poor distribution of wealth and power, and high human population growth rates which will increasingly stress their plant cover, among other things. The population of dry lands will rise from the present 850 million people to 1.2 billion by the year 2000. This growth rate is in part due to immigration of people from humid climates to drier ones. An increasingly large percentage of this population will come totally ignorant of the water constraints in their new home. They will expect the arid regions to feed them as well as their humid parent-lands have. Yet their land clearing, fuelwood use, grazing and urbanization will continue to deplete the very plants which have the genes to make their food economy more water-use efficient.

Instead of utilizing drought-hardy plant resources, arid lands dwellers are attempting to squeeze more water out of the deserts than the deserts have. Remaining riparian and oasis plants will be adversely affected. Pockets of plants that still survive around springs, artesian seeps, floodplains and canyon streams will be threatened by plans for dams and aquifer mining.

As with the tropical forests, botanists have offered the deserts' genetic resources as a reason to preserve such places, for they offer potential benefits to human welfare. Yet there may be differences in the relative contributions to food versus chemical industries that the deserts and moist tropics offer.

The intermediate arid lands are somewhat richer in herbaceous annual and perennial seed plants that are closely related to field crops already grown on several continents. There are already public repositories of such germ plasm, and their benefits are likely to be partially passed on to the small-scale farmer.

The rainforests are richer in plants capable of rapid vegetative propagation, particularly specialty fruits and pharmaceutical precursors. Multinational genetic engineering firms have already funded private expeditions to obtain these tropical materials in order to see if they are suitable for laboratory tissue culture. Any patented medicines or high-value fruits that suit themselves to such biotechnological endeavors are less likely to benefit indigenous tropical peoples, from whose lands this germ plasm has been obtained, than to benefit multinational corporations. Some tropical organisms may permanently lose their home in the rainforest for a life confined to the petri dish.

In my opinion, the hidden utilitarian treasures of these plant communities should not be the major argument for preserving them. Following ecologist David Ehrenfeld, I feel we must stress the intrinsic right of any lifeform to exist regardless of its perceived worth. We must also reiterate the life-support services offered by these ecosystems as wholes, including their role in climatic stabilization, watershed buffering from floods and erosion, and other less-tangible functions.

Currently, there are less than 50 Biosphere Reserves of any size in either the desert or the rainforest. These are not enough to adequately represent the various habitat and community types found within these biomes. They are entirely inadequate to conserve even a small percentage of the genetic variation found within the most useful, widespread plant species, let alone the obscure, localized endemics.

If we have any obligation to future generations of our species or of others, it is to protect all sizable tracts of desert and rainforest that remain. These lands need to be managed in a way that allows plant evolution to continue. This cannot happen if we simply collect the remaining representative species and lock them up in a liquid nitrogen gene bank. Unless we want to see ourselves swept away with the draining of their gene pools, we must become the plugs that keep the fullness of this planet's life from being emptied.

Ed. note: More recent studies suggest that we will lose far more than a million species by the turn of the century if present trends continue.

DO WE REALLY WANT DIVERSITY?
Litha 1986
by Reed Noss

Diversity is a byword of the conservation movement, and is cherished unquestioningly by Audubon members and Earth First!ers alike. But the attraction to diversity is a trait not confined to bird-watchers and tree-huggers. Everybody likes diversity. A life of sameness is hardly worth living. Psychologists confirm that humans need variety of experience to be mentally healthy. We share this need with other creatures. But whereas the ordinary American looks for diversity in shopping opportunities, social occasions and VCR tapes, the conservationist is seemingly more altruistic. S/he seeks diversity of life.

But what is this diversity of life that conservationists seek? Perhaps it is the pleasure of experiencing a variety of species and habitats in a stroll through a nature reserve. Few could deny the attraction of such a diversion from the insanity of our machine society. But if a pleasurable jaunt is all we seek, are we any less self-serving than the average Yuppie? To be worthy of a cause, the enchantment with diversity must involve more than esthetics.

Conservationists often speak loftily of preserving "biological diversity" and "genetic diversity," as if the meaning and application of these concepts were self-evident. In reality, the scale and content of biological diversity are often unclear, and this is where we get into trouble. "Managing for diversity" is the code of today's land manager, but in many cases "managing for weeds" would be a more accurate description of what goes on in the field. Our love for diversity can be an ecological trap.

Some conservationists have been horribly surprised when the concept of diversity has been used against them by those who would convert the Earth's last natural areas into economic production units. The US Forest Service has been preparing land and resource management plans for all National Forests. The Forest Service says that maintaining a diversity of wildlife in the forests is a major objective of the forest plans, and indeed it is. But curiously, the "preferred alternative,"—which invariably calls for more roads, more intensive silviculture, and increased timber harvest—is also considered the best for wildlife diversity.

Is the Forest Service lying to us again? In this case, probably not. When a forest is fragmented by roads and clearcuts, the resulting patchwork of habitats is almost always richer in species (in the short term, at least) than the original, unfragmented forest. In addition to climax forest species (many but not all of which dwindle away after fragmentation), species dependent on early successional habitats often thrive under intensive forest management regimes. This is the perverse logic of the maximum diversity concept: bring in humans, roads, and machines; rip apart the old growth; and we will have more species. Human progress and wildlife working together!

But the story is much more complicated than FS officials and other manipulative land managers would have us believe. We cannot deny that human disturbance will often increase the number of species within single management units or even entire forests. But what about the identity of those species? The species that benefit from human disturbance are primarily plant and animal weeds. They are opportunistic generalists that thrive in the human-dominated agricultural and urban landscapes that surround our remaining natural areas. Opportunistic weeds do not need protected forests or parks for survival.

On the other hand, species that disappear from fragmented and human-disturbed habitats are those most in need of protection. These are wilderness species, wide-ranging animals requiring big areas, and organisms sensitive to human intrusion. These sensitive species cannot usually survive without large nature reserves.

Examples of weedy species proliferating in disturbed areas and increasing overall diversity abound. A recent study in the New Jersey

Pine Barrens focused on the effects of water pollution from residential and agricultural development. More species of aquatic macrophytes (vascular plants) were found in the polluted sites than in the unpolluted sites. But the polluted sites were dominated by marginal or non-indigenous species that are common to wetlands throughout the eastern US. The unpolluted sites—although less diverse—contained a unique and distinctive Pine Barrens flora that is disappearing as the region is developed.

Human trampling in the vicinity of trails is another diversifying factor. Many studies have documented that trails create new microhabitats in their vicinity, leading to an increase in the number of plant species. (Many new species "hitch-hike" in as burrs or "ticks" on the pant legs of hikers.) But what about rare and attractive orchids plucked by hikers who gained access by the trail? Should we trade one rare orchid species for a dozen cosmopolitan weeds? And what about animals disturbed by the frequent presence of hikers on the trail? In conservation generally, it is a mistake to treat all species as equal. We must focus on those species that suffer most from human disturbances. Without radical changes in the way we treat the land, many of those species will soon be gone.

The notorious edge effect is a classic example of the maximum diversity concept gone awry. Wildlife biologists early in this century (particularly my ideological hero, Aldo Leopold) noticed that edges— the places where distinct habitats meet—are often richer in species than either of the adjoining habitats. This was explained by observations that edges contain animals from both of the adjoining habitats, in addition to animals that need both kinds of habitat for their life functions, and other animals that actually "specialize" on edges. Edges were found to be especially productive of certain favored game species like rabbits, Ring-necked Pheasants, and Bobwhite Quail.

Seeing these tantalizing benefits of edges, wildlife managers set out to create as much edge habitat as they could. "Managing for diversity" usually meant managing for edge, and the accompanying huntable wildlife. But species of artificial edges tend to be weeds, and species in habitat interiors tend to disappear when habitat area is reduced to favor high edge-interior ratios. Managing for edge is simply one more form of habitat fragmentation, the most serious threat to wilderness and natural areas on Earth.

Human-induced edge effects include many insidious processes. Edge habitat, often drier and denser than interior habitat, typically extends a considerable distance into the forest interior. Weedy species invade from the edges to alter species composition throughout a small forest block. Forest birds suffer reduced reproductive success when nest predators (e.g., grackles, jays, crows, and small mammals) and brood parasites (e.g., Brown-headed Cowbirds) move in from the edges. People and their domestic animals also invade natural areas from the perimeters. Aldo Leopold would not be pleased to see how his edge effect concept has been used to justify the fragmentation of natural areas.

A study I conducted in an Ohio nature reserve surrounded by suburbs and agricultural land found an extraordinarily high diversity of breeding birds. Unfortunately, the dominant species in this 500-acre reserve were the same ones that dominated the surrounding developed land. Typical forest interior birds of the region had small populations in the reserve and were in danger of local extinction. Management for habitat diversity, heavy human visitation, and especially the maintenance of artificial grasslands and numerous edges along absurdly wide trails within the reserve intensified its biological deterioration. Since my 1978 study, many of the forest-interior bird species have disappeared from the reserve.

Disturbance, of course, is fundamentally a natural phenomenon that provides suitable niches for a variety of native species. Fire, windthrow, floods, landslides, and other natural disturbances maintain the natural patchiness of vegetation characteristic of big natural areas. Many wildlife species depend upon early successional habitats, created by disturbance, for food, shelter, and other critical needs. Some native species are "fugitives" that cannot compete in climax communities and survive only by dispersing among recently disturbed patches of vegetation in the forest mosaic. Even the climax forest is diversified by small-scale disturbances such as treefalls. Many of the "shade-tolerant" tree species we associate with old growth habitat actually require multiple treefall gap episodes in their lifetimes in order to reach the forest canopy. Other old growth forest types require more catastrophic disturbances, such as crown fires, to replace themselves.

But the ecological mosaic created by natural disturbance is a far cry from the checkerboard of isolated habitats created by modern humans. The natural mosaic is interconnected; the artificial patchwork is fragmented. This is an important distinction for species that require large systems of continuous habitat for survival. Additionally, artificial habitat manipulation generally requires roads. Nothing is worse for sensitive wildlife than roads. Roads bring vehicles, guns, noise, and weeds. A bear (Smokey notwithstanding) can usually deal with fire, windthrow, and flood—but is in trouble when surrounded by drunken redneck poachers in ORVs.

The critical point is that the diversity concept does not prescribe straightforward recommendations for conservation. A more diverse system, in terms of number of species or habitats, is not necessarily more valuable than a simpler system. A relatively depauperate system may be the natural system for the area of concern. Another important consideration is scale. Manipulative management for edge and habitat interspersion may increase the number of species at the scale of an individual forest or nature reserve, but decrease the number of species in the biogeographical region. This switch occurs when the managed area simply perpetuates those species that are common in the developed landscape, while the species most in need of reserves for survival are lost from the region. Species dependent upon large blocks of unfragmented habitat—wilderness—disappear first.

If we carry this fragmentation process to its logical extreme, we end up with a bland biosphere composed of only those species that can adapt readily to human development: opportunistic weeds. Eventually every place of similar climate has virtually the same set of cosmopolitan species. Local character disappears. Diversification tragically becomes homogenization.

Ecologists are becoming aware of these diversity problems. But many foresters, wildlife biologists, park managers, and naturalists are being sucked into the trap of maximum diversity. Conservationists have been fooled and confused about what diversity means. They are unable to argue with the Forest Service's management plans which ostensibly maximize both hard commodities and wildlife. They are unaware of the divergent effects that a land management regime can have at different spatial and temporal scales. They think they are getting diversity, but they are really getting impoverishment.

To answer the question posed in the title of this essay: yes, conservationists do and should want diversity. We should allow every species to exist unmolested in its natural habitat, and assure each species the potential to evolve as conditions change. In some situations this will necessitate active ecological management and restoration projects, whereas in other cases it will mean simply leaving areas alone. But for any given area, number of species or habitats alone is a poor criterion for conservation. Diversity can be a license for managers to over-manipulate natural areas. What we want is the full complement of native species in natural patterns of abundance. Call that "native diversity," or "naturalness." Demand that from the land managers before it's too late, and tell other well-meaning but misinformed conservationists about it.

ROGUE GRIZ SANCTUARY PROPOSED
Samhain 1987
by Doug Peacock

In brief, the Rogue Griz Sanctuary would consist of a large, secured area in the lower 48, preferably adjacent to public lands including designated Wilderness, where Grizzly Bears sentenced to death by bear managers would be placed. A minimum average of 26 Grizzlies a year are killed by humans in the Yellowstone and Glacier ecosystems; 41% are females. These are only the known dead; many more are poached. Most of the mortality results from management actions in Yellowstone, and management and hunting in the Bob Marshall ecosystem.

The success of the Rogue Griz Sanctuary will depend upon help from big conservation groups. At least in private, some have expressed interest. Their support is essential due to monetary requirements—first, a large, private piece of Grizzly habitat is required; and second, release of condemned Grizzlies to Earth First! or anyone else will entail liability, hence extensive legal support must be on call. These bears, who would otherwise be dead, may have to be intensively monitored (as they already are in Yellowstone National Park and on the Rocky Mountain Front), and occasionally returned to the Sanctuary if they roam away from public land. The offspring of the condemned Grizzlies would be genetically intact and used for augmenting dwindling populations such as the Cabinet-Yaak, or for reintroduction.

Should one of our bears kill a rancher's sheep or destroy an outfitter's camp, let them sue away. This litigation may be a blessing in disguise and that's why we need preservation lawyers' help. The sooner the issues of fear of litigation, limit of agency responsibility, and delineation of individual right to risk, are resolved in the courts, the better. The government, especially the National Park Service, is afraid to touch the issue of liability for natural hazards— which reveals the inherent contradiction involved with the management of Grizzlies, avalanches, lightning strikes—and they will always try to settle out of court or win on technicalities. They fear that the same ruling that might protect them from liability will strip them of their authority to manage the wilderness. Along with six to eight new Grizzly Bear cubs a year, this windfall judiciary clarification could be the greatest value of establishing the Rogue Griz Sanctuary.

Editor's update: The National Park Service in Yellowstone and Glacier National Parks, especially Yellowstone, continues to manage bears rather than humans. This is resulting in the deaths of more bears than the populations can sustain (directly through shooting, indirectly through deportation and habitat disturbance). Doug Peacock's superb book Grizzly Years *has greatly enlarged the constituency for bears in this country, making the idea of a rogue bear sanctuary more and more feasible.*

YELLOWSTONE: OUT OF THE ASHES
Yule 1988
by George Wuerthner

The summer of 1988 set a number of records for the northern Great Plains and Rocky Mountains. It was one of the driest ever recorded. Rivers shrank and crops died. Heat waves blasted the land for months. But above all, the summer of 1988 will be remembered as the summer when Yellowstone National Park burned. Within the Greater Yellowstone Ecosystem, the perimeter of the charred acreage totaled 1.38 million acres. Not since the summer of 1910, when wildfires swept through 3 million acres of northern Idaho and western Montana, has the region seen fires on such a scale.

At the beginning of the summer, the National Park Service in Yellowstone National Park, as well as the US Forest Service in adjacent National Forests, allowed lightning caused fires to burn unhindered, as had been policy for more than a decade. However, as the number of fires grew, both agencies faced increasing criticism of their lack of containment or suppression actions. Eventually, the entire "let burn" policy came under attack.

The fires became a daily news item on TV and in the papers and the impression given by most reports was that Yellowstone, the nation's first National Park, was in cinders. The call for suppression rose to firestorm proportions. In response, 10,000 firefighters were brought in from all over the country to battle the flames, and eventually both the Army and the Marines were called in to supplement and relieve civilian workers. In the end, more than 120 million dollars were spent in a vain attempt to control the flames. As with all large fires ever recorded, it was a change in weather, not firefighting efforts, that stopped the fires. On September 11, snow fell over much of the Park, quelling the fires sufficiently that firefighters were able to contain most Park blazes.

Acrimonious editorials and letters of indignation flooded local and national newspapers. Most of the nation, it seems, felt the Park Service had failed to protect Yellowstone. Congress threatened to investigate the agency's fire plans. (The NPS's "let burn" policy should be called a "natural fire policy"; for under the plan, all human caused fires are suppressed immediately, as are any fires which threaten life or property.) Even President Reagan was drawn into the fray as he admonished National Park Service Director William Mott for supporting the let burn policies.

Yet when the smoke cleared in September, it appeared that much less of the Park had actually burned than at first surmised. Also, despite the large acreage within the burn *perimeter*, the fires, in typical fashion, jumped about, resulting in a mosaic with many areas only lightly singed or even untouched.

Many critics have called for expanded logging so as to prevent future conflagrations. This, despite the fact that most of the Yellowstone Plateau is off limits to logging by virtue of its Park status, and that most of the mountainous country surrounding Yellowstone is so steep and the trees so slow growing that logging is economically unfeasible. As it is, even in more accessible areas, timber sales regularly cost the federal government more than it receives in stumpage fees—even by the distorted accounting methods the government employs to justify its continued road-building and wilderness destruction in this region.

Was the National Park Service indeed negligent as critics suggest? If not, what happened in 1988 to make it such a spectacular year for fires? To answer these questions requires a review of fire ecology as it pertains to the Yellowstone Ecosystem.

Research has demonstrated that the Greater Yellowstone Ecosystem periodically, but infrequently, experiences episodic fires that burn vast acreages. In between these ecologically significant blazes, many small fires occur, most burning less than an acre. Under conditions of high humidity, cool temperatures, no wind, and little fuel, nearly all fires go out on their own. In these situations, sending in firefighters is nothing more than a make-work program for college students. The weather and fuels control fires, not people.

Nevertheless, the Yellowstone Ecosystem is a fire-adapted landscape. It is created by fire, not the small fires that occur nearly every year, but the large fires which may burn once every century—if that often. When tourists gaze at the Park's aspen fringed meadows and rolling forested plateaus, they see the successional results of massive wildfires of the distant past. The fact that 80% of the Yellowstone Plateau is covered by Lodgepole Pine, a fire tolerant species, indicates the previous occurrence of fires.

The high elevation of the Yellowstone Plateau—average elevation over 8000 feet—and its extensive and almost monotonous forest cover, influence fires in several ways. First, the high elevation, along with low summer precipitation, inhibits biological decomposition of dead plant material. As a result, litter gradually builds on the forest floor. However, because the cool temperatures on the plateau limit plant growth, it may take 200–300 years before a significant amount of fuel accumulates.

Second, due to the plateau's elevation, annual precipitation rates are high, generally from 30–80 inches a year. In most summers, Yellowstone's high country is simply too wet to burn well.

Nevertheless, because of the extensive and nearly continuous forest cover, when the fuels are finally ignited, the possibility exists for fires to burn substantial acreages, as they did in 1988. These infrequent large fires provide an energy and nutrient pulse through the Yellowstone Ecosystem. Fires release nutrients bound up in litter, as well as changing their chemical structure, so that they are more available for plants.

Events such as the Yellowstone fires appear destructive only because of our human tendency to view them within the narrow confines of our lifetimes. Furthermore, resource management, as practiced by the National Park Service, US Forest Service, and other land management agencies, focuses on populations or individual species instead of ecological processes. Most people believe that to "save" Yellowstone it is necessary to prevent the "destruction" of trees. Yet, trees are only one manifestation of the forest ecosystem, and in order to preserve the forest it is necessary to preserve ecological processes, including fire. Failure to identify and preserve ecological processes dooms most resource management (whether it attempts to maximize the number of deer to shoot, number of trees to harvest, or some other variable) to eventual failure.

Thus, on the Yellowstone Plateau, in order to preserve the forest, it is necessary to tolerate large wildfires. Small prescribed burns will not work (although they may be useful in lowering fuel accumulations, hence fire danger, near developed sites or towns, if that is a goal).

The exception to these general statements about periodic large fires in Yellowstone concerns the lower elevation portions of the Park between Gardiner and the Lamar Valley. Here, arid conditions of less than 10 inches of precipitation a year enable grasslands to dominate. In coves and on shaded slopes grow Quaking Aspen and Douglas-fir. Fire intervals of 20–25 years were common here prior to fire suppression.

Under normal circumstances, Yellowstone's high elevation Lodgepole Pine forests don't burn well. Out of 233 lightning caused fires between 1972 and 1987, 205 went out without burning even an acre. Unlike Lodgepole forests elsewhere in the Rockies, there is no developed shrub layer beneath the trees for the first 100 or more years after the Lodgepole stands are established. And because young Lodgepole Pines are shade intolerant, they cannot successfully regenerate in the shade of their parents' canopy. So, fire that sets back succession to bare soil tends to be followed by even-aged Lodgepole stands that develop into tall "doghair" stands with little ground cover. In fact, under many forests, as much as 85% of the ground is bare dirt. Except for a light litter of pine needles and branches, there is not much to burn. Fires that do burn in such forests tend to creep along slowly, barely producing a flame.

After a period of 100–300 years, depending on the site, the Lodgepole Pine forests begin to break up due to various factors including susceptibility to pine beetle attacks. Pine beetles only successfully attack trees greater than 8 inches in diameter. Since growth on the cold Yellowstone Plateau is slow, most Lodgepole stands 8 inches or larger are at least 100 years in age. The pine beetle can only success-fully attack and kill weak, sick trees. Most pine beetle attacks focus on Lodgepole stands that have not burned in a long while, for the stands eventually become too crowded and hence too weak to repel beetle attacks. However, if thinned, whether by pine beetles themselves or by fires, the resulting healthy forests can repel beetle attacks.

As the beetles kill trees, the canopy is opened and light penetrates to the ground. This stimulates the growth of young Lodgepole as well as shade tolerant Subalpine Fir and Engelmann Spruce, which often begin to grow in the understory of mature Lodgepole forests. Understory trees, particularly the fir and spruce, form a "ladder" that allows fire to climb into the canopy and crown out. Thus, old mature stands are more likely to burn and especially to crown out than young stands. In addition, the dead snags and blowdowns that normally accompany an aging Lodgepole stand provide more fuel than is in the younger Lodgepole stands, again ensuring that these are most likely to burn.

To anthropomorphize a bit, Lodgepole Pine does not want to be replaced by fir or spruce. Hence, it is to the advantage of the Lodgepole if something eliminates the mature trees as well as the young fir and spruce in the understory. Only fire does this.

If a stand-replacing fire occurs, the Lodgepole is ideally suited for successful regeneration on the site. The tree has two kinds of cones—open and serotinous. The scales of the former open with cone maturity, thereby providing a steady supply of seeds to shower down on the forest floor. If beetles open the canopy, then open cones pro-vide the seeds that develop into the occasional young Lodgepole. Unlike the open cones, serotinous cones have a waxy covering that only melts if temperatures rise above 113 degrees—which never hap-pens on the Yellowstone Plateau except in a fire. If a burn occurs, serotinous cones open within 24 hours and reseed the site.

If Lodgepole seeds successfully germinate, the precocious young trees can begin producing cones when barely five years old. Subalpine Firs, in contrast, may not produce cones until 50–60 years old. To give the Lodgepole another advantage, cone serotiny is not expressed until the tree is between 30 and 60 years of age. Immediately after a fire, when another fire is highly unlikely and there is thus no advantage in having serotinous cones, the Lodgepole only develops open cones, thereby ensuring plenty of seeds for domination of the site.

For these reasons, Lodgepole Pine is the most likely tree to grow on a recently burned site. Since extensive fires occur with some regularity in Yellowstone, Lodgepole dominates the Park.

Quaking Aspen is also common in Yellowstone, but it tends to grow in the drier part of the Park on the edge of the grassland zone. Aspen usually regenerate by suckering—producing new shoots from existing root stock, rather than from seeds. If the above-ground aspen boles are destroyed by fire, avalanche, or insect attack, the roots send forth new suckers. Nearly all aspen groves survive for generations by this method. Though aspens produce a large quantity of seeds, they have very precise germination requirements, hence scientists believe that nearly all Rocky Mountain aspen groves have existed since the end of the last Ice Age by suckering rather than by establishment from seed.

Going into this summer, most of Yellowstone's aspen groves were decadent and in danger of dying out. There was almost no aspen regeneration in the park, even though aspen are well adapted to fire and most aspen live in a zone where fire frequency is estimated to be on a 20–25 year interval. Large populations of Elk and other ungulates are one reason for lack of aspen regeneration.

In addition to discouraging aspen regeneration by browsing heavily on aspen suckers, Elk and other ungulates have reduced the amount of flammable grasslands and shrubs in the Park's northern rangelands through excessive grazing and browsing. (Yes, in the absence of predators, wildlife commonly overgraze a range just like livestock; and humans long ago eliminated Gray Wolves from Yellowstone.) In most years, the range can no longer carry a fire. Also, since this open area is the most accessible portion of the Park, fire suppression has been most successful here.

Researchers have studied the relationship between Elk, fire and Quaking Aspen near Jackson Hole just south of Yellowstone Park. They have found that although fires may stimulate the production of as many as 30,000 aspen suckers per acre, if Elk browsing is heavy, the number of suckers is reduced to pre-burn levels in three years.

However, if fires stimulate aspen regeneration over an extensive enough area, Elk herds may not crop all groves intensively enough to prevent sucker development into pole sized young trees. In essence, "swamping," as biologists refer to prey reproduction exceeding the capacity of predators to limit prey population, enables the aspen to regenerate. One of the expected benefits of this summer's fires is widespread aspen regeneration in the Park. Given their high numbers, though, Elk may still severely crop all new growth. We'll know in about three years.

Impacts of fires on wildlife were minimal. Only 244 large mammals are known to have died in the fires, most from suffocation. Impacts to wildlife in the years following the fires will be temporary. Some Elk may starve this winter, since 11% of the Park's total winter range was burned. In addition, the drought severely reduced plant production in unburned areas, so overall there is a significant reduction in forage. However, given the inflated Elk numbers, starvation of a large proportion of the herd would benefit the ecosystem.

Grizzly Bears may be affected since some Whitebark Pine burned. Whitebark pine nuts are an essential fall food for Yellowstone's Grizzlies, so a reduction could adversely impact them. However, salvaging of dead Elk and other carrion next spring could provide bears with a major protein addition to their diet.

Perhaps the greatest changes will occur in Yellowstone's famed fisheries. Sedimentation, particularly in the Upper Lamar River Valley where the Clover Mist fire perimeter encompassed 390,000 acres, could adversely impact trout by smothering fish eggs and aquatic insects. How much sedimentation occurs depends on many variables including the size of the snowpack this winter and how fast it melts in the spring. Usually within three years of a fire, revegetation is sufficient to prevent further sedimentation problems.

In contrast to the negative effects on wildlife, *benefits* to wildlife from fire are many. Regeneration of aspen, willow and other shrubs (provided the Elk don't eat them all) will increase passerine bird nesting habitat. Cavity nesters will find the numerous fire-killed snags ideal home building sites. If sufficient aspen are regenerated, potential for reestablishment of Beaver in the Park will increase. Although there is still debate about their disappearance, Beaver were likely eliminated by excess Elk browsing. The return of Beaver and their dams would slow sedimentation problems in streams because fine soil particles would settle out in their ponds. Their ponds would raise the water table, creating healthier riparian zones and wet meadows—favorite foraging grounds for Grizzlies, Elk, and other grazers. Whether the National Park Service will reintroduce Beaver remains to be seen, but there is no question that at one time they were abundant in the Park.

The most important factor in causing the 1988 fires to grow so large was drought. Not since officials began keeping records in the Park 112 years ago has there been such a dry summer. The previous winter in Yellowstone was relatively mild with below average snowpack in the mountains. Although rainfall was higher than normal in April and May, it was low in June, and during July and August there was no measurable rain. Instead, uncharacteristic heat coupled with high winds dried the landscape. By late July, the moisture content of litter on the forest floor was as low as 2–3%. (Kiln-dried lumber has a 12% moisture content.) Significantly, every major wildfire in North America's recorded history can be traced to severe drought.

The first blaze in Yellowstone during 1988 occurred on May 24 when lightning struck a tree in the Lamar Valley and it burst into flames. But as usually happens, the fire went out—without suppression. Fires from lightning strikes in late June and early July, however, grew slowly. Nine fires were burning in the Park on July 15, most having charred less than 100 acres.

Then, on the 15th, winds expanded the Clover fire overnight from 4700 acres to 7000 acres. Several other fires increased as well. On this date, the perimeter of fires in the Park totaled 8600 acres and the Park Service, under pressure from critics, decided that new natural fires would be suppressed.

But lightning was igniting blazes at a unusual rate. On average, lightning causes 22 fires a year in Yellowstone. In 1988 it caused more than 50.

High winds fanned the flames and enabled individual fires to burn hundreds of thousand of acres in a single spectacular "run." For example, winds of 80 miles per hour on August 20—called "Black Saturday" by firefighters—sparked new life in nearly exhausted fires. The Hellroaring fire, in the Absaroka-Beartooth Wilderness north of the Park, burned through 10 miles of timber in three hours.

It takes the convergence of high winds, low humidity, severe drought, sufficient fuel and an ignition source to cause a large fire complex. The chances of all these ingredients coming together in one year are exceedingly small, which is why fires such as seen in Yellowstone this year are unusual.

Despite the fires, the Park remained open throughout the summer. Only on September 10, when a firestorm threatened to run right over Park headquarters in Mammoth, was the entire Park closed. Visitors expected a special opportunity to see wildfire in action. For most, it was a disappointment.

Although on rare occasions, such as Black Saturday, high winds may propel fires to great heights, ordinarily wildfires merely creep and sputter along—producing great quantities of smoke, but not much flame. One can easily walk away from the advancing fire front, and wild animals do so. A fire is analogous to a volcano. During a major eruption, a great volume of magma may be spewed from the crater, but most volcanic eruptions are more smoke and cinders than lava flows.

It is only when an understory of fir or some other fuel exists to ladder flames into the canopy, and winds are strong enough to propel the flames rapidly from tree to tree, that large acreages are burned and the walls of flames we imagine actually exist.

However, when these conditions do develop, no power on Earth can stop them. This summer, high winds threw firebrands a mile or more ahead of the advancing fronts. Sparks leaped across roads, across the Grand Canyon of the Yellowstone, across lakes—all considered excellent fire breaks. Those who claimed the NPS could have stopped the fires if bulldozers had been freely employed did not see the firestorms that whipped flames across 35 miles of the Park in early September. When winds are pushing fires, it is insane to put anyone in front of them.

To its credit, the National Park Service resisted using the bulldozers except as a last ditch effort. Research suggests that bulldozers, by scraping away all soil layers, do more long-term damage to the landscape than the fires themselves.

Most firefighting is, to borrow a phrase from Shakespeare, more "sound and fury—signifying nothing." Yellowstone spent $120 million on fire suppression, not because anyone who knew about fires thought they could stop them, but because the Park had to put on a good show. For political reasons, the Park had to appear that it was trying to contain the fires.

Despite the power of this summer's blazes, remarkably few people were hurt (one man was killed by a falling snag outside the Park) and few structures burned. Nevertheless, some property owners whose cabins outside the Park were burned have filed suit against the government.

Because of the bad press, the public's lack of understanding of fire's role in Yellowstone, and lawsuits by adjacent landowners, "let burn" policies not only in Yellowstone but throughout the West are in jeopardy. Though the Park Service has been misguided in some of its other policies, such as its management of Grizzly Bears (as evidenced by its failure to close the Fishing Bridge facilities), the agency deserves support for its fire management policies.

Yellowstone was not destroyed by fire. Of the 1.38 million acres within the fire perimeter, only 400,000 acres are thought to have actually burned. Of these, half were only lightly singed. By next spring, a new generation of Lodgepole Pine will be sprouting on the newly opened forest floor. By next summer, green grass, not charred stumps, will greet tourists. The charred snags will provide new homes for cavity nesting birds; new fallen logs in streams will provide fish habitat.

Fire is as essential to the ecological health of the Greater Yellowstone Ecosystem as rain is to the health of tropical rainforests. Yellowstone cannot be preserved in a static form; it can only be preserved if the ecological processes that shaped it are preserved.

1988 FIRES AND LARGE MAMMALS

by Doug Peacock

The 1988 fires in the Yellowstone Ecosystem will benefit the ecosystem's large mammals. The plants that come back after a typical fire that goes through Lodgepole Pine and doesn't destroy the soil are grasses, forbs, small bushes, and in wet areas sedges. Grass, sedges and forbs are the foods that ungulates need most. The Yellowstone fires will especially benefit Moose. Moose are colonizers, not herd animals, and they will colonize essentially all the burned areas until they are stopped by some natural population regulating mechanism. The Elk population will explode in the next few years because the fires will give way to more meadows, which are what Elk need most. This is a problem because there are too many Elk in the Yellowstone Ecosystem already. Bison will also do well.

In the long run, Grizzly Bears will benefit. However, for a couple years there will not be as much food in the Park, and that means the bears will wander out of the Park into the National Forests, especially during dry periods when they'll go down to wet bottoms. That's where the people are, and without a lot of education and law enforcement, Grizzly Bears will be killed in conflicts with humans.

The same is true with Black Bears. The Black Bear is more of a forest animal than the Grizzly, but Black Bears habituate much more readily to humans and human food than do Grizzlies. Grizzlies seem not to like much about us except our garbage.

What all these benefits for wildlife mean for National Park Service policy is that the let-it-burn policy is right. People who want to protect Yellowstone should defend the policy.

These people should also work for wolf reintroduction in Yellowstone. Yellowstone is an ecosystem without all its members. The most obvious of the absent species is the Gray Wolf. This is an ideal time to reintroduce wolves to the Yellowstone Ecosystem, because by popular assessment there are too many Elk and Bison already. The wildfires will bring more Elk, Moose, Bison, and Mule Deer than the ecosystem can support. These animals no longer have predators. Coyotes take some deer, even a few Elk, but they're not effective predators. Grizzlies also kill a few winter-weakened animals in the spring, but again they are not effective predators. So the ungulates have no mechanism to limit their populations except for severe winters. We haven't had a severe winter in a long time, and perhaps given current weather patterns, there's no such thing as a typical winter anymore, so the ecosystem needs a predator right away to limit the ungulate explosion.

Editor's update: The real tragedy of the 1988 fires may be the partial suppression of the National Park Service's natural fire policy. After the fires ended, the federal government appointed a task force to study the policy. Its report basically confirmed the wisdom of the "let burn" policy, yet recommended less tolerance for natural fires in the future.

POTENTIAL FOR RESTORING OLD-GROWTH FORESTS IN THE SOUTHERN APPALACHIANS
Yule 1989
by Robert Zahner

This paper discusses the potential for restoring some of the indigenous landscape we have lost here in the southern mountains. It addresses the requirements, limitations, and challenges for our society to commit large areas of the Southern Appalachian second-growth forests to continue recovery toward old-growth ecosystems. We have the resource already established on the landscape: millions of acres of second-growth forests under the long-term stewardship of our National Forests. We also have the vision. But we do not yet have the plan. Nature has a strategy for rehabilitation of old-growth forests, but the forest managers do not.

Background

The case has been established for large contiguous areas of old-growth. Isolated fragments do not meet the imperative for biological diversity. We must no longer think in terms of old-growth forest stands, but in terms of old-growth forest landscapes, and the requirements of forest interior species, both plants and animals, who depend on uninterrupted mature forest, that is, high quality old-growth forest landscapes.

Restoration to primeval or pre-disturbance condition of forest habitats in the Southern Appalachian Mountains is, of course, impossible. Many plant and animal species have been extirpated. Soils on some sites have been degraded by erosion or depletion of minerals and organic matter, so that productivity of natural biotic communities has been permanently altered. Introduced insect and disease pests continue to take their toll on native forest trees. Perhaps most importantly, acid rain, ground level ozone poisoning, and climate change due to carbon dioxide enrichment of the atmosphere will continue to disrupt life support systems at every ecosystem level.

Reservoirs of genetic diversity for forest interior species will become more essential for the survival and migration of species as man-caused stresses become more severe. The potential exists at the species level for many forest interior communities to be restored to at least a semblance of their predisturbance biota. The potential also exists at the habitat level for virtually all major natural forest types to be represented in a large-scale landscape restoration effort. Thus it is still possible to integrate large contiguous areas of diverse habitats that can be restored to biological maturity, and in time to old-growth forests.

Southern Appalachian land use history determines the potential for restoration of old-growth, and this in turn is defined by the magnitude of past damage to a given ecosystem, the time lapsed since man altered the system, and the degree of recovery to date. Current forest ages, current rehabilitation status, landscape ownership patterns, and future management plans all impose challenges to old-growth restoration. Future old-growth forests will have a unique composition and a structure as yet unknown.

Old-Growth Characteristics

Before we can assess the potential for old-growth, we must define what we hope to restore. There are few scientific records of the nature of the Southern Appalachian primeval forest. Ecologists have documented relics such as Joyce Kilmer Memorial Forest, Linville Gorge Wilderness Area, and the boreal forests of the Great Smoky Mountains. We have descriptions of plants and animals, especially birds, by early naturalists. The turn-of-the-century logging companies published descriptions of large standing timber for sale. But most of the forest history of our mountains records only the massive destruction of the old-growth forests. Today we must piece together the scraps of information gleaned from these sources and from modern ecological interpretations of second-growth forest dynamics to estimate the kinds of plant and animal communities that existed in pre-settlement forests.

Because of the immense diversity of potential habitats in the Southern Appalachians, it is easier to define what old-growth is *not* than what it is. It is not a forest that has grown beyond economic or commercial timber maturity. It is not decadent. It is not limited to virgin or ancient forest. It is not just a forest that contains very big trees. It is not synonymous with "wilderness."

Let's try a simple definition: *Old-growth forests are forests having a long, uninterrupted period of development,* or scientifically speaking, they are the end point of an ecosystem's development without disturbance by modern man.

A regime of recurring natural disturbances gives old-growth forests their essential character, that of "canopy gap patchiness," or to use the technical term, that of a "shifting mosaic steady state." As old trees are lost from the canopy, by such natural causes as lightning strikes, ice breakage, and blowdowns, younger replacement trees maintain an uneven-aged canopy structure. Looking at the forest as a whole, these small patches of shifting canopy ages comprise a heterogeneous steady state, or mosaic.

An old-growth forest always contains trees in all stages of aging, including senescence, as well as dying, standing dead, and fallen dead trees. With a few exceptions, most tree species that comprise the Southern Appalachian forests today reach senescence between 150 and 300 years. Because old-growth forests contain many species, ages of individual dominant trees in such a stand may vary between mature 100–year old trees just growing into canopy gaps and dying 400–year olds. Both the size of old trees and the average life expectancy for dominant trees vary considerably with site, however, thus leading to a descriptive criterion for age rather than a quantitative one.

"Age" of an old-growth stand must also include the length of time fallen dead trees have been decaying. The micro-habitats provided by old wind-thrown trees, standing dead snags, and rotting logs are essential to the integrity of old-growth. Down trees and large debris are even more important in streams than on the ground, indispensable to restoration of aquatic habitats in old-growth forests. Thus natural processes that eventually achieve such restoration may require centuries to reach true indigenous condition. Most ecologists agree that a semblance of old-growth structure and composition is developed in many hardwood forest types of eastern North America at age 150–200 years, with another 50–100 years to achieve the down-timber habitats.

Many primeval forests were not ancient forests when Europeans first encountered them, but were in varying stages of successional development toward a stable, end-point condition. In the pre-settlement Southern Appalachian Mountains, periodic wildfires prevented the long-term stabilization of forest composition on some sites, in particular south-facing slopes and ridges. Such fire-maintained sub-stable communities are a natural part of the mosaic of old-growth landscapes. The "age" of these sub-stable forests in a primeval landscape, however, must include that of the previous forest, because the residual standing charred snags and decaying remnants of burned down timber are integral parts of the evolving biotic community.

A restored old-growth forest cannot be delineated as a forest "stand," in modern inventory terminology. There can be no clear boundaries drawn where old-growth stops. There must be a gradual transition to other communities or land uses, because requisite for the protection of interior species from "edge effects" is freedom from man-caused disturbances in the surrounding area. There are no sharp "edges" in an old-growth landscape, because the entire area is a mosaic of canopy gaps. Even natural wildfires, ice storms, and wind blow-downs do not leave abrupt edges. Thus forest management activities outside old-growth preserves must be carefully assessed for their impacts on the rehabilitation processes of the interior communities under restoration.

Biological Potential

There are three classes of "potentials" for the restoration of old-growth landscapes in the Southern Appalachians: 1) the biological potential, 2) the land ownership potential, or potential for long-term commitment, and 3) the ethical potential, or potential for acceptance by society.

A forest that has been disturbed by timber harvesting can be a candidate for restoration to an old-growth forest. Although the indige-nous condition has been altered by logging, some old-growth characteristics may be retained and many more may be restored over time. Most present-day timber management activities in second-growth forests do not irreversibly alter the potential for old-growth restoration. These transient management disturbances, probably more properly termed "interferences," include the suppression of natural dis-turbances such as wildfire, and the removal, termed "salvage," of dead and dying trees. So-called "timber stand improvement" and "vegeta-tion management" alter only temporarily the species composition in many forest stands by discriminating against those tree and shrub species that have little or no commercial value.

Ecologists agree that restoration to near pre-disturbance condi-tions, with the exceptions of extirpated species and the presence of introduced exotic species, can in time be accomplished on previ-ously cut-over forestlands that have regenerated a second-growth forest of native species. Exceptions to this in the Southern Appalachians are plantation forests and some second-growth natu-rally seeded forests established on lands that were previously converted to agriculture. Soil degradation on such land in many cases has so modified habitats that recovery to pre-disturbance con-dition will require thousands of years.

In most second-growth forest stands that have recovered through protection from logging abuse early this century, significant restoration has already occurred. After 60–100 years of natural rehabilitation, such stands are approaching biological maturity. Because of their origin, which is regrowth from massive disturbance, many of these stands are even-aged. Canopy gap patchiness has not yet become established, and will be slow in emerging because all dominant trees are the same age. As genetically different dominant trees succumb to environmental stresses, and as lightning and ice take their toll, younger trees, usually of shade tolerant species, will begin to fill canopy gaps. Tree species diversity thus will increase along with age diversity.

During the four or five decades between the massive logging early this century and the beginning of clearcutting in the 1960s, selection harvesting and high-grading of mature timber removed some commercially important trees from many stands, thus establishing canopy gaps without the accompanying fallen dead boles. Over hundreds of thousands of acres of National Forest, however, second-growth has developed relatively free of further man-caused disturbance. In some remote sites without access for salvage operations, a component of dying, dead, and down trees is beginning to develop. Natural disturbances continue to create canopy gaps for more varied tree species to assume dominance.

Most importantly, many plant and animal species are gradually migrating from adjacent refuges, that is, from fragments of ecosystems that escaped devastation, into surrounding habitats that are becoming habitable. As more of these mature forest interior species become established, there is an acceleration of essential recovery processes, such as a build-up of soil organic matter, the creation of more varied micro-habitats and niches, and a proliferation of lowest trophic level organisms.

Land Ownership Potential

Where are second-growth forests located in the Southern Appalachians that are suitable for restoration to old-growth? Because of the long-term commitment required, only two possibilities exist: 1) preserves created by such private organizations as The Nature Conservancy, and 2) public federal lands, especially the National Forests and National Parks. The private preserves are exemplary, and serve an urgent need to protect rare and uncommon habitats; but such preserves are fragmentary, almost always small isolated tracts surrounded by the abrupt edges of a modified landscape. They are not an integral part of an old-growth or mature forest landscape.

Great Smoky Mountains National Park encompasses the largest remaining area in the Southern Appalachians of old-growth forest landscape, 165,000 acres of contiguous forest habitats that retain most characteristics of old-growth, free of significant physical disturbance by European man. Much of this old-growth lies in the unique high elevation spruce-fir forest, currently being degraded biologically by the man-introduced balsam wooly adelgid. The remaining two-thirds of the Park, about 335,000 acres previously cut-over, farmed, grazed and otherwise disturbed prior to the establishment of the Park, meet all requirements for the restoration of old-growth landscapes. The protected status of the Park allows these forests to eventually be restored to near pre-disturbance conditions.

The six National Forests of the Southern Appalachians in North Carolina (Pisgah, Nantahala), Tennessee (Cherokee), Georgia (Chattahoochee), South Carolina (Sumter), and Virginia (Jefferson) presently contain 30 separate tracts of congressionally designated Wilderness, totaling 275,000 acres. It must be remembered that Congress sets aside these areas for *people*, as recreational commodities. The needs of biota are only of secondary consideration, as evidenced by the hundreds of thousands of people visiting these areas annually, creating severe impacts on biota, especially stresses on birds and large mammals. However, the long-term legal commitment for preservation does in effect secure Wilderness Areas for the restoration of old-growth.

The five largest of these National Forest Wilderness Areas average about 22,000 acres, or 35 square miles each, areas sufficiently large for restoration of complete old-growth landscapes. The remaining 25 areas average only 5200 acres each, with the ten smallest averaging less than 3500 acres. The small sizes of these Wilderness Areas come into perspective when we realize that the home range of a single male Black Bear is well over 25 square miles of contiguous forest. Unless protected by large additional acreages of surrounding mature forest with a long-term old-growth commitment, all but the five largest National Forest Wildernesses in the Southern

Appalachians serve little purpose in restoring the integrity of the old-growth forest landscape.

Aside from the small and fragmentary sizes of this potential old-growth in designated Wilderness, such areas were selected largely for their scenic beauty and their unsuitability or inaccessibility for timber harvest. Many of these Wilderness habitats are high ridges and deep gorges, excellent examples of uncommon forest communities and critical to regional diversity. Only the Cohutta Wilderness in Georgia, the Citico Wilderness in Tennessee, and parts of the Joyce Kilmer/Slick Rock Wilderness in North Carolina contain large contiguous areas of forest with significant second-growth timber potential. Yet it is those very habitats with good timber potential that contain the species mix and site capabilities to provide the old-growth forest communities that are now most lacking and are most needed in a restored old-growth landscape.

The greatest limitation to old-growth restoration lies in current National Forest management plans, which make little or no provision for any rehabilitation of old-growth outside designated Wilderness and Research Natural Areas. Plans call for new road construction into and clearcutting of large acreages, a continuation of policies that are rapidly fragmenting these forests into small blocks of young regeneration, setting back natural forest succession by at least six decades. The potential gained for restoration of old-growth, that is, the rehabilitation that has occurred since the National Forests were established as watershed preserves in the mid-1920s, is rapidly diminishing. Every year the six National Forests of the Southern Appalachians plan to clearcut over 24,000 additional acres of second-growth commercially mature timber.

Timber management for commercial sawlog rotations is designed to maintain oaks, as well as introduce more planted pine, on the south-facing slopes and ridges. Timber management on the north-facing slopes and coves is increasing Yellow Poplar to the point of eliminating many other, less economically important, mesic species. National Forest plans include harvesting 2,000,000 acres of such forest eventually, redesigning it to produce more commercially desirable timber and game species. This immense acreage includes virtually all National Forest lands that would be required to restore the old-growth habitats in a balanced landscape, i.e., to provide contiguous habitat for interior species and to provide corridors of mature forest for migration and genetic exchange among old-growth communities.

What is the potential composition of tree species in biologically mature forests of the Southern Appalachians as they grow undisturbed toward old-growth? Ecological research tells us that the second-growth oak-hickory forests currently occupying many south-facing slopes and ridges will probably perpetuate themselves as climax forest, and in time develop directly into old-growth. Associated tree species will include White and Yellow Pines, Red Maple, Black Gum, Sourwood, and occasional Black Locust and Black Cherry. With the elimination of vegetation management that reduces undesirable timber species, a total of perhaps 20 canopy old-growth species should eventually occupy such south-facing and ridge sites.

On the other hand, second-growth oak-hickory stands currently occupying many north-facing slopes and coves, mixed with varying amounts of Yellow Poplar and other hardwoods, will eventually be replaced by a more mesic species composition. The current predominance of oaks and hickories on these sites is due to the violent disturbances wrought by early logging and burning, and this forest type now represents a late successional stage. As the present oaks, hickories, Black Locust, Black Cherry, Sourwood, and Sassafras mature toward senescence and die, mid-story species, including Red and Sugar Maples, American Basswood, Eastern Hemlock, Yellow and Sweet Birches, Beech, Yellow Buckeye, and Silverbell, will gradually work their way up into the canopy to take their places beside large Yellow Poplar and White Pine already there. A stabilized old-growth forest on these sites will probably contain over 30 species of canopy trees, including a few old residuals of the present oak and hickory species.

The Society of American Foresters' task force on old-growth has stated the situation clearly (adapted from the *Journal of Forestry*, 1984): There is a compelling need to preserve and to rehabilitate old-growth forests throughout the United States and the world. Further, it is not possible to hasten the processes by which nature creates old-growth. The best way for management to restore old-growth is to conserve an adequate supply of present second-growth stands and leave them alone. Most forest scientists agree that there is little silvicultural potential for "speeding up" the restoration of old-growth. It is a matter of educating National Forest managers and policy-makers to the responsibility of defining, identifying, and inventorying adequate large areas of present forestland, and then making the long-term commitment to preserve and monitor it as it matures toward old-growth. This must be done despite strong pressures for resource production.

Here on the National Forests of the Southern Appalachians we are well on our way toward the 150–200 year-old stands that begin to stabilize as old-growth. This rehabilitation has occurred in my lifetime, in the 65 years since the Southern Appalachian National Forests were established. We are halfway to the youngest old-growth condition. My grandchildren can experience the initial phases of restored old-growth forests across large landscapes. This will take a commitment longer than the life span to date of the agency we are asking to allow these old forests.

How much old-growth is enough? Accepting that old-growth forest landscapes are required for the restoration of biological diversity in the Southern Appalachians, minimum sizes must be sufficiently large to embrace several adjacent entire watersheds. Species migration and genetic exchange require, in addition to large preserves, corridors of old-growth forests linking preserves together. Preserve Appalachian Wilderness (PAW) has a vision of a wildlife corridor linking mature forests along the Appalachian Trail from Maine to Georgia, utilizing much of the mountain National Forests to provide large preserves. The six Southern Appalachian National Forests would play a major role in realizing such a vision. Such a concept offers a framework on which to build policy and reform National Forest land use planning.

Ethical Potential

In addition to the biological and land allocation potentials for the restoration of old-growth forests in the Southern Appalachians, we must address a third factor: What is the ethical potential that such large-scale restoration of forest landscapes can be established on our public lands? What are the social and legal possibilities?

Strong biocentric sentiments have flowered intermittently throughout recorded history, in such thinkers as St. Francis of Assisi, Albert Schweitzer, and Henry David Thoreau, all of whom saw God in every living animal and plant, and called for an end to the dominance of man over nature. By contrast, the earliest National Forest policies were based on the land stewardship concept of Gifford Pinchot, that of the conservation and management of our natural resources for the use of society. Aldo Leopold added a more biocentric aspect to land management with his call for a "land ethic" that included respect for and preservation of all species, whether or not they were of economic value.

Leopold's land ethic is receiving much attention today among professional land managers. Indeed, in the 1988 and '89 surveys of its membership, the Society of American Foresters found overwhelmingly that Leopold's *A Sand County Almanac* is the most important book relating to their profession. Further, the Society recently released a position statement that there are ethical reasons, among others, for preserving and rehabilitating old-growth forests throughout the world. The Society is currently encountering much pressure from its membership to add a "land ethic" to its official code of human ethics. I conclude, therefore, that many professional foresters are part of an ethical movement to grant rights of existence to all types of natural systems. However, the Leopold ethic has not yet found its way into widespread practice.

What is the potential for such a movement to gain legal status for the "rights of nature"? Legislative history in America suggests the potential is good, at least legal rights for natural habitats. Since the Declaration of Independence established America's desire for the rights of citizens (at least for male citizens) many acts of the US Congress have established an evolving concept for the legal rights of other entities: In 1863 the Emancipation Proclamation extended legal freedom to slaves; in 1903 the National Wildlife Refuge Act protected certain public lands as sanctuaries for specified wildlife; in 1920 the Nineteenth Amendment gave female citizens equal rights with males; in 1924 the Indian Citizenship Act gave native Americans equal rights; in 1938 the Fair Labor Standards Act freed blue collar workers in the workplace; in 1957 the Civil Rights Act put legal teeth into the other acts that had established equal rights for all citizens; in 1964 the Wilderness Act opened the way for the preservation of large wild landscapes on public lands, and permitted legal defense of these preserves; in 1966 the Animal Welfare Act, in 1972 the Marine Mammal Protection Act, and in 1973 the Endangered Species Act all gave particular legal rights to certain animals, rights that were later extended even to certain plants.

The Endangered Species Act, the Multiple Use Sustained Yield Act of 1960, and the National Forest Management Act of 1976 have mandated that public agencies protect certain biotic habitats. These laws establish legal ways for humans to defend some of the "rights of nature" against man's infringements. A next stage in this legal evolution is the passage of the proposed Biological Diversity Bill and the World Environmental Policy Act now in Congress. Such a clear federal mandate should give natural diversity the same legal status now enjoyed by individual Endangered species. This means that uncommon *combinations* of species that comprise a biotic community will have legal protection, and further, that federal land managers will have an obligation to not only protect such existing communities but also to restore such communities where the potential exists. Since old-growth forests comprise many habitats in short supply in the Southern Appalachians, National Forest management plans will be revised to accommodate this new law.

Congress still operates from the conservative philosophy of Gifford Pinchot which espouses good stewardship in the management of our National Forests for the production of goods and services for people. Many preservationists today, however, are embracing a more biocentric view of nature. Norwegian philosopher and naturalist Arne Naess proposed in 1973 a new environmentalism that he termed "deep ecology." This concept has caught on strongly in America over the past decade, and many recent writings are espousing the intrinsic rights of all species and all habitats, in fact, all nature, to exist unmolested by humans. Such a philosophy is essential to success in the movement for restoration of old-growth forest landscapes.

Conclusion

All the potentials are in place for the restoration of large old-growth forest landscapes across the Southern Appalachian Bioregion. Although these old-growth forests will not be the same as those of pre-disturbance landscapes, within another 75–150 years many habitats can be restored to a semblance of their primeval condition. The land base and partially rehabilitated second-growth forests exist on our mountain National Forests; the long-term commitment to bring it about is possible in federal land management policy. Finally, public and congressional sentiments have evolved to recognize the scientific and moral necessity to provide old-growth habitats where all levels of biological diversity can evolve naturally in response to the expected environmental changes of the next century.

A national crusade is arising for preserving and restoring old-growth forests in every forest region. A recent conference of the Natural Areas Association, for example, hosted 12 papers on the old-growth temperate deciduous forests of the southern United States. Scientific journals, environmental reports, and even national media are giving the subject unprecedented attention. The case for restoring old-growth has been well established. We are beyond the debating stage. As now urged by the Society of American Foresters, it is time to conserve an adequate supply of second-growth forest, and *leave it alone*. Forever.

PARTIAL LIST OF REFERENCES
relative to restoration of Eastern old-growth forests

- Barnes, Burton V. 1989. Old-growth forests of the Lake States: A landscape perspective. *Natural Areas Journal* 9(1).
- Blockstein, David E. 1988. US legislative progress toward conserving biological diversity. *Conservation Biology* 2(4).
- Bolgiano, Chris. 1989. A case for eastern old growth. *American Forests Magazine*, May/June.
- Braun, E Lucy. 1950. *Deciduous Forests of Eastern North America*. Macmillan Pub, NY.
- Cooley, James L, & June H Cooley, editors. 1984. *Natural Diversity in Forest Ecosystems: Proceedings of the Workshop*. Institute of Ecology, University of Georgia, Athens.
- DiGioia, Harriet. 1989. Cohutta: A Wilderness-to-order. *American Forests*, July/Aug.
- Ehrlich, Paul R. 1987. Biodiversity and the public lands. *Wilderness Magazine*, Spring.
- Ehrlich, Paul R. 1989. Facing the habitability crisis. *Bioscience* 39(7).
- Forman, Richard T. 1983. An ecology of the landscape. *Bioscience* 33(9).
- Harris, Larry D. 1981. *The Fragmented Forest: Island Biogeographic Theory and the Preservation of Biotic Diversity*. University of Chicago Press.
- Heinrichs, Jay. 1983. Old growth comes of age. *Journal of Forestry* 81.
- Hunter, Malcolm L. Jr. 1989. What constitutes an old-growth stand? *Journal of Forestry* 87.

• Jackson, Laura E. 1989. *Mountain treasures at risk: The future of the Southern Appalachian National Forests.* The Wilderness Society, Washington, DC.

• Juday, Glenn P. 1988. Old-growth forests and natural areas: An introduction. *Natural Areas* 8(1).

• Jones, Steven M. 1988. Old-growth forests within the Piedmont of South Carolina. *Natural Areas* 8(1).

• Ledig, E. Thomas. 1988. The conservation of diversity in forest trees. *Bioscience* 38(7).

• Leopold, Aldo. 1949. *A Sand County Almanac.* Oxford University Press, Oxford.

• Maser, Chris. 1988. *The Redesigned Forest.* R & E Miles, San Pedro, California.

• Myers, Norman. 1989. The heat is on: Global warming threatens the natural world. *Greenpeace Magazine* 14(3).

• Nash, Roderick F. 1989. *The Rights of Nature: A History of Environmental Ethics.* University of Wisconsin Press, Madison.

• Norse, Elliot A. 1986. *Conserving biological diversity on our National Forests.* The Wilderness Society.

• Norton, Bryan G. editor. 1986. *The Preservation of Species: The Value of Biological Diversity.* Princeton University Press, Princeton, New Jersey.

• Noss, Reed F. 1983. A regional landscape approach to maintain diversity. *Bioscience* 33(11).

• Noss, Reed F. 1987. Protecting natural areas in fragmented landscapes. *Natural Areas* 7(1).

• Odum, Eugene P. 1969. The strategy of ecosystem development. *Science* 164.

• Odum, Eugene P. 1977. The life support value of forests. In *Forests for People.* Soc. Amer. Foresters 1977 National Convention, Washington, DC.

• Parker, George R. 1989. Old-growth forest of the central hardwood region. *Natural Areas* 9(1).

• Pelton, Michael R. 1986. Habitat needs of black bears in the East. In *Wilderness and Natural Areas in the Eastern United States: A Management Challenge,* ed. by D. L. Kulhavy and R. N. Conner. Austin State University, Nacogdoches, Texas.

• Shen, Susan. 1987. Biological diversity and public policy. *Bioscience* 37(10).

- Sheppard, Paul R. and Edward Cook. 1988. Scientific value of trees in old-growth natural areas. *Natural Areas* 8(1).
- Smith, Thomas L. 1989. An overview of old-growth forests in Pennsylvania. *Natural Areas* 9(1).
- United States Congress. 1988. *Technologies to Maintain Biological Diversity*. Office of Technology Assessment, Washington, DC.
- US Dept of Agriculture, Forest Service, Southern Region. Atlanta, GA. Land and Resource Management Plans and Final Environmental Impact Statements. 1985, Chattahoochee–Oconee National Forests (GA); 1986, Cherokee NF (TN); 1987, Nantahala and Pisgah NFs (NC).
- Wharton, Charles H and Harvey L Ragsdale. 1983. The values of unmanaged National Forests in the Southern Appalachians. Report to the Georgia Conservancy, Atlanta.
- White, Peter S. 1987. Natural disturbance, patch dynamics, and landscape pattern in natural areas. *Natural Areas* 7(1).
- Whitney, Gordon G. 1987. Some reflections on the value of old-growth forests, scientific and otherwise. *Natural Areas* 7(3).
- Wilcove, David S. 1988. Protecting biological diversity. The Wilderness Society, Washington, DC.
- Wilson, E.O. editor. 1988. *Biodiversity*. National Academy Press, Washington, DC.

Editor's note: Particularly valuable for activists among the sources above is The Wilderness Society's Mountain Treasures At Risk, available free from TWS, 1400 Eye St. NW, Washington, DC 20005.

FROGS TO REINTRODUCE BISON
Mabon 1989
by Mary Davis

In 1919 a poacher on the Polish-Russian border killed the last European Bison in the wild. Because a few individuals were protected in zoos, however, the species has been able to make a comeback. In 1952 nine European Bison were reintroduced to the 308,750 acre Bialowieza Forest in Poland and the USSR, the largest virgin forest in Europe. By 1980, 411 bison lived in this forest, and bison also inhabited the Beskides in Poland and, in small numbers, several other sites in the Soviet Union. This fall, 1300 years after the bison's disappearance from France, the species will be reintroduced to the Margeride in the Massif Central as the beginning of a program in green tourism.

[The European Bison (*Bison bonasus*), or Wisent, is closely related to and similar in size to the American Bison (*Bison bison*), or Buffalo. Its habitat preferences are closer to those of the Buffalo subspecies known as the Wood Bison than to those of the Wood Bison's Western counterpart, the Plains Bison.]

The reintroduction plan is the creation of animal ethologist Gilbert Maury, who, since childhood, has explored the Margeride, 494,000 acres of mountains, forests, and farmland, west of Le Puy-en-Velay. Most of the area's farms have been abandoned. It has less than 20 human residents per square mile.

In 1984 Maury visited the Beskides in the Massif of Tetra in the south of Poland. He was struck by the similarity of the Beskides to the Margeride in soil, plants, and climate. The ground in both areas is basically granite; the mountains are of moderate height, with the tallest in the Beskides being 4416 feet and in the Margeride 4921 feet; beech and spruce are the dominant trees; and snow comes early and stays late but averages less than 20 inches in depth. It seemed to Maury that in the Margeride as in Poland, bison would feel at home.

His research over the next 4 years confirmed his initial insight. The Margeride was the only area of Western Europe suitable for bison, because it was the only area with the granite base the bison require and of sufficient size and low human population density.

In 1988 Maury held a meeting on the reintroduction of European Bison. To his surprise 75 interested people came. Eventually all three departments and the two regions in which the Margeride is situated agreed to subsidize the initial operating expenses of the park.

To win supporters, Maury spoke of the value of helping wild animals live free and of the importance of establishing a bison colony in Western Europe in case disease should wipe out the bison in the East. (Bison are subject to the same illnesses as farmers' cows.) He emphasized, however, the economic benefits that bison would bring to the region.

Human society is dying in the Margeride, because the region's farms have become unprofitable. In France, sooner or later deserted land is discovered by entrepreneurs wanting to construct vacation villages and ski areas and by families seeking second homes. (The English are gobbling up French land, because they look forward to the completion of the tunnel under the English Channel; and the Dutch, because they fear the greenhouse effect will result in the flooding of their homeland.) Landowners may plant trees on former farmland—in France 3 trees are planted for every 1 that is cut—but, for financial reasons, the land is much more likely to become an evergreen plantation than a mixed forest. Furthermore, intensive hunting usually prevents the fauna from recovering.

Maury thinks bison reintroduction will enable the region's remaining people to earn a living while maintaining their traditional way of life and preserving the environment. The bison will draw visitors. In 1986, 370,000 people visited the bison in Poland. The French hope that 200,000 people a year will come to the Margeride. Visitors who stay overnight will be put up at farms. Farmers, moreover, will be encouraged to sell their produce to tourists.

Poland agreed to donate to the project as many bison as the French wished. Maury requested 15. They will be shipped this fall in a truck that will be flown from Poland to France on a French military plane. In the Margeride they will be placed in a 617 acre enclosed park. Since European Bison each weigh 1000–2000 pounds and can jump 6 feet high, the enclosure will be formed by a 10 foot wall lined with a ditch.

European Bison normally live in herds of 7–15 animals. Maury hopes that in 10 years, 5 herds with a total of 40 bison will roam free outside the park. Fifteen bison will always be kept in the enclosure for viewing by tourists. No bison will be freed until 7 young have been born and weaned, a stage that Maury thinks will take 3–4 years. The 7 youngsters will be the first to be let loose.

European Bison are herbivores, each eating 50 to 100 pounds a day of grass and bark. Their direct competitors for food are the Red Deer (cerf) and the Roe Deer (chevreuil), both of which live in the Margeride, the latter in large numbers. Since roughly 2500 acres of land are required to support a single bison under natural conditions, the bison (including in winter those outside the enclosure) will be fed to keep them from destroying their surroundings. Their food will be hay, corn, barley, and wheat, some of it grown inside the park.

Farmers in the region have accepted the reintroduction plan. The freed animals will have radio emitters in their ears, and the society managing the park will reimburse farmers for any damage they do. In the Beskides bison roam freely among farms without causing problems.

The bison will be observed during their first months in the park, and the park will not be open to the public until at least next spring. When visitors do come, they will be taught about bison. Before seeing any live animals, they will tour a bison museum located in an old stone farmhouse. They will enter the park on foot or on horseback. A biologist will accompany to observation towers those who walk. Horseback riders will be able to go nearer to the bison, because the horses will mask the humans' scent.

The biggest uncertainty in the project is the bison themselves. Maury warns that since European Bison have not previously been reintroduced into Western Europe, an error is always possible. If they adapt, he does not expect financial problems. With 100,000 visitors annually, the park would begin to profit in its third year.

Maury would like the bison reintroduction to become the first step in establishing in the Margeride a reserve where a variety of extirpated animals again roam freely—the Aurochs, Tarpon, Prejewalski Horse, and even Reindeer. The Margeride is cold enough for Reindeer.

And what if an entrepreneur decides to erect a hotel near the park? Maury will refuse to work on the project if hotels loom on the horizon; and, since he is the only French expert on the bison and essential to the project, he believes the authorities will heed his views.

CHAPTER 6

Matters Spiritual

THOSE READERS WHO FIND RELIGIOUS and spiritual talk repugnant need not be dismayed by this chapter's title. We use the word 'spiritual' here in a very broad sense. This chapter is our representation of poetic, artistic, and ritualistic writings.

It deals with extra-rational matters, right brain thinking. According to such deep ecology theorists as Arne Naess and Bill Devall, deep ecology is compatible with, but not dependent upon, many spiritual paths.

Moreover, creative expression, such as music, drawing, poetry, and humor, has been essential to the EF! movement's success. Indeed EF!ers' sense of humor long ago distinguished them from other environmental groups—whose members cannot boast the level of depravity EF! achieved!

The EF! movement has attracted people of numerous spiritual persuasions and dissuasions, ranging from practising witches and neo-pagans to incorrigible empiricists and atheists, with a few Christian clerics in between! It has also attracted many outstanding artists, musicians, and poets, whose works we cannot include here but who richly deserve thanks: artists Helen Wilson, Roger Candee, Jim Stiles, Robert Waldmire, Sky Jacobs, Peggy Sue McRae, Bob Cremins, Claus Seivert, Marcy Willow, Lourdes Fuentes-Williams, Christoph Manes, and the late John Zaelit; musicians Dana Lyons, John Seed, Glen Waldeck, Bill Oliver, Cecelia Ostrow, Joanne Rand, Peg Millett, Mavis Muller, Scotty Johnson, Greg Keeler, Dakota Sid Clifford, Walkin' Jim Stoltz, Susan Stoltz; poets Art Goodtimes, Gary Lawless, Mary de La Valette; and many others. If you wish to support art in defense of Earth, seek these names.

SONG OF THE TASTE
Samhain 1984
by Gary Snyder

Eating the living germs of grasses
Eating the ova of large birds
the fleshy sweetness packed
around the sperm of swaying trees
The muscles of the flanks and
thighs of soft-voiced cows
the bounce in the lamb's leap
the swish in the ox's tail
Eating roots grown swoll
inside the soil
Drawing on life of living
clustered points of light spun
out of space
hidden in the grape.
Eating each other's seed
eating
ah, each other.
Kissing the lover in the mouth
of bread:
lip to lip.

—Gary Snyder, New Directions, 1970
Copyright 1970 by the author

On "Song of the Taste"

The primary ethical teaching of all times and places is "cause no unnecessary harm." The Hindus, Jains, and Buddhists use the Sanskrit term *ahimsa*, "non-harming." They commonly interpret this to mean "don't take life," with varying degrees of latitude allowed for special situations. In the eastern traditions "cause no unnecessary harm" is the precept behind vegetarianism.

Non-vegetarians too try to understand and practice the teaching of "non-harming." People who live entirely by hunting, such as the

Eskimo, know that taking life is an act requiring a spirit of gratitude and care, and rigorous mindfulness. They say "all our food is souls." Plants are alive too. All of nature is a gift-exchange, a potluck banquet, and there is no death that is not somebody's food, no life that is not somebody's death.

Is this a flaw in the universe? A sign of a sullied condition of being? "Nature red in tooth and claw?" Some people read it this way, leading to a disgust with self, with humanity, and with life itself. They are on the wrong fork of the path. Otherworldly philosophies end up doing more damage to the planet (and human psyches) than the existential conditions they seek to transcend.

So again to the beginning. We all take life to live. Weston LaBarre says, "The first religion is to kill god and eat him" or her. The shimmering food-chain, food-web, is the scary, beautiful, condition of the biosphere. Non-harming must be understood as an approach to all of living and being, not just a one-dimensional moral injunction. Eating is truly a sacrament.

How to accomplish this? We can start by saying Grace. Grace is the first and last poem, the few words we say to clear our hearts and teach the children and welcome the guest, all at the same time. To say a good grace you must be conscious of what you're doing, not guilt-ridden and evasive. So we look at the nature of eggs, apples, and ox-tail ragout. What we see is plenitude, even excess, a great sexual exuberance. Millions of grains of grass-seed to become flour, millions of codfish fry that will never—and must never—grow to maturity: sacrifices to the food-chain. And if we eat meat, it is the life, the bounce, the swish, that we eat. Let us not deceive ourselves; Americans should know that cows stand up to their hocks in feed-lot manure waiting to be transported to their table, that virgin forests in the Amazon are clearcut to make pasture to raise beef for the American market. Even a root in the ground is a marvel of living chemistry, making sugars and flavors from earth, air, water.

Looking close at this world of one-ness, we see all these beings as of our own flesh, as our children, our lovers. We see ourselves too as an offering to the continuation of life.

This is strong stuff. Such truth is not easy. But hang on: if we eat each other, is it not a giant act of love we live within? Christ's blood and body become clear: The bread blesses you, as you bless it.

So at our house we say a Buddhist verse of Grace:

"We venerate the Three
Treasures"
(Buddha, Dharma, Sangha)
"And are thankful for this meal
The work of many people
And the sharing of other
forms of life."

Anyone can use a Grace from their tradition, if they have one, and infuse it with deeper feeling and understanding, or make up their own, from the heart. But saying Grace is not fashionable in much of America now, and often even when said is mechanical and flat, with no sense of the deep chasm that lies under the dining table. My poem "Song of the Taste" is a grace for graces, a model for anyone's thought, verse, song, on "the meal" that the fortunate ones on earth partake of three times a day.

Copyright 1984 by the author

GAIA MEDITATIONS AT THE COUNCIL OF ALL BEINGS
Samhain 1986
by Joanna Macy and John Seed

What are you? What am I? Intersecting cycles of water, earth, air and fire, that's what I am, that's what you are.

Water—blood, lymph, mucus, sweat, tears, inner oceans tugged by the moon, tides within and tides without. Streaming fluids floating our cells, washing and nourishing through endless riverways of gut and vein and capillary. Moisture pouring in and through and out of you, of me, in the vast poem of the hydrological cycle.

Earth—matter made from rock and soil. It too pulled by the moon as the magma circulates through the planet heart and roots suck molecules into biology. Earth pours through us, replacing each cell in the body every seven years. Ashes to ashes, dust to dust, we incorporate and excrete the earth, are made from earth.

Air—the gaseous realm, the atmosphere, the planet's membrane. The inhale and the exhale. Breathing out carbon dioxide to the trees and breathing in their fresh exudations. Oxygen kissing each cell awake, atoms dancing in orderly metabolism, interpenetrating. That dance of the air cycle, breathing the universe in and out again, is what you are, is what I am.

Fire—from our sun that fuels all life, drawing up plants and raising the waters to the sky to fall again replenishing. The inner furnace of your metabolism burns with the fire of the Big Bang that first sent matter-energy spinning through space and time. And the same fire as the lightning that flashed into the primordial soup catalyzing the birth of organic life.

You were there, I was there, for each cell of our bodies is descended in an unbroken chain from that event. Through the desire of atom for molecule, molecule for cell, cell for organism. In that spawning of forms death was born, born simultaneously with sex, before we divided from the plant realm. So in our sexuality we can feel ancient stirrings that connect us with plant as well as animal life. We come from them in an unbroken chain—through fish learning to walk the land, feeling scales turning to wings, through the great migrations in the ages of ice.

We have been but recently in human form. If Earth's whole history were compressed into 24 hours beginning at midnight, organic life would begin only at 5:00 P.M. . . . mammals emerge at 11:30 . . . and from amongst them at only seconds to midnight, our species.

In our long planetary journey we have taken far more ancient forms than these we now wear. Some of those forms we remember in our mother's womb, wear vestigial tail and gills, grow fins for hands.

Countless times in that journey we died to old forms, let go of old ways, allowing new ones to emerge. But nothing is ever lost. Though forms pass, all returns. Each worn-out cell consumed, recycled . . . through mosses, leeches, bird of prey. . . .

Think of your next death. Will your flesh and bones back into the cycle. Surrender. Love the plump worms you will become. Launder your weary being through the fountain of life.

Beholding you, I behold as well all the different creatures that compose you—the mitochondria in the cells, the intestinal bacteria, the life teeming on the surface of the skin. The great symbiosis that is you. The incredible coordination and cooperation of countless beings. You are part of a much larger symbiosis, living in wider reciprocities. Be conscious of that give-and-take when you move among trees.

Breathe your pure carbon dioxide to a leaf and sense it breathing fresh oxygen back to you.

Remember again and again the old cycles of partnership. Draw on them in this time of trouble. By your very nature and the journey you have made, there is in you deep knowledge of belonging. You have earth-bred wisdom of your interexistence with all that is. Take courage in it now and power, that we may help each other awaken in this time of peril.

THOUGHTS ON AUTUMN EQUINOX ABOUT THE IMPORTANCE OF RITUAL
Mabon 1989
by Dolores LaChapelle

All these autumn weeks I have watched the great disk going south along the horizon of moorlands beyond the marsh, now sinking behind this field, now behind this leafless tree, now behind this sedgy hillock dappled with thin snow. We lose a great deal, I think, when we lose this sense and feeling for the sun. When all has been said, the adventure of the sun is the great natural drama by which we live and not to have joy in it and awe of it, not to share in it, is to close a dull door on nature's sustaining and poetic spirit.[1]
—Henry Beston

Moreover, it becomes apparent . . . that ritual is not simply an alternative way to express certain things, but that certain things can be expressed only in ritual. Ritual is without equivalents or even alternatives . . . I take ritual to be the basic social act . . . social contract, morality, the concept of the sacred, the notion of the divine, and even a paradigm of creation are intrinsic to ritual's structure.[2]
—Roy Rappaport

Most primal or indigenous societies around the world had three common characteristics: they had an intimate, conscious relationship with their place; they were stable "sustainable" cultures, often lasting for thousands of years; and they had a rich ceremonial and ritual life culminating in seasonal festivals. They saw these three as intimately connected. Out of the hundreds of examples, consider the following:

- The Tukano Indians of the northwest Amazon River basin, guided by their shamans, use various myths and rituals that prevent over-hunting or over-fishing. They view their universe as a circuit of energy in which the entire cosmos participates. The circuit consists of "a limited quantity of procreative energy that flows continually between man and animals, between society and nature." Colombian anthropologist Reichel Dolmatoff notes that the Tukano have little interest in exploiting natural resources more effectively but are greatly interested in "accumulating more factual knowledge about biological reality and, above all, about knowing what the physical world requires from men."[3]

- The Kung people of Africa's Kalahari Desert have been living in the same place for 11,000 years! They have very few material belongings but their ritual life is one of the most sophisticated of any group.[4]

- Roy Rappaport has shown that the rituals of the Tsembaga of New Guinea allocate scarce protein for the humans who need it without causing irreversible damage to the land. Ritual dictates the proper ways and times to hunt the pigs which supply their protein.[5]

- The longest inhabited place in the United States is the Hopi village of Oraibi. At certain times of the year the Hopi here may spend up to half their time in ritual activity.

- About ten years ago the old *cacique* of San Juan Pueblo in New Mexico died. The young man elected to take over as the new *cacique* will do nothing for the rest of his life but take care of the ritual life of the Pueblo. All his personal needs will be taken care of by the tribe, but he cannot travel more than 60 miles or one hour from the Pueblo. The distance has grown with the use of cars but the time remains one hour. His presence is that important to the life of the Pueblo.

Our Western European industrial culture provides a striking contrast to all these examples.* We have idolized ideals, rationality and a limited kind of "practicality," and have regarded the rituals of these other cultures as at best frivolous curiosities. The results are all too evident. We've only been here a few hundred years and already we have done irreparable damage to vast areas of what we call the United States. As Gregory Bateson notes, "mere purposive rationality is necessarily pathogenic and destructive of life."

We have tried to relate to the world around us through only the left side of our brain, and we are clearly failing. If we are to reestablish a viable relationship, we must rediscover the wisdom of these other cultures who knew that their relationship to the land required the whole of their being. What we call their "ritual and ceremony" was a sophisticated social and spiritual technology for such a relationship

The Industrial Growth Society (IGS) has caused us to forget so much in the last 200 years that we hardly know where to begin. It helps to begin by remembering. All traditional cultures, even our own Western European ancestors, had seasonal festivals and rituals. The true origins of most of our modern holidays date back to these seasonal festivals.

The purpose of seasonal festivals is to periodically revive the topocosm. Gaster coined this word from the Greek topo for place and cosmos for world order. Topocosm means "the world order of a particular place." The topocosm is the entire complex of any given locality conceived as a living organism—not just the human community but the total community—plants, animals and soils. The topocosm is not only the present community but also that continuous entity of which the present community is but the current manifestation.[6]

Seasonal festivals make use of myths, art, dance and games. Each of these aspects of ritual serve to keep open the essential connections within ourselves. Festivals connect the conscious with the unconscious, the right hemisphere with the left hemisphere of the brain, and the cortex with the older three brains (including the Oriental tan tien, four fingers below the navel). They also connect the human with the non-human—earth, sky, animals and plants.

I'm often asked, "What relevance does this kind of ritual have for people who live in the city?" The modern city of Siena in Italy provides a good answer. Siena with a population of 59,000 has the lowest crime rate of any Western city of comparable size. Drug-addiction and violence are virtually unknown. Why? Because it is a tribal, ritualized city organized around the contrada (clans)—with names such as Chiocciola, the Snail, Tartule, the Turtle, etc.—and the Palio (the annual horse race). Each contrada has its own territory, church songs, patron saint and rituals. Particular topographical features of each contrada's area are ritualized and mythologized. The ritualized customs of the city extend back to the worship of Diana, the Roman goddess of the moon. Her attributes were taken over by the worship of Mary when Christianity came in.

Such famous writers as Henry James, Ezra Pound and Aldous Huxley sensed the energy of the city and tried to write about it, but none of them even faintly grasped the year-long ritualized life behind it. About one week before the day of the Palio race, Siena workmen begin to bring yellow earth (*la terra*) from the fields outside Siena and spread it over the great central square, the Campo, thus linking the city with its origins in the earth of its place. Anytime during the year when someone needs to be cheered up, the sad person is told not to worry because soon there will be "la terra in piazza."

The horse race serves two main purposes. In the intense rivalry surrounding the race, each *contrada* "rekindles its own sense of identity." The Palio also provides the Sienese with an outlet for their aggression, and as such is a ritual war. The horse race grew out of games that were actually mimic battles used to mark the ends of religious festivals in the old days.

The Palio is truly a religious event. On this one day of the year the *contrada's* horse is brought into the church of its patron saint. In the act of blessing the horse, the *contrada* itself is blessed. This horse race is the community's greatest rite.[7]

If we want to build a sustainable culture, it is not enough to "go back to the land." That's what our pioneering ancestors did and, as the famous Western artist Charles Russell said, "A pioneer is a man who comes to virgin country, traps off all the fur, kills off the wild meat, plows the roots up . . . and calls it civilization."

If we are to truly re-connect with the land, we need to change our perceptions. As long as we limit ourselves to rationality, we will be disconnected from the deep ecology of our place. As Heidegger explains: "Dwelling is not primarily inhabiting but taking care of and creating that space within which something comes into its own and flourishes." It takes repeated rituals through the years for real dwelling. Likewise, as Roy Rappaport observes, "knowledge will never replace respect in man's dealings with ecological systems, for the ecological systems in which man participates are likely to be so complex that he may never have sufficient comprehension of their content and structure to permit him to predict the outcome of many of his own acts." Ritual is the focused way in which we both experience and express that respect.

Ritual is the pattern that connects. It provides communication at all levels—communication among all the systems within the individual human organism; between people within a group; between groups within a city; and throughout all these levels, between the human and the non-human in the natural environment. Ritual provides us with a tool for learning to think logically, analogically and ecologically. Perhaps most important, during rituals we have the experience, unique in our culture, of neither *opposing* nature nor *trying* to be in communication with nature; but of *finding* ourselves within nature.

NOTE: Most of these primitive groups' cultures have been virtually destroyed in the last 20 years by the Industrial Growth Society, but they are our only sources of information on what constitutes a sustainable culture.

BIBLIOGRAPHY

1. Henry Beston, *The Outermost House*, Viking Explorer Books, 1961 ed.

2. Roy Rappaport, *Ecology, Meaning and Religion*, North Atlantic Books, 1979.

3. G. Reichel-Dolmatoff, "Cosmology as Ecological Analysis," in *Man: Journal of the Royal Anthropological Institute* (9–78).

4. Richard B. Lee, "What Hunters Do for a Living," in Lee and DeVore, *Man the Hunter*, Aldine Publishing Co, 1968.

5. Rappaport, *Pigs for their Ancestors*, Yale University Press, 1968.

6. Theodore Gaster, *Thespis: Ritual, Myth and Drama in the Ancient Near East*, Norton and Co, 1977 ed.

7. Alan Dundes and Alessandro Falassi, *La Terra in Piazza: An Interpretation of the Palio of Siena*, University of California Press, 1975.

THE PRAIRIE SHIELD
August 1990
by Daniel Dancer

Elements of Place

An old farmhouse burning down, a turtle skeleton and a handmade wind ornament were the elements of place I encountered one spring day in the Flint Hills of Kansas. I was there scouting a site for the creation of an eco-sculpture that would celebrate the native Tallgrass Prairie—my bioregion and home for the last 16 years. Actually, it would be more than just a sculpture. It would be, as well, a shield of sorts, sacred ground from which to rally and rail against Fort Riley's proposed acquisition of the region for tank training maneuvers.

I discovered the wind ornament blowing in triplicate on the front yard fence posts of a small house in Burdick, a sleepy farm community that would be rocked by exploding shells should the military's bid for expansion be granted. I stopped here to ask for directions. An old woman of the self-sufficient Kansas backcountry variety was bidding farewell to her son's family when I pulled up. She gave me directions and asked if I was "one of them government people." I said, "no." She said "good." Then I commented on her cut-out plastic bottles twirling in the wind. "Ya want one?" she asked. "Sure," I replied and headed down the road with one on the seat beside me. American prayer wheels, I thought, thinking of Tibet, though in this case the wind does the turning.

I quickly forgot her directions, as I usually do after becoming engaged with an unusual personality. It was ok though. I had my map, sent to me by the Preserve Rural America Society which had organized communities against the expansion. There were four areas selected as possible zones for government acquisition, each about 100,000 acres in size. I had chosen to explore the southernmost zone, about 50 miles from Ft. Riley.

Most of it was prime Flint Hills grassland and I was anxious to find an auspicious site for the sculpture that was beginning to take shape in the events of the day.

As I usually do when I want to find the wild spaces of a region, I began turning off on progressively smaller dirt roads; roads that headed away, into the hills; signless, wireless, houseless—the more rutted and rocky the better. It was on one of these, after forging a river, that I rounded a bend and discovered an old farmstead burning to the ground. No one was around. The fire was in its early stages and flames danced almost playfully from the upstairs windows. I photographed the scene and marveled that this 100 plus year old house had awaited my precise arrival to burn to the ground. Memories set in wood of children laughing, late night lovemaking and dinner table arguments were set free in the smoke that wafted up through the immense cedars that once shaded the grounds. The barn was burning also and I noticed the backroad I was following wound between it and the house and up a steep hill out of sight. I smiled inwardly and knew, with the certainty such events claim, that I was about to enter *sacred ground*.

After watching the buildings climax in flames I threaded my way between them, their heat blasting my old Subaru for a moment. Once up the hill I discovered the source of the fire. As anyone from the prairie lands knows, "burnin' pasture" is a spring rite, and this particular prairie fire had worked its way into the domain of the abandoned farm below. I followed the track through the freshly burned landscape to a rickety fence gate. I knew from past experience in the hills that this was what I was looking for. This gate would open onto a 10 or 20,000 acre pasture of native tallgrass prairie hills, valleys, glades, creeks and sky that descends everywhere to your very toes. Wild space. Private land of course, but owned by folks who understand the craving of the odd naturalist to stretch out in a land that has the feel of heaven and the taste of 100 years ago. And best of all, the cows hadn't been turned out yet.

I cruised 30 miles across the giant pasture that afternoon, most of it freshly burned and exuding the clean smell of ash. I found the skeleton of a turtle, its bleached white bones set upon the black prairie like a beacon on a dark night. I gathered it up and headed eastward to a high point of land that protruded over the surrounding terrain, presenting a sweeping panorama of the prairie world. Here was a forever view. Sunrise, sunset, the four directions—all seemed to converge here. It was one of those places—perfect for the sculpture which at that moment I knew I would call "The Prairie Shield."

Refuge for the Imagination

Few Americans have heard of the Flint Hills. Even fewer have been there. They are not the home of still wild and dangerous predators nor do they contain rivers with adrenalin pumping rapids or vistas of mind numbing spectacle. Devoid of hype, no indicators on your map will direct you here for this land is not the widest, deepest or longest of anything. It is the last of something though. The Flint Hills are the last large reserve of the native Tallgrass Prairie that once covered a quarter billion acres of this continent.

Here and there along roads are prairie islands—patches of Big Bluestem, tallest of the prairie grasses, reaching over 8 feet tall. Safe from munching cows, these lonely stands hark back to not so long ago when this was an inland sea of grass supporting one of the Earth's largest concentrations of mammals. Passing these haunting remnants I often slip into a dreamtime of Buffalo infinity, lurking Gray Wolves, and teepees nestled in cottonwood coves. No sooner am I there than a bend in the road or a deep rut yanks me back into these troubled times and the sad realization that the Tallgrass Prairie is the world's most damaged ecosystem, in terms of percentage of land lost.

Today, only about 1% of the original Tallgrass Prairie persists, and most of that is here in the Flint Hills of eastern Kansas, a rough ellipse 40 miles east and west at its widest and some 200 miles north and south. Protected from the sodbuster's plow by its flinty subsoil, the Flint Hills prairie survived the onslaught of western advancement. This is a lost land, a refuge for the imagination where *less* often turns out to be *more*. Hill after hill, gentle sculpted curves swell and crest as far the eye can see in shades of green or tan, painted with windblown snow or rainbows of wildflowers, depending on the season. The Bluestem ecology of this area is without parallel. Biologists have identified over 300 species of birds, some 80 species of mammals and 600 species of plants, many found nowhere else. It is one of Earth's most complex and endangered ecosystems.

Lemons on the Prairie

It is here that the government proposes to "acquire" (through our tax dollars) 100,000 acres of land to blast, compact, uproot and other-wise destroy in the name of weapons training for the M1 Abrahms Tank and Bradley Fighting Vehicle. A look at the effectiveness of these weapons would be almost humorous were it not for the excesses and stupidity they represent. *US News and World Report* portrays the M1 as rolling into battle but then running out of gas before the fight is over (1 tank division needs 600,000 gallons of fuel a day, twice as much as Patton's entire Third Army used when it raced across Europe!). In research tests the M1 broke down for more than 1/2 hour every 58 miles, thus requiring a separate maintenance team traveling with the crew, presumably prepared to get out and make repairs during battle. As for the Bradley, it is made of aluminum which is inflammable and often explodes when hit. The world's leading experts in tactical tank warfare, the Israelis, refuse to use the Bradley because its huge size makes it an easy target. The army wants to loose these lemons on the prairie.

It is not the army's sad absurdity, however, nor the plight of the many farm families who would be uprooted by the fort's expansion that attracted my attention as an environmental artist. Multitudes of angry Kansans have already rallied upon this ground. Few, however, have spoken for the prairie itself.

A Kind of Virginity

We have no sizable portion of native Tallgrass Prairie protected in this country. Sure, we have our token preserves managed by The Nature Conservancy (10,000 acres in Kansas; 15,000 acres in South Dakota; 50,000 acres in Oklahoma), but nothing on the scale of what Ft. Riley wants to acquire for weapons training. The once heated battle for a Prairie National Park has all but died in the Midwest. Its last gasp lies in an Audubon sponsored effort to buy, from a willing seller, the beautiful 11,000 acre Flint Hill's Z Bar Ranch and turn it into a Prairie National Monument.

Although I dream of one day taking my daughter into a vast, presettlement style, mid-continental "big open" with thousands of square miles of restored prairie, complete with Bison, Grizzly, and Elk; the region in its current state *is* a kind of refuge already—one for the imagination. The Flint Hills have few people, abundant space, a fair amount of wildlife and almost no tourism. Naturally, I'd rather see Bison on the prairies than cows, but until the world realizes that it makes more sense to eat grains and vegetables than to eat beef, the landowners here will continue to graze cattle. Unlike BLM lands in the West, this country is meant to be grazed, albeit by Bison; and aside from burning too much (annual fires decrease the diversity of the forbs), most Flint Hills ranchers do an adequate job of caretaking the prairies.

I'm as anti-grazing as the next environmentalist but during the battle for a prairie park some years ago, I could never quite come to terms with the virtue of removing ranchers and cattle from a big chunk of ground and replacing them with Buffalo, Elk, rangers, parking lots, interpretation centers and hordes of gas guzzling, wrapper spewing, ozone depleting tourists. I had no trouble with the Elk or Buffalo, of course, but the rest of the package made me uneasy. Kansas has a kind of virginity when it comes to tourists, and I couldn't help but feel a little protective of it. In a sense, these hills are a sort of national park already, one that preserves a special reality and *kind* of wild—an endangered way of life without hype, glitter or signs pointing the way. In other words, it is a *real* place for the adventurous to discover and enjoy.

I find it easier to imagine a herd of cows as Buffalo than a parking lot full of RVs as a camp of tipis. As others have argued, the integrity of the hills is perhaps better protected as it is, with cows (God help me), rather than Bison; ranchers rather than tourists. It's a point well taken, for Kansans would rather see travelers, on their way to Colorado or Missouri, than tourists. It's not that they aren't friendly; they are among the most welcoming folk you will find, and they'll assure you that Kansas is a great place to live . . . but you wouldn't want to visit there.

Turtle Island

I can say with a fair degree of certainty that no tourist had ever shared the Elysian prairiescape in which I began to build the shield. Deep in the hills, miles from the nearest road, I gathered large white rocks and formed a circle about 12 feet in diameter. I aligned the four directions with the two significant features rising above the land-scape—a pair of huge cottonwoods to the west, and a lone, monolithic hill to the north, Ft. Riley way. I marked the directions with cedar stakes tied with owl feathers. From the small, brown, shiny flint rocks lying helter skelter across the prairie, I arranged a turtle like the one whose bones I had found. From the shield's north point, its head emerged open-mouthed emitting a rock spiral which wound to the precipice of the hill. Spinning on a stake at the spiral's center was the homemade prayer wheel adorned now with prayers and prairie affirmations. I applied black ash from the burned farmhouse to the direction lines and the turtle's back to highlight it from the native grass. And finally, I pounded a pipe, taken from the fire site, into the center of the turtle's back to function as a lightning rod.

In the course of four trips to the hills needed to complete the shield, I experienced the prairie in many facets. One of the wildest, most awesome sounds in nature often accompanied my work—the extraterrestrial-like deep whirring of a nighthawk breaking the vortex of its dive above me. Some 100 feet from the site, and an initial omen for the spot, was a nest of curlew eggs. I often observed the parents attempt to lead me away from the nest with their broken wing routine. I made hurried descents from camp at night to escape the deadly lightning bolts, called grave diggers in these parts, and lay awake till the

storms passed, giddily enjoying the light and sound shows for which
the prairie is famous. And then there was the disappearing Coyote—
the trickster. He was 200 feet away. I turned around to grab my
binoculars and when I looked back he was gone—no trees to hide
behind, no gullies to descend into, just plain gone. This was prairie
primeval almost, and for awhile its magic was my own.

Common in Native American mythology is the notion that all
life exists on the back of a giant turtle, thus they call the Earth *Turtle
Island*. This is wise counsel, for it depicts the Earth as a living finite
being—a being that must be protected and used wisely so its life may
continue. The turtle, whose skeleton I found upon the blackened
prairie and which took life again in the center of the shield, was a trib-
ute to this concept. There was a second death however, and the
turtle's ultimate fate can be viewed as a metaphor for our time.

The Lesson of a Thousand Cows

On my final trip to complete the shield I encountered the white
man's prairie, a prairie I had nearly forgotten. So far I hadn't been both-
ered, but when I reached the site I knew man's favorite beasts had been
there. The circle of white stones had been broken—the turtle barely
recognizable. Shit was at the center and all about me the earth was
trampled. The air reeked with the acrid stench of a thousand cows.

At first I was furious. They were still in the area and when a maver-
ick bunch came over to investigate I lashed out at them with a mixed
flurry of insults and stones until my arms and lungs gave out. And then
I sat down and laughed. How could I have been so stupid? This was,
after all, no pristine prairie; just a giant cow pasture. What did I expect?
Create a piece of Earth art and if the Earth is filled with cattle . . .

It took an hour or so to rebuild the shield and by nightfall I was
nearly finished, waiting only for the sunrise to add the ash and lightning rod. When morning dawned I was surrounded by
cattle—hundreds of them. I leaped out of bed and took action. I
whooped and flailed my purple windbreaker as I ran through the dewy
morning grass. My retriever quickly realized what I had in mind. It was
to be a one man–one dog, cattle stampede. Kona, whose main talent
until then had been retrieving frisbees, suddenly became an expert
cow getter. With me flagging my jacket and Kona barking and biting
heels we quickly moved the stinking beasts across the draw, a good

mile from the shield.

So began a day of fasting and final completion of the project. I photographed the site and stayed up late into the night sitting beside the circle. I sang and beat the drum a bit but mostly I just thought. I realized that after I left, the cows would soon return and claim the shield. They would chew the feathers from stakes, urinate on the stones, trample the ash and knock down the prayer wheel. Nothing intentional, it would just be their cow way. All that would remain would be a lightning rod amongst a scattered assemblage of rocks. And, an idea. An idea that by setting in action a notion, a prayer; by honoring an ecosystem as sacred ground, the universe would respond with healing power. It was an idea as old as thought itself and I hoped it was true.

To protect the shield in its finished form would have taken eternal vigilance, a ridiculous notion in that cow pasture. In the larger sense however, that is exactly what is called for in the protection of Turtle Island's remaining wilderness and biodiversity. My encounter with one of the "killing C's" (cars, cattle and chainsaws) is a metaphor for the task at hand for Earth Patriots now and always—declare and protect sacred ground. This must be done eternally and with a high degree of vigilance for there will always be those who will want to take it down, grind it up and turn it into something else.

The Final Metaphor

The prairie flowers were in full bloom when I returned to the site a few weeks later with my wife and child. As we crossed the open grasslands I told Christine that the Plains Indians considered the turtle to be a symbol of long life and how it was customary for new mothers to seal their baby's umbilical cord into a beaded, turtle shaped pouch to insure the child's longevity. As we neared the hilltop, I expected to find the shield ravaged by cattle; after all, they were a part of this "art." A small part of me, though, held on to the notion that perhaps the shield had "hexed" them—that they had left it alone. I was wrong on both counts, for what I found was beyond mere cow destruction. The iron lightning rod, the feathered stakes and the prayer wheel were totally gone. I scoured the area and found only a few feathers and bits of twine. Large stones had been moved aside here and there—the turtle was far from recognizable, the hoop broken.

We repaired the circle and piled all the stones inside it with a tall cairn in the north adjoining the still intact spiral. It looked good in its new form and we left feeling strong yet bewildered about what had happened.

Weeks later the mystery ended in a letter by Jack and Nancy Methvin—the owners of the land who had given me permission to do my art. Someone, it seemed, had been watching me through binoculars from a far hill. There had been a few cattle thefts in the area and evidently he thought he was on to something. When he investigated the site he figured it to be the doings of a satanic cult. The sheriff was called and together they gathered "the evidence." The determined duo contacted Jack and Nancy and proudly presented them with their findings. Despite the duo's fervor to bust a band of satanic cattle thieves, the Methvins managed, at last, to convince the disappointed prairie detectives that it was only "eco-art."

Sure it's funny, but what does it say about our species? It was Man himself, the wielder of the killing Cs who gutted the turtle shield. Humankind, so anxious to protect our beliefs, at any cost, that we kill our fellow men and women and the Earth in the process. The toxic nature of our ideologies weaves the bloody fabric of human history. How many have died, how much of the Earth has been ravished in the name of this or that religion, this or that ideology? It is beyond reckoning and there is little real sign of change. We hold on to our beliefs like a drowning man his gold.

Beliefs are dangerous and indeed toxic to the degree they separate us from the sacred web of nature. They have led us to a great forgetting—to the very edge of a fatal abyss of separation from the wondrous nurturing and sustaining being of which we are a part. The one grand and timely healing for all Earthlings and our sacred planet home is the remembering, finally, that we must simply love (protect, nurture, celebrate) *First, The Earth!* This is not an ideology. It is common sense. Continuing evolution. The spark of life itself.

Five Ways You Can Help Protect the Prairie

1. Move to the Flint Hills of Kansas. Land is cheap out here, the air clear, the storms beautiful, and the open space—healing. Buy or rent an old farm with native prairie, preserve it and restore more land to its original condition. Get a few Buffalo, some Elk, and stay awhile.

2. Join the Flint Hills National Monument Association. Your support is critical now as they move to convince Congress that there is widespread interest in preserving the native Tallgrass Prairie. No need to send money—your name is what they most need now. After you get their material, write your representatives regarding the establishment of the National Monument. Write: Flint Hills National Monument Association, POB 423, Strong City, KS 66866 or phone 316-273-6803.

3. Join The Nature Conservancy. Request that your money be used to purchase native prairie land.

4. Give up beef! Join the building wave of people who understand the Earth killing nature of beef addiction. This is the first step to dreaming back the Bison.

5. Write Congresspersons insisting they oppose all military expansion efforts, especially into intact Tallgrass Prairie ecosystems in the Flint Hills. Representatives are at US House of Representatives, Washington, DC 20515; senators at Senate, Washington, DC 20510.

—Daniel Dancer

Editor's note: Biologists have recently found that grasslands have been grossly underrated as carbon dioxide sinks. Native grasslands may be as important as primary rainforests in counteracting the greenhouse effect, yet no sizeable Tallgrass preserves have been established. The Nature Conservancy is obtaining land for a preserve in the Osage Hills of Oklahoma, but the Flint Hills remain unrepresented in preserve systems.

Some Summary Thoughts on Earth First!

ONE OF THE MAIN FUNCTIONS OF EARTH FIRST! has been to act as an environmental gadfly, criticizing mainstream environmental groups' excessive centralization and willingness to compromise, trying to force those groups to take stronger stands in defense of wild lands and waters. Constructive criticism of established groups—including Earth First!—can strengthen the environmental movement.

As Earth First! expands and divides, it is wise for its adherents and erst-while adherents to assess the movement and its tactics. Hence, this chapter deals with the role of Earth First! and the tactics for which EF!—rightly or wrongly—became best known, monkeywrenching and civil disobedience. The juxtaposition here of articles from the early 1980s with some from the last two years helps show the evolution EF! has undergone.

It is important to emphasize that the division (or speciation) of Earth First! does not mean the end of no-compromise wilderness defense. Rather it means a further decentralization of the radical wing of the conservation movement, which should serve to strengthen that aspect of the movement. The Earth First! ideal is alive and mushrooming.

EARTH FIRST!'S PROPER ROLE
Grizzly Den, Eostar 1982
by Howie Wolke

Earth First! has its roots deeply embedded in the wilderness of the western U.S. We've recognized that wilderness preservation is the most urgent necessity on Earth. Once wilderness is gone, in most places geologic time will be needed for nature to restore it. And once the living organisms that depend on wilderness become extinct, they're gone forever.

I don't mean to downplay the importance of other aspects of the environmental struggle. But eventually, the gears of this civilization will likely grind to a halt under the immense weight of its own blundering and greed. And when this glorious day occurs, the sky will gradually return to blue, our imprisoned and polluted waters will once again begin to run free, and suburbs will turn to dust as our population is forced—one way or another—to return to a manageable level. But it will all be for naught, unless we've had the vision and determination to save wilderness and the wild things dependent upon it.

So, speak out with passion against the mindless insanity of nuclear proliferation; against killer acid rain; against toxic chemical wastes; against air you can see, water you can't drink; and above all, against the Earth-raping power-brokers of the multinationals and their governmental cohorts. But let Earth First! always concentrate its efforts on the wilderness battleground. It's where we can do the most good.

ED ABBEY TO EARTH FIRST!
Mabon 1983
(Originally read to a gathering of EF!ers that Ed was unable to attend)

The undersigned deeply regrets that he cannot be here in the flesh—or what there is left of it. Pressing moral obligations and inescapable spiritual duties require my physical presence elsewhere—namely, floating down a river with some old cronies and a few dozen cases of beer in a godawful place called Desolation Canyon, Utah. Rejoice that you are here instead, under the blazing sun (or drenching rain) of the fairgrounds in Salt Lake City, Shithead Capital of the Inter-Mountain West. Although my feet, head, belly, etc., are out yonder, my heart is here with all of you posie-sniffers, toadstool worshippers, eco-freaks, earth-lovers, anti-nuke hardheads, environmental blowflies, FBI agents, innocent onlookers, Mothers for Peace and Winos for Ecology. You are the new salt of the Earth.

I am with you in spirit, whatever that means. And it does mean something. It means first of all that I wish to salute everyone who took part in the recent EF! road-blocking operations in the Kalmiopsis wilderness of Oregon. You are heroines and heroes and no praise for your courage, daring, and irrepressible good-will can express the admiration that we feel. I would like to name names, read the entire roll of honor, and if it were not for fear of overlooking somebody, I would do so. But you know who you are, and your pride in what you have accomplished should fill your hearts with a golden glow for the rest of your lives.

It is not enough to write letters to Congressmen, deliver sermons, make speeches, or write books. The West we love is under violent attack; the Earth that sustains us is being destroyed. Words alone will not save our country or ourselves. We need more heroes and more heroines—about a million of them. One brave deed, performed in an honorable manner and for a life-defending cause, is worth a thousand books. At some point we must draw a line across the ground of our home and our being, drive a spear into the land, and say to the bull-dozers, earth-movers, government and corporations, *thus far and no farther.* If we do not we shall later feel, instead of pride, the regret of Thoreau, that good but overly-bookish man, who wrote, near the end of his life, "If I repent of anything it is likely to be my good behavior. What demon possessed me that I behaved so well?"

Yes, we must continue to talk with one another and with our fellow citizens. We must continue to take part in political action, to reason with our adversaries, to think and meditate and develop a philosophy that gives moral justification to what we believe. But we must also be prepared to put our bodies on the line. Philosophy without action is the ruin of the soul.

We must stand up, speak out, talk back—and when necessary, fight back. The great powers ranged against us—industrial, governmental, military—may seem omnipotent. But they are not. If enough of us resist, fiercely enough and for long enough, the huge concrete wall of the Corporate State will begin to crack. Its dams are already beginning to crack—the very bedrock beneath them is crumbling—and someday soon, if the river of the water of life continues to flow, the State's dams will go down like dominos.

Concrete and asphalt and iron are heavy, oh, so terribly massive and heavy—but water is stronger, grass is stronger. So long as the light of the sun continues to shine, the green tough grass of life will continue to grow and to break through the dead heavy static oppressive barriers of the industrial prison-house. If we are on the side of life then life is on our side. And if we are wrong we might as well get down on our knees and crawl into our little separate cells in the Beehive Society of the Technological Superstate. But we are not wrong; the grass will overcome the cement. The continuity is all.

Meanwhile, a final homily: Let's keep our bodies strong and enjoy the world. Eat more crunchy granola. Climb those mountains, run those rivers, explore those forests, investigate those deserts, love the sun and the moon and the stars and we will outlive our enemies, we will piss on their graves, and we will love and nurture and who knows—even marry their children.

Turn on, tune in, take over. Let's keep our minds, our senses and our common sense strong also. Who's in charge here? We're all in charge: every man his own guru, every woman her own gurette. Who is our leader? We are all leaders. What is our program? Earth first, life first; power and profits and domination last.

Down with Empire! Up with Spring! We stand for what we stand on! I thank you, partners.

—Ed Abbey

THOUGHTFUL RADICALISM
Grizzly Den, Yule 1989
by Howie Wolke

Author's note: The description below of a felony is pure fiction and is for entertainment purposes only. For the discussion that follows, "radicalism" means monkeywrenching (ecological sabotage), various forms of civil disobedience (road blockades, illegal occupations, tree sitting, etc.), and even legal demonstrations that promote protecting all remaining wildlands and restoring much that has been degraded.

Three men in a rusty foreign car drank a warm sixpack of Pabst as they drove down the Limestone Creek Road in Wyoming's Bridger-Teton National Forest. Behind them were the peaks of the Gros Ventre Range, glowing in the late afternoon sun. Earlier, the three men and a 7 year old boy had stood among those peaks baked by the intense June sun in a world of wet snowbanks, meltwater, bare rock and glacier lilies: a "Sierra Club Calendar wilderness" of glaciated brilliance, one that even the Forest Service concurred to protect.

The driver, a slightly overweight university professor, was a thoughtful man and the father of the boy, now asleep beside them. As the pitiful machine lumbered down the gravel road, all three were admiring the adjacent rich habitat of Mountain Sagebrush, grass, Douglas-fir, Subalpine Fir, Lodgepole Pine, and Quaking Aspen. This was the unprotected roadless country beneath the peaks; the land of multiple use where the Forest Service proposed logging, oil rigs, and new roads.

In 1980 the blasting of seismic crews was ubiquitous in western Wyoming. Roads and oil rigs followed the seismic crews deep into the wilds; the rigs pierced the earth by pulverizing thousands of feet of sedimentary rock. Big oil was looking for natural gas in the Wyoming wilds. But this day was Sunday and local seismic workers were off, hungover from a typically drunken Saturday night in Jackson.

At once, the two young men noticed the "Doghouse" a hundred or so yards from the road. The small building contained a seismic crew's "nerve center," where high tech devices recorded the rumblings of a bruised Earth and translated those rumblings to a potential bottom line calculated in some sterile boardroom hundreds or thousands of miles distant—in horrible places such as Houston, New York, and Casper. The devices inside the locked building were worth hundreds of thousands of dollars. The young men told the professor to stop the car, let them out, continue down the road and then return to pick them up in a half hour. With little hesitancy, he obliged. In broad daylight with little forethought and no planning, with stealth but no tools, the two men committed a felony. They broke into the building and attacked the computers, switches, dials and data with the appropriate available technology: rocks. Within minutes, the damage was done; the ecoteurs crossed the shadowed sagebrush meadow, met the nervous professor along the road, and were in the tourist mecca of Jackson by dark.

As ecological calamity unravels the living fabric of the Earth, environmental radicalism has become both common and necessary. But if lacking a sound ethical and biological basis, environmental radicalism can be a double-edged sword: a threat to the enemy, yes, but a danger to its wielder, too. In order to avoid self-defeating radicalism, I suggest a commitment to what I'll simply call "thoughtful radicalism." The 4 cornerstones of thoughtful radicalism are: 1) **Thwart.** 2) **Protect.** 3) **Restore.** 4) **Educate**.

It is admittedly impossible for all radical actions— legal or not— to always build upon all 4 cornerstones. Sometimes, all you can hope for is to thwart, or perhaps to contribute to long-term protection for an area. But it is possible to always avoid regression. That means we should consider both the short and long term consequences of our actions. For instance, generally avoid monkeywrenching a project if a legal victory to stop it seems at hand. Monkeywrenching in that situation might impair public support for long term protection. Don't damage any cornerstones.

Education is the most fundamental of the cornerstones, and it's the one most important when we look beyond the short term crises that so often co-opt our efforts. It's also the easiest cornerstone to neglect or subvert. Any action, however radical or illegal, should avoid unnecessary, juvenile or thoughtless acts that might prevent open-minded people from heeding our message. Remember, we want to convince the populace (70% of whom now consider themselves to be "environmentalists," according to pollster George Gallup), or at least elicit their sympathies. The stupidest thing that radical activists can do is to appear as common criminals. That's the fastest way to negate education.

For instance, when carrying out civil disobedience or monkeywrenching, don't dilute your message by committing extraneous illegal acts. There are great philosophical differences among radical environmentalists regarding laws and lawbreaking in general. Regardless of those differences, though, getting busted for grass, getting stopped for DUI, or getting caught shoplifting will only convince the public that radical activists are a bunch of anarchist hooligans with no sense of decency or respect for others. Regardless of how badly you'd like to rip off that store with the anti-wilderness sign; regardless of how badly you'd like to slip out of the Exxon Valdez station with a full tank *and* a full wallet, do it on your own time if you must; avoid such temptation when carrying out or preparing to carry out radical environmental defense. Consider the impact upon those we're trying to reach. Focus.

Moreover, we want the public to focus not on our style but on the substance of our message. With substance in mind (not the controlled kind), it is often good strategy for radical activists (this generally does not pertain to monkeywrenchers) to wear fairly conventional attire. Again, the public needs to learn about the ecological atrocity; we don't want undue attention diverted to the unusual dress or lifestyle of action participants. Swallow your pride and leave your hippie or 1830s mountain man duds at home. Ecosystems are more important than your personal identity. Again, focus.

Furthermore, since we want the public to get the message, don't confuse the issue at hand with other issues, no matter how dear to your heart they may be. In Earth First! the issue is wilderness/biodiversity/planetary survival. At radical actions promoting natural diversity, don't confuse the issue by promoting legalization of dope, the right to burn a flag, women's rights, racial equity, tax protests, nuclear disarmament, or anything else extraneous to the particular issue. Do we have legitimate feelings about these things? Certainly. Are nuclear weapons, unfair taxes, and racism symptoms of a thoroughly corrupt and destructive system? Of course they are. Nonetheless, do we want those who might politically differ from us but agree with us on wilderness and planetary survival to jump on our bandwagon? Emphatically yes! Once more, just say "No" to your ego. Focus.

Thoughtful radicalism means that spokespersons (and ideally all who are involved) must be knowledgeable. Quoting biologists is often effective. Even better is to include a reputable biologist as a spokesperson. Publicize the "why" as well as the "what." Prepare an informative packet for demonstrations. Thoughtful radicalism will create public support for wildness and natural diversity. Occasionally that will contribute to thwarting a project or to gaining long term protection for an area. Thoughtful radicalism can also lay the groundwork for future restoration of damaged wild places. Again: *Thwart, Protect, Restore and Educate*. Whenever and however we decide to break the law in defense of the planet, we must do so without egocentrism, and with clarity of purpose. That is, focus. Understand the issue and leave your baggage at home.

How does the episode at the beginning of this essay relate to the 4 cornerstones of thoughtful radicalism? On that June afternoon the 3 radical activists *thwarted*, at least for a while, destruction—oil exploration in roadless habitat. Moreover, monkeywrenching in general can thwart many destructive but economically marginal projects by adding significantly to their costs (read *Ecodefense* for a discussion of this topic). In itself, the men's act of planetary defense was probably neutral regarding long term wilderness restoration. The action, however, certainly helped incite a polarized atmosphere which contributed to the eventual designation of an incomplete but substantial Gros Ventre Wilderness. Moreover, social polarization regarding wilderness in the Jackson Hole area has created at least some diffidence in the Forest Service's desire to wreck habitat. Regarding protection, I give the monkeywrenchers a slight plus. Unfortunately, though, the local media reported the act as "vandalism." The ecoteurs should have carefully and anonymously publicized why they demolished the "Doghouse." Crudely put, seismic exploration had opened the door for the throbbing organ of an industrial dragon planning to rape the Gros Ventre roadless area. Though they could have said it more gently, the saboteurs failed to educate.

The monkeywrenchers who thwarted the seismic operation acted spontaneously. They had simply been hiking. There was no planning and little consideration of the potential consequences. But the men knew the intent of the industrial dragon, and they acted with a focused purpose: to damage a vulnerable appendage of the monster; to emasculate its lust for unprotected wilderness. Spontaneous monkeywrenching is ok. Dragonian claws are everywhere, suddenly emerging at unexpected times and places. Occasionally, ecodefenders have little choice but to seize the moment and act.

Should illegal acts of environmental defense be undertaken only as a last resort when all methods of legal resistance fail? Not just no, but *Hell no!* Again, the claws of the mutated beast are everywhere. To neutralize opposition, a primary strategy for agencies such as the Forest Service and BLM is to wear us out with *process*. Assaults on natural diversity are so overwhelmingly common, so multidimensional that it is impossible for activists to monitor—let alone resist—more than a tiny fraction of threats to wildlands. Hearings, negotiating sessions, EISs, appeals, lawsuits, and informational (propaganda) workshops are time consuming and expensive for volunteer activists, yet represent bread and butter for bureaucrats and corporate officers. Remember that Thursday night when you wanted to read at home after a hard day's work or maybe watch your kid play basketball, but instead you went to that wilderness meeting? You got the shaft, but the Freddie got overtime pay. And you wrote the check!

By submerging ourselves in the process; indeed, by making an effort to exhaust the process prior to conducting illegal but moral resistance, we guarantee more fodder for the dragon. Yes, we need more people working within the system because occasionally that succeeds. But we also need more focused monkeywrenching and more civil disobedience to fend off the dragon, even when the individuals involved make little or no attempt to spar with the beast in its own arena.

Also, there's an inherent danger in committing civil disobedience or monkeywrenching after staggering through the confusing maze of the "legitimate" process. Chances are, after you've spent time, energy and money on meetings, phone calls, and appeals *ad nauseum*, all to no avail, you'll be quite justifiably angry. If you're like me, you'll be thinking REVENGE. Such a mindset, though natural and occasionally stimulating, is not conducive to clarity of purpose: that is, to conducting a well-focused effort to thwart, protect, restore, and educate. Though I'm not certain of this, I suspect that serious radical activists—monkeywrenchers in particular—should generally avoid working within the system altogether.

In 1986 I spent 6 months in a county jail. I was a convicted remorseless monkeywrencher who had gone through all available legal channels in a futile attempt to thwart an oil drilling and logging project in Wyoming's Grayback Ridge roadless area. The final straw was a meeting at which Bridger-Teton National Forest Supervisor Reid Jackson refused Chevron Oil's offer to restore and reclaim the new road and drillsite if the well proved dry. The supervisor wanted access for future below cost timber sales in the wildlife-rich area. This situation illustrates the pitfall of "frustration monkeywrenching." On the day I got busted, my cohort and I had spotted the full-time guard (the project had already been de-surveyed twice, though, of course, not by me!) before he spotted us. Nonetheless, we unwisely decided to continue to monkeywrench. We should have waited until night. Or until Sunday, when the guard's hangover would have impaired him. Or until we had another cohort to monitor the guard. But I was angry. I remembered the time consuming sessions, the paperwork, the late night phone calls, and the Forest Service's stubborn refusal to compromise. Pure anger can result in a lack of focus on the 4 cornerstones of thoughtful radical activism, and that can be dangerous. A pissed off monkeywrencher can be careless. That mindset cost this one 6 months.

There is, of course, a bigger question that I've thus far avoided. Implicit in my plea for thoughtful radicalism is an assumption that there are limitations on what ecodefenders can accomplish. If, however, we see ourselves as a rising power capable of bringing the industrial system to its knees before it squelches all that remains wild, then perhaps we should do as follows: Lash out at every offensive aspect of society at once. Decry all laws as unjust and blatantly break them. Be wild and radical to encourage rebellion for its own sake. Dress like punks, hippies, or Neanderthals at demonstrations because conventional attire is worn by land-raping pillagers. Most important, because everything is connected to everything else, and because planetary demise is the result of a complex tangle of greed, injustice and overpopulation, lash out at everything—attack the whole enchilada because it's all equally rotten. That's one way of emphasizing our disgust with the insanity of a world paradigm based upon consumption, greed, and growth for its own malignant sake.

But if we assume, as I do, that for a while at least we're stuck with the dragon, an insatiable force that can be slowed but not entirely subdued, then focus where it is occasionally vulnerable, and where its slime-encrusted claws are directly assaulting nature. Convince our fellow humans by being thoughtful yet unyielding that we must radically alter the way our species treats its embryonic home, the wilderness, and the rest of this beleaguered planet.

Quite honestly, I doubt that anything, including thoughtful radicalism, can bridge the gap between saving some wilderness today and creating a society that lives within its ecological means: humans as members, not outlaws, of the biotic community. I doubt even more strongly, though, the ultimate effectiveness of unfocused organized tantrums. Thoughtless radicalism will save little that remains wild now. Despite the insanity of modern consumerism, shopping mall "puke-ins" don't educate; they alienate. A bunch of naked anarchists smoking dope at a wilderness demonstration will neither speed the demise of the industrial dragon nor save a besieged roadless area. Neither will militant vegetarians who won't work with us omnivores to save wild country.

The demise of the beast will, I venture, occur via the ungodly weight of its own momentum. Education today will increase the chance of creating an ecologically sustainable society after the inevitable demise of today's biological aberration. What will eventually replace today's dragonian madness is anybody's guess. It's my guess, though, that thoughtful radicalism will save some biotic diversity in the short term, and allow more to be saved and restored for the longer run. Then, when the floundering beast finally, mercifully chokes in its own dung pile, there'll at least be *some* wilderness remaining as a seedbed for planet-wide recovery. Maybe even some Griz; some Flat-spired Three-toothed Land Snails, some Pallid Bats; some man-eating Tigers; some wild humans; and some living canyons like the Colorado's Glen. Some hope. And maybe even some human wisdom.

MONKEYWRENCHING: AN APPRAISAL
Brigid 1990
by CM

Our duty is to destroy billboards.
—Doc Sarvis

Over the past year or so, a number of groups and individual activists associated with Earth First! have distanced themselves from the radical environmental banner, ostensibly over the issue of ecotage. They argue that they can more effectively inform and influence the public if they don't have to bear the spike-ridden cross of vindicating this controversial practice. There is no point in disputing this reasoning. The field of environmental activism is broad enough to let each plow his or her own plot (though some of us would rather put the farm out of business and encourage natural succession). No one is quarreling with the goal of informing the American public on the environmental cataclysm now taking place, and doing so without getting bogged down in arguments about property rights, law and order, and violence, if this is possible.

Nevertheless the fact that monkeywrenching looms so large in these considerations calls for an appraisal of its effectiveness, a report card to compare with less direct methods of expressing environmental discontent.

The controversy over monkeywrenching is nothing new. In 1982 the editor of *Earth First!* (then the mildly named *Earth First! Newsletter*) resigned over EF!'s sympathetic coverage of monkeywrenching. Gary Snyder, an early supporter of EF!, also criticized ecotage. Over the years disputes have flared up intermittently during particular campaigns between those committed to civil disobedience and those using ecotage. The controversy is likely to stay with us until industrial society crashes to the ground and happily makes the question moot.

Meanwhile, it's fair to ask: what has monkeywrenching accomplished? The answer is, a great deal more than is obvious.

Oddly enough, until recently no one, either in government or industry, kept track of the cost of ecotage. The Forest Service, always on the cutting edge of lethargy, simply lumped ecotage incidents with vandalism and other crimes. The timber industry, already beset by insurance problems because of its shameful safety record, was reluctant to give the insurance companies another category of risk for raising rates. All this is changing. The Forest Service law enforcement division in Washington is overhauling its reporting methods, and they expect this will allow a more accurate accounting of ecotage. Moreover many Forest supervisors are now going back and reevaluating reports of "vandalism" to see if environmental motives were involved. According to Eco-Media Toronto there are also a half dozen "Pinkerton-like" private groups starting to monitor ecotage, as well as to infiltrate radical environmental groups. One of these, the ultra-conservative Mountain States Legal Foundation (once headed by the glabrously messianic James Watt), is now in the ambitious process of cataloguing all incidents of monkeywrenching nationwide, with the stated purpose of informing the public and the rumored aim of bringing a class-action suit against Earth First!

Bad accounting aside, reliable estimates do exist for the cost of ecotage to the industries and government agencies now in control of our public lands. A forest policy analyst for the Association of Oregon Loggers and its unintentionally self-defining alter ego Prevent Ecological Sabotage Today—PEST—estimates that the average monkeywrenching incident causes $60,000 in damages, including equipment loss and downtime (but not law enforcement investigation and insurance). This accords with what most newspaper accounts, Forest Service special agents, and ecoteurs say. In a typical incident last Labor Day weekend, for example, a bulldozer and two skidders were siltated and mangled, causing $45,000 in property damage plus about $15,000 in downtime.

According to a timber industry spokesman, an average tree-spiking incident costs about $15,000 assuming the spikes are found and removed, or, more likely nowadays, marked with tape to allow loggers to cut around them (thus many small nails placed in a helix pattern around the tree are more effective than a few large ones). The above estimate also includes the value of the wood in the larger stumps the loggers have to leave to avoid the spikes. The cost goes up astronomically if a spike hits a bandsaw in the mill, as several did last summer in southern Oregon. Though the timber industry is loath to talk about it, one timber industry spokesman called this a "monthly" occurrence. The saws themselves typically cost $1500–5000. A damaged saw can be changed in an hour or so (assuming a replacement is on hand). The big expense comes if the saw shatters and shrapnel flies into the head-rig. Head-rig repairs can cost $20,000.

The actual cost of an average monkeywrenching incident climbs to well over $100,000 when you figure in police investigation, private security, insurance hikes, and the fatuous efforts of groups like the Mountain States Legal Foundation (whose lawyers, if they follow the usual practice of double billing, will run up an account of over half a million dollars on this public-spirited project, subsidized in part by taxpayers, since the Foundation has tax exempt status—which should be challenged in court!). When you consider that the typical monkeywrenching incident probably costs the ecoteur no more than $100 and a night's sleep, this is a remarkably cost-effective way to register one's disapproval of present resource industry practices.

How much monkeywrenching is happening? Again, until recently no one was keeping count. According to industry and Forest Service officials in southern Oregon, there were "dozens" of reported incidents last summer alone, and most of these can be tallied from newspaper accounts. As already mentioned, however, the timber industry often avoids reporting sabotage or lies about the cause of the damage so as to keep their insurance companies in the dark (their natural element). Timber industry spokesmen suggest that 1 out of every 2 monkey-wrenching incidents goes unreported. According to Forest Service agents in region 5 (California), at least a dozen tree-spikings occurred in their jurisdiction last year. These tend not to get into the papers since monkeywrenchers realized a while back that once the incident reaches the media the Forest Service will stop at nothing to go through with the sale in order to show that it is in control of the pub-lic lands. And, of course, this estimate doesn't include incidents on private and state land, which, as the Maxxam battle indicates, are significant in California. In Washington monkeywrenching is so rife that special agent Ben Hull simply won't talk about it. Several years ago, Hull did a survey of Forest supervisors across the nation to get an estimate of how common monkeywrenching was. He has refused to release the information, despite demands by environmentalists under the Freedom of Information Act. He admits he doesn't want to give ecoteurs the satisfaction of knowing how much havoc they're causing.

Admittedly Oregon, northern California and Washington are "hot spots" with an unusual amount of ecotage. However, the number of such hot spots itself is increasing: Montana, Wyoming, Arizona, Alaska, New Mexico, Idaho.

Moreover there are many "hidden" costs associated with ecotage, in particular legislative action. For instance, the anti-tree spiking rider in the 1988 Drug Act (18 USCA Sec. 1864) came about only after a long process in which the Forest Service, at the behest of that cham-pion of deforestation, Senator McClure of Idaho, submitted several draft bills. Never satisfied with halfway measures at repression, McClure has continued to clamor for even more strident legislation. Last June, US Representative Pashayan of California sponsored a bill that calls for 20 years in prison and a $100,000 fine for repeat offend-ers. Following the lead of this rogues' gallery, Oregon passed its own anti-spiking act last session.

All this legislative activity costs money. Lawyers write these bills. Consultants and researchers are usually involved. A small, uncompli-cated bill like the foregoing, therefore, may cost $50,000 before getting to a committee of Congress or of a state legislature, where it will probably (4 to 1 odds against any given bill) languish and die.

Taking all this into consideration, ecotage in the United States today is probably costing government and industry $20–25 million annually. This represents money industry was not able to use to deforest public lands, sink oil wells in the backcountry, invest in more destructive equipment, influence politicians with campaign contributions. . . . It represents money the FS was not able to use to build new roads, or hide deficit sales, or hire more sub-brutal special agents.

People argue that corporations can simply pass this cost on to their customers and continue their destructive practices. Since no market is completely elastic, this isn't entirely true. But even if it is substantially so, a higher cost for wood products will inevitably mean that fewer wood products are bought—according to the vast and sublime free-market paradigm we are all withering under— which is ultimately the point. Furthermore, sometimes monkeywrenching as an economic weapon is completely effective: When in 1985 ecoteurs firebombed the $250,000 wood-chipper in Hawaii that was grinding rainforest into fuel for sugar mills (without a permit and in violation of a court order), the company went bankrupt.

Thus if the sole purpose of ecotage is to make an adverse financial impact on government agencies and their resource industry clientele, it must be judged a success. This is true even if it is looked at in isolation from a larger strategy involving civil disobedience, legal remedies and public outreach. When the woodsy Leroy Watson (any relation to Paul?) first brought tree-spiking to the attention of Earth First! in these very pages in 1981, he probably had no idea it would ever become the headache to CEOs and Forest supervisors it now represents.

Monkeywrenching has also accomplished other aims. In at least two cases the Forest Service has quietly withdrawn timber sales after learning they were spiked. There are probably more such recisions; the FS refuses to elaborate on the subject. Now that the risk of ecotage is publicly known, we can also speculate that timber company CEOs are taking the cost of ecotage into consideration when a sale of old-growth or other controversial ecological matter comes before the board. Failure to do so could get them in trouble with their stockholders. The ability of monkeywrenching to intimidate and unnerve the bureaucratic and the plutocratic mind cannot be measured but likely is significant.

Where ecotage isn't saving biological diversity directly, it is at least making biodiversity an issue. It can therefore be an important part of a larger campaign. The radical environmental message, whether concerning old-growth or dolphins, would not be receiving the widespread coverage it is today were it not for the "publicity value" of monkey-wrenching. Most of the coverage EF! has received over the years—in *Esquire, The Amicus Journal, The Nation,* local newspapers, etc.—has concentrated on ecotage, often favorably or at least without overt condemnation. Monkeywrenching seems to strike a cord with many modern Americans who, for different reasons probably, would also like to get back at the arbitrary powers that dominate their lives.

Regardless of sentiments pro and con, by its very controversial nature, ecotage makes biodiversity a matter of public interest and debate. It takes seemingly obscure environmental issues out of the dark of scientific calculations into the limelight of individual passion and commitment. Even when the media distorts ecotage by emphasizing its unlawfulness rather than its motives, it has been, like civil disobedience, an important element in the broader campaign to rally public opposition to wilderness destruction. For instance, in news coverage of the old-growth controversy, the subject of ecotage inevitably comes up, along with civil disobedience, and this activism clearly attracted the coverage in the first place.

This is what monkeywrenching is doing right now. Whether it should be doing more or less or something different is another topic. Unquestionably it has over the past 10 years revolutionized the way public lands policy is made in this country. It has upset the unhealthy *modus vivendi* that had developed among industry, moderate environmental groups, and the government agencies in charge of our wildlands. No longer can the Forest Service or BLM act like a band of medieval forestmeisters without fearing the bad publicity (a bureaucrat's one unforgivable sin) of a tree-spike or a de-flagging. The timber industry is now criticizing the FS for not acting even more one-sidedly for the corporations' interest. The mainstream environmental organizations are beginning to be embarrassed into addressing issues their professional leaders would never have broached if left to their own devices (martini glass, three-piece suit, and half a loaf).

What monkeywrenching isn't doing is hurting people, despite its media image. Whether ecotage is "violent" in itself is an ethical question best left to an individual's own conscience. The ethical rationales for ecotage have been thoroughly discussed by others, so I won't repeat them. But it is a fact that there has not been one authenticated incident in which ecotage caused significant injury to a person. The case inevitably reported as the evil fruit of ecotage is the infamous spike that seriously injured a Louisiana Pacific mill-worker in northern California two years ago. There is, however, no evidence monkeywrenchers were involved. On the contrary, eco-teurs would have notified the company, and no notification was given. Possibly a disgruntled LP employee—and there are many of them—put the spike in; or possibly LP itself did to get publicity, which it certainly got, often of the most exaggerated kind (I talked with a woman who said the spike killed 5 people). Or, ironically, as one newspaper suggested, a radical Republican, whose libertarianism was outraged by logging near his property line, may have done it. How many bad motives can dance on the head of this problematical spike? No one knows.

Jay Hair, executive director of the National Wildlife Federation, once said he couldn't tell the difference between destroying a river and destroying a bulldozer. Blessed with a more conventional sense of values, ecoteurs can, and as the record indicates, they have also fastidiously respected the difference between destroying property and hurting innocent people.

This isn't to say ecotage is a panacea, or that we don't need other people doing other things. No one knows for sure what it will take to save the natural world from the juggernaut of industrialism. But one thing is sure: if we fail and the fragile web of the biosphere unravels, it will not be because there were too many ecoteurs pounding spikes into trees, burning bulldozers and making the guilty squirm.

GOOD LUCK, DARLIN'. IT'S BEEN GREAT."
September 1990
by Dave Foreman and Nancy Morton

Dear friends

We feel like we should be sitting at the bar of a seedy honky-tonk, drinking Lone Star, thumbing quarters in the country-western juke-box, and writing this letter on a bar napkin.

Breaking up is never easy to do, whether it's with a lover or an organization that's been the central focus of your life for a decade. But people and groups change over time, and the Earth First! movement seems to be changing in such a way that we don't feel comfortable sharing a name with it any longer.

So it's time to sit down and write a "Dear John" letter to Earth First!. This isn't a sad letter, but it's not a happy letter either. It's a letter that remembers the good times, but recognizes we and Earth First! are on separate trails. It's bittersweet, with fond memories and glad anticipations.

From the beginning, Earth First! has straddled a wide slice of the environmental movement. It seems to us that we've had three major strains: monkeywrenching, biocentrism and ecological wilderness preservation/restoration, and confrontational direct action both legal (demonstrations) and illegal (civil disobedience). Different personalities have been attracted to Earth First! by each of these strains and the dynamic among them has contributed to the vigorously positive impact Earth First! has had on the environmental movement.

A good metaphor, we think, for Earth First! over the last decade is that of a generalist species in a new habitat with many available niches. (Say, a finch blown over to the Galapagos.) Slowly, different populations of that generalist species adapt to more effectively exploit the different niches and evolve into separate species. Oftentimes, external environmental stresses push a generalist species toward faster differentiation into separate, specifically adapted sister species.

This is what has happened to us in Earth First!. Those given to better exploiting the different niches of monkeywrenching, direct action, and conservation biology have been diverging.

For several years we've recognized signs of these changes and Dave has tried to point them out in articles and speeches. Sensing an influx into our gene pool by those more adapted to a social and economic justice worldview than an ecological one, Dave offered his perspective on what defined the Earth First! species in a speech at the 1987 Grand Canyon Rendezvous and later in an article for the *Earth First! Journal* entitled "Whither Earth First?"

However, the divergence continued and has been hastened by increased predation from the FBI and others. Unless we can adapt to both this changed environment and this divergence within our gene pool we will become extinct as a species.

Our personal choice for adapting is to declare that the Earth First! movement has been a success, that it has accomplished far more than any of us dreamed possible ten years ago, and then retire the name "Earth First!." We should then regroup under different names to continue the work to which we are individually best adapted and with those we are most closely related. In ecological terms, then, to declare our generalist species extinct because of evolution into separate sister species that are specifically adapted to different niches. Of course, this is unlikely to happen because many remain attached to the Earth First! name for various reasons and others are loath to give up the tribal sense of belonging inherent to the Earth First! movement.

So be it.

Both of us have smoked a lot of cigars and downed a lot of beers trying to figure out what to do. But we cannot escape the fact that we are uneasy with much in the current EF! movement. We therefore have come to the irrevocable decision to leave. This letter announces that decision. We do not henceforth represent what has become Earth First! and we are not represented by it.

We do not wish to go into some unfortunate matters of recent rhetoric directed against us (Dave in particular) and the original ideals of Earth First! by some who would lead the movement to a new niche, nor belabor the specific trends and tendencies within EF! that cause us concern. And we wish to make it abundantly clear that for the most part these are honest differences between decent people who respect one another.

In short, we see happening to the Earth First! movement what happened to the Greens in West Germany—an effort to transform an ecological group into a Leftist group. We also see a transformation to a more overtly counterculture/anti-establishment style, and the abandonment of biocentrism in favor of humanism.

Mind you, we are not opposed to campaigns for social and economic justice. We are generally supportive of such causes. But Earth First! has from the beginning been a wilderness preservation group, not a class-struggle group. For us, we still believe in Earth First!. We are uncompromising advocates for the process of evolution and the non-human world. We stand by the guidelines Dave offered in 1987 in

"Whither Earth First!?" Moreover, we are conservationists. We are not anarchists or Leftists. We are biocentrists, not humanists.

Yes, we do believe that overpopulation is a fundamental problem. William Catton in *Overshoot* restates Malthus's dictum in ecological terms as *The biotic potential of any species exceeds the carrying capacity of its habitat.* That is exactly the case with human beings on this planet today. We believe that human overpopulation has led to overshooting the carrying capacity of the Earth and will result in a major ecological crash. We do not think that believing this means one is racist, fascist, imperialist, sexist or misanthropic even if it is politically incorrect for cornucopians of the Left, Right and Middle.

So, what does our leaving Earth First! mean? First of all, we will not exit in a rancorous or angry way. We wish those who remain in Earth First! the best and we wish campaigns like Redwood Summer every success. We will not attack the evolving Earth First! organization or individuals in it. We will not encourage anyone to leave Earth First! with us. We will not tell anyone they have to make a choice between EF! and us. We will not claim we are right and the class-struggle Left/counterculture approach of the "new" Earth First! is wrong. We are merely different and have our own separate strengths and roles to play. We continue to admire and respect many of the people and local groups in Earth First! and have no reason to criticize them.

We will continue with the fight. Dave plans to begin work on thoroughly revising and updating *Ecodefense* into a Third Edition. And, along with others who emphasize biocentrism, we will be starting a new organization to work on concrete proposals for ecological wilderness identification, preservation and restoration.

Some will ask, "Why not stay and fight to return Earth First! to its original ideas and goals? Why abandon the movement to those who would transform Earth First! into an environmental reincarnation of the New Left?" We can only reply that we have never seen a fight for control of an organization achieve anything positive. We all have better things to do than engage in a sectarian donnybrook that will take us away from the real battle and result only in hard feelings. Also, as we've pointed out, we think that the Earth First! name and movement have outlived their usefulness for us. One reason for this is that we no longer manipulate the media. The media manipulate us and establish our style for us. It is time to regroup, refocus our energies, confuse our enemies, and do whatever we can do best to impede the destruction of our precious Earth. Moreover, a number of conservationists to whom we are very attached and with whom we wish to work in the future have already left or are planning to leave Earth First!. Finally, we do not want to discourage the courageous actions of those remaining in Earth First!.

In closing, let us thank all of you for your friendship and fellowship whether you are in the Earth First! movement or outside of it. These last ten years have been the best of our lives although we expect the next ten to be even better. We do not ask anyone to follow us out of Earth First! nor do we plan to offer competition to Earth First!. There is considerable room in the no-compromise environmental movement, many niches to fill, and a need for many groups working separately and/or harmoniously in defense of the great dance of life. Too much diversity within one group can become counterproductive. When that occurs, energy and time is wasted debating contrasting styles, philosophies, worldviews, priorities and strategies. It is far better to recognize the differences, accept that one is not right and the other wrong, that we're simply different, kiss a last time, file a no-fault divorce, and say to the other, "Good luck, Darlin'. It's been great."

Splitting the sheets is not pleasant but staying together with irreconcilable differences is worse.

Happy Trails
—Dave Foreman and Nancy Morton

AUTHORS

We wish to give special thanks again to all the writers who made this book possible. Most of these authors will be writing for *Wild Earth* in the future, and some of them will be serving on our editorial advisory board, so they will continue to share their wisdom with us. Below, they are arranged in alphabetical order.

Ed Abbey is the late and legendary writer who inspired Earth First! in its early years. His books include *Desert Solitaire*, *The Monkey Wrench Gang*, *Journey Home*, *A Fool's Progress*, and *Hayduke Lives!*.

Jasper Carlton is the coordinator of the Biodiversity Legal Foundation (POB 18327, Boulder, CO 80308), and a conservationist of 25 years' experience. He was a key figure in the victory for the Snail Darter in the 1970s, which victory was later stolen by Congress. Jasper has helped gain ESA listing for the Desert Tortoise, Cahaba Shiner, Northern Spotted Owl, and numerous other species. He won notoriety back in his old state of West Virginia when he stopped a major development by showing that it would do irreparable harm to the Flat-spired Three-toothed Land Snail.

CM is a widely published writer and scholar whose career dictates anonymity.

Leon Czolgosz is the pseudonym for Ron Kezar. Ron was one of the five who co-founded Earth First!, in 1980. He is now one of approximately the same number of Great Basin wilderness activists. When not working, he spends his time exploring that region's wildlands and waiting for a cataclysm to end the industrial machine's assault on them.

Daniel Dancer is a photo-journalist and artist based near what little remains of the Tallgrass Prairie biome in Kansas. He works with Project Lighthawk, documenting environmental abuses from the air. Daniel is working on a book about the role of Earth Art, ancient and modern, in healing ourselves and the Earth. He would like to hear of others doing work in a similar vein and on ancient sites not in the common literature. Write him at Sleeping Beauty Ranch, Oskaloosa, KS 66066.

Mary Davis is the author of *The Green Guide to France* and *Going Off the Beaten Path: An Untraditional Travel Guide*. She is a scholar of the Romantic poets of 19th-century England, and of the nuclear technicians of 20th-century France.

Bill Devall is an influential deep ecology proponent, and a retiring sociology professor. His books include *Deep Ecology* (with George Sessions) and *Simple in Means, Rich in Ends*. Bill is a longtime defender of the Coast Redwood forests, and the Marble Mountains and Trinity Alps of northern California.

Barbara Dugelby was an early leader of Texas Earth First! and a driving force behind that group's famous and successful campaign to win Endangered Species Act protection for central Texas cave bugs threatened by development. She is a longtime rainforest defender, and is now studying for a Ph.D. in tropical ecology and conservation at Duke University in North Carolina.

Suslositna Eddy is a former Earth First! leader from Maine who now homesteads in Alaska.

R. Wills Flowers is an entomologist at Florida A&M University. He has recently been involved with a national biodiversity research project in Costa Rica (*EF! J*, 11–90). Pursuing environmental ethics as an avocation, he has explored in writing the possibilities for extending rights to the natural world.

Dave Foreman is one of the EF! co-founders and was the editor of *Earth First!* from 1983–1988. His books include *The Big Outside* (with Howie Wolke), *Ecodefense* (with Bill Haywood), and *Confessions of an Ecowarrior*.

Mitch Freedman is a former Washington EF! leader who founded the Greater Ecosystem Alliance, which is working for ecosystem management—large Wilderness Areas, buffer zones, corridors, etc.—of the North Cascades and other ecosystems. To this end, Mitch edited *Forever Wild: Conserving the Greater North Cascades Ecosystem*, and publishes *Northwest Conservation: News & Priorities* (POB 2813, Bellingham, WA 98227).

Cindy Ellen Hill is an attorney in Massachusetts. Since writing "White Hats," she has begun working almost full-time, without pay, for Preserve Appalachian Wilderness (PAW). With Cindy's help, PAW has slowed the chemical poisoning of tributaries of Lake Champlain (with lampricide) and of ponds in the Adirondacks (with rotenone). Cindy has also been working on the dam relicensing hearings in the Northeast, trying to force dams to shut down or at least accommodate the needs of Atlantic Salmon and other imperiled fish. Cindy is also a poet.

Lynn Jacobs is the coordinator of the Grazing Task Force (POB 5784 Tucson, AZ 85703). He is perhaps the activist most hated by ranchers, in part because of his new book, *The Waste of the West,* which looks askance at welfare ranching. Lynn is also active with Arizona Earth First! He eschews beef.

Clive Kincaid worked as a resource professional for the BLM for five years, including over two years as the wilderness specialist for the Phoenix District in Arizona. He devoted over a year and 18,000 miles on back roads to examining the BLM inventory in Utah. He helped the Southern Utah Wilderness Alliance become the strongest voice for BLM wildlands in Utah.

Dolores LaChapelle is a deep ecologist and teacher at the Way of the Mountain Learning Center (POB 542, Silverton, CO 81433). She is the author of *Earth Festivals, Earth Wisdom,* and *Sacred Land Sacred Sex.* Dolores was a world-class alpinist and powder skier many years before climbing and skiing became fads.

Leslie Lyon is a wilderness activist, animal rights proponent, and environmental educator for children. She has worked with Southern Utah Wilderness Alliance to seek Wilderness protection for BLM roadless areas in Utah.

Joanna Macy is the author of the highly acclaimed book, *Despair and Empowerment in the Nuclear Age.* In addition to conducting Councils of All Beings throughout the world, she is promoting the nuclear guardianship concept—which seeks a permanent solution to the problem of nuclear waste: Stop production of the waste; place existing waste in above-ground structures, which would be eternally guarded and would serve as monuments to man's folly.

Christopher Manes is a student of Old and Middle English, Norse literature, and deep ecology, who was active with Oregon EF! in its formative years. He is also a former Fulbright scholar, a philosopher, and the author of *Green Rage.* He is now working on his second book and getting another degree, this time in law.

Mollie Matteson is a wildlife biologist and wilderness explorer based in Montana, whose travels have taken her to Wildlife Refuges throughout the country. Recently she has been studying Gray Wolves in Montana's Glacier National Park.

Stephanie Mills is an oft-published writer and the former editor of *Not Man Apart* and *CoEvolution Quarterly.* She is the author of

Whatever Happened to Ecology?, and is active in the bioregional movement. She now makes her home in northern Michigan.

Miss Ann Thropy is the pseudonym given by John Davis to a philosopher and deep ecologist whose literary career required anonymity.

Nancy Morton is a former Sierra Club leader in California, who gave up that life to work for Earth First! Nancy gave not only her house, but almost a decade of her life to the movement. She is now a nurse and wilderness activist in Arizona.

R. F. Mueller, a former NASA scientist, is the coordinator of Virginians for Wilderness, through which he has helped force the George Washington National Forest bureaucrats to scale back their clearcutting and road-building plans. Bob lives on a small farm near Staunton, Virginia, where he carefully guards a buckbean refugium.

Gary Nabhan is a co-founder of Native Seeds/SEARCH, in Tucson, Arizona, and an expert on plants and Papago (now Tohono O'odham) peoples of the Southwest. His books include *The Desert Smells Like Rain* and *Gathering the Desert*. He recently was awarded a MacArthur grant for his ethnobotanical research.

Arne Naess is a world-renowned Norwegian philosopher. He coined the term 'deep ecology' in 1973, thereby initiating the deep, long-range ecology movement. In his seventies, Arne can still leave younger folk in the dust on long hikes.

Reed Noss is a former EPA official and widely published conservation biologist. His works have appeared in *Natural Areas Journal, Bioscience,* and *Conservation Biology.* His specialty is community ecology, though his expertise extends to island biogeography and other fields. Under the name "Diamondback," Reed wrote the central article in the widely circulated "Killing Roads" tabloid that *EF! Journal* produced in 1990 to combat the road-building mania in this country.

Doug Peacock is a living legend. Inspiration for Ed Abbey's beloved character George Hayduke, former Green Beret, survivor of the Vietnam War and of over 20 Grizzly Bear charges, world wildlands explorer, husband of Lisa Peacock, and highly acclaimed writer, Doug is a good cook. His new book *Grizzly Years* is a provocative exploration of bear biology and war psychology.

Jamie Sayen is the founder and coordinator of PAW—Preserve Appalachian Wilderness. A Princeton graduate, he wrote the celebrated

Einstein in America, then tossed to the wind a promising literary career to work instead, impecuniously, for habitat in the Northern Appalachians. With PAW, he writes, lobbies, protests, and otherwise endeavors to restore large wild areas first in the Appalachians, and eventually from the Florida Keys to Hudson Bay. Jamie publishes PAW's journal the *Glacial Erratic* (RFD 1, Box 530, N Stratford, NH 03590).

John Seed is an Australian EF! contact and a world leader on rainforest issues. His group, the Rainforest Information Centre (POB 368, Lismore, New South Wales 2480 AUSTRALIA), publishes the *World Rainforest Report.* When not touring the globe doing rainforest gigs, John is often engaged in direct action to defend Australia's remnant rainforests.

Joanna Macy Seed and John are co-authors, along with Arne Naess and Pat Fleming, of *Thinking Like a Mountain: Toward a Council of All Beings* (New Society Publishers, 1988), in which their Gaia Meditations appear.

George Sessions is a leading international deep ecology theorist who teaches philosophy at Sierra College in California. He co-authored (with Bill Devall) *Deep Ecology.* George is also a Spinoza scholar and rock climber.

Gary Snyder is a Pulitzer-prize-winning poet and author. His numerous books include *The Old Ways, Good Wild Sacred,* and *Practice of the Wild.* He inhabits and defends the Shasta Bioregion (northern California).

Carole King Sorensen, best known as a singer, is an Idaho resident and a champion of its wildlands. Recently she has been working for introduction in Congress of the Wild Rockies Land Conservation Act. She has even convinced some politicians, no less, that this is a conservative, or *status quo* bill, as it would leave all of Idaho's and Montana's roadless areas as they are: wild!

Chant Thomas is a long-time old-growth defender and llama wilderness expeditions outfitter in the Siskiyou Mountains of northern California and southwestern Oregon, of which the Kalmiopsis is a part. He participated in both the 1983 and the 1987 direct actions.

Dale Turner is the former assistant editor of *EF! Journal.* He is also a longtime leader of the Arizona chapter of the Sierra Club and of Arizona EF! A genuine desert rat, he complains when the temperature drops below 90, and has a predilection for horned lizards.

Paul Watson is the founder of Sea Shepherd Conservation Society and captain of their vessel the *Sea Shepherd II*. One of the founders of Greenpeace, he left that group because it was too moderate. He is feared worldwide by ocean exploiters, yet operates with impunity because he is enforcing existing international environmental law.

Howie Wolke is another of the Earth First! co-founders. He was the Wyoming representative for Friends of the Earth in the 1970s but became disenchanted with mainstream conservation efforts after the RARE II debacle. He recently authored a book partly about that debacle, *Wilderness on the Rocks*, and operates a long-standing backpacking guide service, Wild Horizons, out of western Montana.

George Wuerthner is a wildlife biologist and freelance environmental writer based in Livingston, Montana. He has written books on wild areas throughout the country, as well as numerous articles for *Wilderness*, *High Country News*, and other periodicals. George has explored wilderness in almost every region of North America.

Robert Zahner is a retired professor of forestry. He lives near and works for the forests of the Katuah Province (western North Carolina, eastern Tennessee, northern Georgia) of the Southern Appalachian Highlands Bioregion.